HAITI: A BASIC REFERENCE BOOK

General Information on Haiti

Compiled and edited by
Patricia Schutt-Ainé
and the staff of
Librairie Au Service de la Culture

HAITI: A BASIC REFERENCE BOOK
General Information on Haiti

By Patricia Schutt-Ainé
and the Staff of Librairie Au Service de la Culture

Published by: Librairie Au Service de la Culture
                Post Office Box 162236
                Miami, Florida 33116-9998, U.S.A.

                89 Rue Pavée
                PO Box 613
                Port-au-Prince, Haiti

Library of Congress Catalog Card Number: 93-080454
ISBN 0-9638599-0-0   Softcover

Picture Credits
From the collection of Willy Nicolas, Creative Images of Haiti,
P.O. Box 260558, Brooklyn, New York 11226

A Note From the Editors

Haiti: A Basic Reference Book is a preliminary effort to provide relevant information pertaining to Haiti. It is designed to be a reference tool for librarians, scholars, researchers, students and persons interested in Haitian subjects. In compiling this volume the editors have carefully examined and verified every information for accuracy. They selected data which they assumed to be fundamental and essential.

The publisher, **Librairie Au Service de la Culture**, is an organization that has been serving the reading community in Haiti for more than forty years. Its objective in **Haiti: A Basic Reference Book** is to continue the tradition of service by presenting facts and useful information on Haiti to readers in the English language. It is hoped that this publication will be an interesting and rewarding resource.

Patricia Schutt-Ainé
and the staff of
Librairie Au Service de la Culture

To the memory of
Emmanuel Schutt-Ainé
1930-1989

Acknowledgment

The publisher would like to express special thanks to Terence and Fleur Sequeira of **A to Z Word-O-Matics,** Miami, Florida. Terence Sequeira read and edited the manuscript offering comments and many helpful suggestions. Fleur Sequeira proofread the text, designed the style, and prepared, indexed and finalized the book for publication. This edition was made possible because of their guidance, tireless effort and attention to detail.

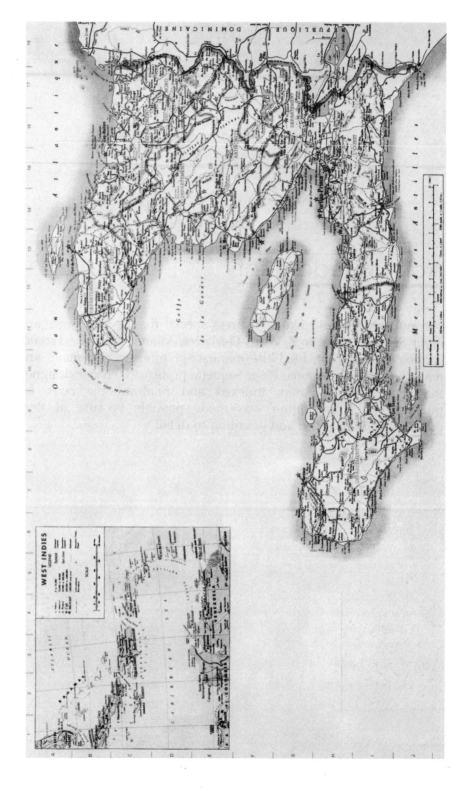

CONTENTS

Chapter 1

COUNTRY SYNOPSIS 1

Chapter 2

GEOGRAPHY 14
Territorial Divisions of Haiti 15
Surrounding Islands 20
Highest Mountains 20
Major Valleys and Plains 21
Major Lakes 22
Major Rivers 22
Average Temperature and Humidity in Port-au-Prince . . . 23

Chapter 3

HISTORY 24
Important Dates in Haitian History
  500 Years of History (1492-1992) 25
The Founding Fathers of Haiti 59
Act of Independence of Haiti
  January 1, 1804 - English Translation 66
National Anthem of Haiti - English Translation 67
Constitutions 69
Rulers and Heads of Government of Haiti 70

Chapter 4

PEOPLE AND PLACES **74**
Population by Cities   75
Historical Sites   79
Holidays   84

Chapter 5

LITERATURE AND ARTS **87**
Haitian Literature   88
Noted Haitian Artists 107

Chapter 6

LANGUAGE **123**
Creole Expressions 124
Creole-English Lexicon 128
English-Creole Lexicon 131
Selected Haitian Proverbs in Creole 142

Chapter 7

ECONOMICS **156**
Major Banks 157
Currency and Exchange Rate 159
Sample of Monthly Salaries in Haiti 162
Flows of Direct and Fixed Investments in Haiti 163

Chapter 8

GOVERNMENT **164**
Administrative Structure of the
   Republic of Haiti   165
Foreigners and the Republic of Haiti   171
Constitution of the Republic of Haiti
   March 29, 1987 - English Translation   173

Chapter 9

SELECTED BIBLIOGRAPHY ON HAITI **256**
General Reference   257
French   258
English   274

Appendices

APPENDIX 1
Acte de l'Indépendance d'Haïti   283
APPENDIX 2
L'Hymne National de la République d'Haïti
         La Dessalinienne   284
APPENDIX 3
Constitution de la République d'Haïti
   29 Mars 1987   285

SOURCES **369**

INDEX **374**

Haiti: A Basic Reference Book

VERTIÈRES – Monument to the heroes of independence.

COUNTRY SYNOPSIS 1

History of Name / 2

Climate / 3

Population / 4

Haitian Representation in
Foreign Countries / 6

Foreign Diplomatic Missions
Accredited to Haiti / 6

Private Development Organizations / 7

Principal Political Parties / 7

International Organizations
Represented in Haiti / 8

Exchange Rate / 9

Haitian Music / 11

Official Designation:	République d'Haïti (Republic of Haiti)

History of Name:

Haïti - (Short form name) (1804 to present)
Designation adopted by the blacks and mulattoes who modified the spelling of the original name, Ayiti, in order to symbolize a new era and to break away from the slavery period, after winning their independence from France in 1804.

Saint-Domingue (1697 to 1803)
Name given by the French settlers to the western area (Haiti) of the island of Hispaniola.

Española (1492 to 1696)
Named Española, meaning "Little Spain," by Christopher Columbus, in honor of the Spanish crown. Hispaniola is now internationally used to designate the island which is divided between the Republic of Haiti and the Dominican Republic.

Ancient names: Ayiti, Quisqueya, Bohio
Names given by the original inhabitants who occupied the island before Christopher Columbus. Ayiti means "mountainous land" in the language of the inhabitants of the island. Quisqueya, means "big land" to the natives of the islands surrounding Ayiti. Bohio means "rich in villages." AYTI (or Ayiti) is composed of three roots: "A" meaning flower; "Y" meaning high; TI meaning land or region. AYTI hence means "flower of high land" or "mountainous land" or "land of high mountains."

When Christopher Columbus discovered Ayiti, it was inhabited by the Carib tribe and Tainos of the Arawak tribe. It was also divided into five kingdoms named *Caciquats*: Magua, Marien, Xaragua, Maguana, and Higuey.

Location:	Haiti occupies the western third of the island of Hispaniola in the Caribbean Sea, bound by the Atlantic Ocean on the northern coast and the Caribbean sea on the western and southern shores. Haiti is located between 18° and 20°6 north in latitude, and between 71°58 and 74°30 west in longitude. It is 1h40 minutes flight distance from Miami, USA, 3 hours from Montreal, Canada, and 10 hours from Paris, France.
Total Area:	27,750 sq.km. (10,714 sq.mi.) including the surrounding islands totalling 950 sq.km. comprised of La Gonâve, La Tortue, Les Cayemittes, L'Ile à Vache, La Navase and La Grande Caye. The Republic of Haiti is slightly smaller than Belgium (30,513 sq.km./11,781 sq.mi.), slightly larger than Israel (21,475 sq.km./8,291 sq.mi.) and approximately the size of the state of Maryland (27,091 sq.km./10,460 sq.mi.). Hispaniola (76,484 sq.km./29,530 sq.mi.) is the second largest of the Caribbean Islands.
Topography:	75% mountainous - 21,000 sq.km. of mountains up to 2,680 meters high and 6,750 sq.km. of flat lands.
Climate:	The climate is tropical, semiarid, with two thermal seasons in the year, and temperatures ranging between 70°F-90°F (20°C-30°C). The hot season lasts from March to November with the temperatures at their highest between July and August. The cool season is between December and February. The temperature becomes progressively cooler with elevation in the mountain region. The dry months are December through March. Mountains in the east cut off the trade winds. Frequent thunderstorms occur between May and November but seldom last longer than an hour or two, mostly in the evening.

Population:	6,624,896 (1991) 6,763,745 (1992) 6,902,594 (1993) Rural 65% Urban 25% Overseas 10% Year 2000 estimates: 8 million people The population is approximately 48.5% male and 51.5% female.

Haiti has a young population, with nearly 60% below 25 years of age:

Age range	%
0 - 4 years	14.40
5 - 14 "	24.80
15 - 24 "	19.20
25 - 64 "	35.70
65 + "	5.90

Population Density:	178 people/km2
Population Growth:	1.7% annual (1991)
Capital:	Port-au-Prince: 750,693 (1992)
Major Cities:	Cap-Haïtien: 92,021; Gonaïves: 53,094; Les Cayes: 42,334; Saint-Marc: 41,028; Jérémie: 24,596; Port-de-Paix: 23,246; Desdunes: 14,602; Jacmel: 14,456; Hinche: 11,180; Petite Rivière de l'Artibonite: 11,143.
Independence Date:	January 1, 1804 (from France)

National Slogan:	Liberty, Equality, Fraternity
National Anthem:	"La Dessalinienne" (Song of Dessalines)
National Flag:	Blue and red equally halved horizontally, with the blue on the top and red underneath, exhibiting the Haitian coat of arms in a white square center panel.
National Emblem:	The coat of arms which contains the tree of freedom, a palm, topped by a phrygian cap as emblem of liberty, flanked by flags and two cannons above a scroll bearing the motto: L'UNION FAIT LA FORCE (Unity Makes Strength).
National Calendar:	Gregorian
Ethnic Groups:	Western African descent-95%; Mulatto and European descent-5%
Religion:	Roman Catholic-80%, Protestant-16% (Baptist-10%, Pentecostal-4%, Adventist-1%, other-1%) none-1%, other-3% (1982). Voodoo is also practiced and nationally recognized as a religion in Haiti.
Language:	French is the official language. Creole is spoken throughout the nation.
Literacy Rate:	25%
Higher Education:	The government-controlled State University of Haiti was founded in 1944.

Type of Government:	Republic
Constitution Date:	March 29, 1987
Suffrage:	Universal at age 18
Fiscal Year:	October 1 to September 30

Haitian Representation in Foreign Countries:

Caribbean: Santo Domingo, Nassau, San Juan (Puerto Rico)

North America: Ottawa, Canada; Mexico City, Mexico; Washington D.C.; Haitian Consulates in New York, Los Angeles, San Francisco, Boston, Chicago, Denver, Atlanta, New Orleans, Detroit, Philadelphia, Miami.

Central and South America: Bogotá, Brasília, Lima, Buenos Aires, Caracas, Panama City, Santiago

Europe: Paris, Bonn, Brussels, Vatican City, London, Madrid, and Rome

West Africa: Dakar
East Asia: Tokyo, Seoul
Middle East: Tel Aviv

Foreign Diplomatic Missions Accredited to Haiti:

Embassy of the United States of America, Embassy of France, Embassy of Argentina, Embassy of Spain, Embassy of Israel, Embassy of Italy, Embassy of China, Embassy of Colombia, Embassy of Honduras, Embassy of Germany, Embassy of Korea, Embassy of Liberia, Embassy of Mexico, Embassy of Panama, Embassy of Peru, Embassy of El Salvador, Embassy of Venezuela, Embassy of Brazil, Embassy of Canada, Embassy of Japan, Embassy of the Dominican Republic, Embassy of Chile, Embassy of Ecuador.

Private Development Organizations:

For more than 40 years, numerous private institutions have been engaged in social and economic development in Haiti. These organizations are called (O.N.G.) *Organisations non Gouvernementales;* 400 of them are recorded and 153 are licensed by the Haitian government.

Some of these private organizations are:
Cooperative for American Relief Everywhere (CARE); *l'Organisation Catholique Canadienne pour le Développement et la Paix* (The Canadian Catholic Organization for Development and Peace); *l'Agence Canadienne de Développement International (ACDI)* (The Canadian Agency for International Development); *Le Fonds Français d'Aide et de Coopération (FAC)* (French Funds for Help and Cooperation); *Le Programme Alimentaire Mondial (PAM)* (World Food Program); Haitian American Community Help Organization (HACHO); Church World Service (CWS); Catholic Relief Service.

Principal Political Parties:

Mouvement pour l'Instauration de la Démocratie en Haiti (MIDH)
Movement for the Installation of Democracy in Haiti

Parti Agricole et Industriel National (PAIN)
National Agricultural and Industrial Party

Front National pour le Changement et la Démocratie (FNCD)
National Front for Change and Democracy

Rassemblement des Démocrates Progressistes Nationaux (RDPN)
National Progressive Democrats Rally

Parti Démocrate Chrétien Haitien (PDCH)
Haitian Christian Democratic Party

Mobilisation pour le Développement National (MDN)
Movement for National Development

Parti Social Chrétien d'Haïti (PSCH)
Social Christian Party of Haiti

Mouvement d'Organisation du Pays (MOP)
Movement for the Organization of the Country

Parti Nationaliste Progressiste Révolutionnaire (PANPRA)
Progressive Nationalist Revolutionary Party

Alliance Nationale pour la Démocratie et Progrès (ANDP)
National Alliance for Democracy and Progress

Mouvement de Reconstruction Nationale (MRN)
Movement for National Reconstruction

Union pour la Réconciliation Nationale (URN)
Union for National Reconciliation

Front National de Concertation (FNC)
National Front for Concerted Action

Mouvement pour le Développement Economique d'Haïti. (MDEH)
Movement for the Economic Development of Haiti

Parti Unifié Communiste Haïtien (PUCH)
Unified Haitian Communist Party

International Organizations Represented in Haiti:
The United Nations and some of its specialized Agencies maintain resident representatives in Haiti:
The Organization of American States (OAS)
The Inter-American Development Bank (IDB)
The United Nations Development Program (UNDP)
The International Monetary Fund (IMF)

United Nations International Children's Emergency Fund (UNICEF)

United Nations Educational, Scientific, and Cultural Organization (UNESCO)

International Bank for Reconstruction and Development (The World Bank)

Some International Organizations sponsor visiting missions to support development programs: U.S. Aid for International Development (USAID), The European Economic Community (EEC), World Health Organization (WHO), Food and Agriculture Organization (FAO), The Red Cross and the Salvation Army.

International Clubs: Rotary Club, Boy Scouts, Girl Scouts, Free Masons

Monetary Unit: Gourde (G)

Commonly exchangeable as G.1 = U.S.$ .20 or G.5 = U.S.$1 (since 1919)

Notes issued in denominations of 1, 5, 10, 50, 100, 250, 500 gourdes

Coins minted in denominations of 5, 10, 20, 50 cents

Exchange Rate: An economic crisis started in the 1980s causing the devaluation of the Gourde and daily fluctuation of exchange rate;

February 16, 1993: G.10.60 = U.S. $1

March 9, 1993: G. 13= U.S. $1

May 31, 1993: G. 14.65 = U.S. $1

Free Trade Zones Industrial Sites: There are four Free Trade Zones. The most important one is: **SONAPI-** Société Nationale des Parcs Industriels, located in Port-au-Prince, and owned by the government.

Minimum Wage Rates:	Port-au-Prince: G 15 - G 16.50 daily/ U.S. $3.00 - 3.30/daily Regional areas: G 13.75 - G 14.75 daily/U.S.$2.75 - 2.95/daily
Time Zone:	Haiti is at: EST (Eastern Standard Time - USA); GMT-5 (Greenwich Mean Time) November to March. EST (Eastern standard time - USA); GMT-4 April to October.
Phone Code:	To call from the U.S., dial the access code (011) plus the country code (509), plus the six-digit Haitian number.
Ports:	There are 14 seaports in Haiti. The two most important ones are Port-au-Prince and Cap-Haïtien.
Roads:	Total of 3,700 kilometers, of which 672 are paved, 927 are gravel roads, and 2,089 are mud roads.
Major Airports:	Port-au-Prince International Airport Cap-Haitian Airport
Major Trading Partners:	**Exports:** U.S., France, Canada, Japan, Dominican Republic, Italy, Belgium-Luxembourg, and West Germany. **Imports**: U.S., Japan, France, Canada, Netherlands Antilles, Venezuela, Asia and West Germany.
Imports:	Petroleum, chemicals, machinery, transportation equipment, foodstuffs, livestock, beverages, vegetable and animal fats and oils.
Exports:	Coffee, cocoa, sugar, meat, sisal, bauxite, ropes, light industrial goods and handicrafts.
Industries:	Sugar refineries, textile factory, flour mills, cement plant, rum distilleries, tourism, light assembly industries based on imported parts.

Natural Mineral Resources:	Bauxite, copper, manganese, iron, gold, nickel
Agriculture:	Coffee, mangoes, sugarcane, rice, corn, sorghum, potatoes, sweet potatoes, manioc, dry beans, coconuts, vegetables, melons, oranges, lemons, limes, avocados, bananas, plantains, cocoa beans, tobacco, and sisal.

Major Newspapers:

Le Moniteur - Government owned/weekly/Port-au-Prince
Le Matin - Founded in 1908/private/daily/Port-au-Prince
Le Nouvelliste - Founded in 1898/private/daily/Port-au-Prince
Panorama - Private/daily/Port-au-Prince
Le Septentrion - Private/daily/Cap-Haïtien
L'Union - Private/daily/Cap Haïtien

Major Radio Stations:

Radio Nationale - Government owned/AM & FM
Radio Métropole - Private/AM & FM
Radio Soleil - Catholic/AM & FM
Radio Lumière - Congregational/AM & FM
Radio Haiti Inter - Private/AM & FM
Radio Nouveau Monde - Private/AM & FM
Radio Antilles - Private/AM & FM

Major Television Networks:

Télévision Nationale d'Haiti (TNH): National Television of Haiti (Government-owned)
Télé Haïti: Cable Station with two channels in French and English (Private)
PVS Antenne 16: (Private)

Haitian Music:

Types:
Rara: Early days of Haitian music to present
Méringue: Until 1955
Cadence Rempa: Introduced by Webert Sicot (1950s)
Compas Direct: 1956-60 to present
Musique Racines: Introduced in the 1980s

Haitian Folk Instruments:
Drum, Conga (tambour), chacha, graj, vaksine or vaccines (bambou), kata, sifflet (rara music).

Architects of Haitian Music:
Frédéric Abélard, Dominique Astrée, Louis Astrée Père, Montbrun Basquiat Othello Bayard, Georges Borno, Annulysse Cadet, Lumane Casimir, Geffrard Cesvet, Albert Chancy, Max Chancy, Alain Clérié, Arthur Coupet, Julien Courtois, Michel Desgrottes, Charles Dessalines, Constantin Dumervé, Gérard Dupervil, Lyncée Duroseau, Guy Durosier, Justin Elie, Fernand Frangeul, Nicolas Geffrard, Robert Geffrard, Edner Guignard, Raoul Guillaume, Albert Granville, Nemours Jean-Baptiste, Martha Jean-Claude, Occide Jeanty Fils, Occilius Jeanty Père, Charles Laforestrie, Ludovic Lamothe, Nono Lamy, Micheline Laudun, Toureau Lechaud, Rodolphe Legros, Eugène de Lespinasse, Théramène Ménès, Mauléart Monton, Antalcidas O. Murat, Alexandre Myrtil, Christian Nohel, Ti Paris, Issa Saïeh, René Saint-Aude, Edmond Saintonge, Webert Sicot, Jean Zéphyr.

Earliest Recording Groups:
Super Jazz des Jeunes, l'Ensemble Aux Calebasses, Tropicana, Les Ambassadeurs, l'Orchestre Septentrion, l'Ensemble Méridional des Cayes, Les Difficiles de Pétion Ville, Les Gypsies de Pétion Ville, Shleu-Shleu, Skah Shah, Ibo Combo, D.P. Express, Scorpio, Tabou Combo, Les Frères Déjean, Coupé Cloué, Magnum Band, Bossa Combo, Caribbean Sextét, System Band.

Selected Popular Haitian Dishes:

Bananes Pesées: Fried green plantains.

Grillot: Fried marinated pork, served with a very spicy sauce called "sauce ti malice."

Lambi: Conch meat found inside the sea shells served grilled or boiled.

Riz Djon-djon: Rice with a special kind of local black mushrooms.

Riz National: Mixed rice and red kidney beans.

Salaise: Dried beef served with avocado and plantain.

Sauce Ti Malice: Spicy sauce, made of lemon, sour orange, salt, red pepper, several other spices and seasoning.

Tassot: Goat meat dried under the sun, then marinated before being grilled.

Pain Patate: Sweet potato pudding.

Beverages:

Colas: Soft drinks bottled by local companies, with artificial color of tropical fruit flavors.

Prestige: Local Haitian beer.

Crémasse: Typical Haitian drink during holidays, made of condensed milk and rum or alcohol.

Rhum Barbancourt: Local Haitian rum made of sugar cane.

Sellé-Bridé: Liquor of sweet rum but spicy.

Tafia or Clairin: White brut rum.

GEOGRAPHY 2

Territorial Divisions of Haiti / 15

Surrounding Islands / 20

Highest Mountains / 20

Major Valleys and Plains / 21

Major Lakes / 22

Major Rivers / 22

Average Temperature and Humidity
in Port-au-Prince / 23

Territorial Divisions of Haiti

Haiti is divided into nine Administrative Regions (Départements), 41 Districts (Arrondissements), and 132 Urban Centers (Communes).

The **Urban Center (Commune),** which is the smallest of the territorial divisions, is comprised of the city, the suburban areas, and the rural sections. The Urban Center is autonomous and administered by a council headed by a mayor.

The **District (Arrondissement)** is made of several urban centers (communes), and the **Administrative Region (Département)** is made of several districts (arrondissements).

The nine Administrative Regions (**Départements)** are: West (Ouest), North (Nord), Northeast (Nord-Est), Northwest (Nord-Ouest), Artibonite (Artibonite), Central (Centre), Southeast (Sud-Est), South (Sud) and Grand'Anse (Grand'Anse).

Western Administrative Region
(Département de l'Ouest)
Population (1989) 2,000,000

Districts *(Arrondissements)*	*Urban Centers* *(Communes)*
1. Port-au-Prince	Port-au-Prince, Delmas, Pétionville, Kenscoff, Gressier, Carrefour.
2. Léogane	Léogane, Grand-Goâve, Petit-Goâve.
3. Croix-des-Bouquets	Croix-des-Bouquets, Thomazeau, Ganthier, Fonds Verrettes, Cornillon.
4. Arcahaie	Arcahaie, Cabaret.
5. La Gonâve	Anse-à-Galets, Pointe-à-Raquette.

Northern Administrative Region
(Département du Nord)
Population (1989) 594,509

Districts *(Arrondissements)*	*Urban Centers* *(Communes)*
1. Cap-Haïtien	Cap-Haïtien, Limonade, Quartier-Morin.
2. Acul du Nord	Acul du Nord, Plaine du Nord, Milot.
3. Grande Rivière du Nord	Grande Rivière du Nord, Bahon.
4. St Raphaël	St Raphaël, Dondon, Ranquitte, La Victoire, Pignon.
5. Plaisance	Plaisance, Pilate.
6. Limbé	Limbé, Bas-Limbé.
7. Borgne	Borgne, Port-Margot.

Northeastern Administrative Region
(Département du Nord-Est)
Population (1989) 315,002

Districts *(Arrondissements)*	*Urban Centers* *(Communes)*
1. Fort-Liberté	Fort-Liberté, Ferrier, Les Perches.
2. Trou-du-Nord	Trou-du-Nord, Caracol, Sainte Suzanne, Terrier-Rouge.
3. Vallières	Vallières, Carice, Mombin-Crochu.
4. Ouanaminthe	Ouanaminthe, Capotille, Mont Organisé.

Northwestern Administrative Region
(Département du Nord-Ouest)
Population (1989) 315,002

Districts (Arrondissements)	Urban Centers (Communes)
1. Port-de-Paix	Port-de-Paix, La Tortue, Bassin Bleu, Chansolme.
2. Môle St-Nicolas	Môle St-Nicolas, Jean-Rabel, Bombardopolis, Baie-de-Henne.
3. St-Louis du Nord	St-Louis du Nord, Anse-à-Foleur.

Artibonite Administrative Region
(Département de l'Artibonite)
Population (1989) 777,119

Districts (Arrondissements)	Urban Centers (Communes)
1. Gonaïves	Gonaïves, Ennery.
2. Gros-Morne	Gros-Morne, Terre Neuve, Anse Rouge.
3. St-Marc	St-Marc, Verrettes, La Chapelle.
4. Dessalines	Dessalines, Petite-Rivière de l'Artibonite, Grande-Saline, Desdunes.
5. Marmelade	St-Michel de l'Attalaye and Marmelade.

Central Administrative Region
(Département du Centre)
Population (1989) 380,267

Districts *(Arrondissements)*	*Urban Centers* *(Communes)*
1. Hinche	Hinche, Maissade, Thomonde, Cerca Carvajal.
2. Mirebalais	Mirebalais, Saut-d'Eau, Boucan Carré.
3. Lascahobas	Lascahobas, Belladère, Savanette.
4. Cerca-La-Source	Cerca-La-Source, Thomassique.

Southeastern Administrative Region
(Département du Sud-Est)
Population (1989) 377,015

Districts *(Arrondissements)*	*Urban Centers* *(Communes)*
1. Jacmel	Jacmel, Marigot, Cayes-Jacmel, La Vallée.
2. Bainet	Bainet, Côtes-de-Fer.
3. Belle Anse	Belle Anse, Grand-Gosier, Anse-à-Pitres, Thiotte.

Southern Administrative Region
(Département du Sud)
Population (1989) 521,647

Districts (Arrondissements)	Urban Centers (Communes)
1. Les Cayes	Les Cayes, Torbeck, Chantal, Camp-Perrin, Maniche, Ile à Vache.
2. Port-Salut	Port-Salut, St-Jean du Sud, Arniquet.
3. Aquin	Aquin, St-Louis du Sud, Cavaillon.
4. Côteaux	Côteaux, Port-à-Piment du Sud, Roche-à-Bateau.
5. Chardonnières	Chardonnières, Les Anglais, Tiburon.

Grand'Anse Administrative Region
(Département de la Grand'Anse)
Population (1989) 510,168

Districts (Arrondissements)	Urban Centers (Communes)
1. Jérémie	Jérémie, Abricots, Bonbon, Moron, Chambellan.
2. Anse d'Hainault	Anse d'Hainault, Dame-Marie, Les Irois.
3. Miragoâne	Miragoâne, Petite Rivière de Nippes.
4. Anse à Veau	Anse à Veau, Petit-Trou de Nippes, Baradères, L'Azile.
5. Corail	Corail, Roseaux, Pestel, Beaumont.

Surrounding Islands

The surrounding islands that belong to the Republic of Haiti:

1. **La Gonâve:** (658 sq.km.), located in the gulf of the same name in the western region of Haiti.

2. **La Tortue:** (180 sq.km.), located in the northwest region of Haiti.

3. **L'Ile à Vache:** (52 sq.km.), located at the entrance of bay of Cayes in the southern region of Haiti.

4. **Les Cayemittes:** (45 sq.km.), located in the southwest region of Haiti.

5. **La Navase:** (3 1/2 sq.km.), located west of the south coast of Haiti.

Highest Mountains

Morne La Selle (Western Region)
2,680 meters / 8,793 ft.

Morne Macaya (Southern Region)
2,347 meters / 7,700 ft.

Morne du Cibao (Western Region)
2,280 meters / 7,480 ft.

Morne Bois-Pin (Western Region)
2,235 meters / 7,333 ft.

Major Valleys and Plains

Plains & Valleys	Area Hectares	Square Kilometers	Square Miles
Plateau Central	217,600	2,170	840.15
Plaine de l'Artibonite	80,000	800	308.88
Plains and valleys of surrounding islands	71,300	713	275.29
Plaines du Nord & de Fort-Liberté	38,100	381	147.10
Plaine du Cul-de-Sac	37,000	370	142.85
Plaine du Nord-Ouest	30,000	300	115.83
Plaines des Cayes & de Torbeck	20,000	200	77.22
Plaines de la Grand' Anse & des Abricots	18,500	185	71.43
Plaines des Gonaïves & de Savane Désolée	16,000	160	61.77
Plaine de Léogane	10,500	105	40.54
Plaine de l'Arcahaie	10,000	100	38.61
Plaine de Nippes	10,000	100	38.61
Plaines de Limbé & de Port-Margot	9,000	90	34.75
Plaines des Moustiques, Port-de-Paix & Anse-à-Foleur	8,000	80	30.89
Plaines de Côteaux, les Anglais, Irois	6,500	65	25.00
Plaines de Rochelois, Fonds-des-Nègres, l'Asile	6,200	62	23.94
Vallée de Saut-d'Eau de Mirebalais	6,000	60	23.16
Plaines de Saint-Marc & Montrouis	5,800	58	22.39
Plaines d'Aquin & Côtes-de-Fer	5,000	50	19.30
Plaines de Petit-Goâve & Grand-Goâve	4,500	45	17.37

Major Lakes

Lake Azuei or Etang Saumâtre: (170 sq.km.) is located at the eastern extreme of the Cul-de-Sac Valley. It is 22 km long and 12 km wide.

Lake of Miragoâne: (25 sq.km.) is located at one kilometer southeast of the city of Miragoâne. Its length is 12 km.

Trou Caïman: (Approximately 16 sq.km.), this small lake is located east of the northern part of the Cul-de-Sac Valley. It is 9 km long and 3 km wide.

Major Rivers

	Flow *Cubic / Second*
Artibonite	84.0
Rivière de la Grand'Anse	12.0
Rivière de Cavaillon	8.0
Trois Rivières	6.5
Rivière Momance	6.4
Rivière du Limbé	5.6
Grande Rivière du Nord	5.4
Grande Rivière du Sud	3.9
Rivière du Cul-de-Sac	3.9
Rivière de l'Estère	3.1

Average Temperature and Humidity in Port-Au-Prince

TABLE 1
AVERAGE TEMPERATURE
Port-au-Prince and surrounding areas:
Based on a 10-year period
Degrees Fahrenheit

Average	Jan	Feb	Mar	Apr	May	Jun	Jul	Aug	Sep	Oct	Nov	Dec
Highest	87	88	89	89	90	93	94	93	91	90	88	87
Lowest	68	68	69	71	72	73	74	73	73	72	71	69

TABLE 2
AVERAGE HUMIDITY IN PORT-AU-PRINCE IN %

Average	Jan	Feb	Mar	Apr	May	Jun	Jul	Aug	Sep	Oct	Nov	Dec
Highest	63	66	63	66	71	67	63	65	66	74	67	65
Lowest	57	56	58	60	63	60	58	59	63	60	59	53

HISTORY   3

Important Dates in Haitian History
500 Years of History (1492-1992) / 25

The Founding Fathers / 59

Act of Independence of Haiti / 66

National Anthem of Haiti / 67

Constitutions / 69

Rulers and Heads of Government
of Haiti / 70

Important Dates in Haitian History
500 Years of History (1492 - 1992)

1492

December 6

Christopher Columbus discovers the island named Ayiti, inhabited by Tainos and Caribs. He sails to the northwestern end of the island, now known as "Môle St-Nicolas," takes possession of it on behalf of the Spanish Crown and names it Española (now Hispaniola), which means "Little Spain." The island of Hispaniola is divided today between the Republic of Haiti in the west and the Dominican Republic in the east.

December 24

Columbus' flagship, the Santa María, runs onto a coral reef and is wrecked on the northeastern coast of Haiti.

1503

The first Africans are brought to Hispaniola for labor as the native succumb under the harsh Spanish treatment.

1508

Ferdinand V, King of Spain, officially establishes the African slave trade.

1528

Don Sebastián Ramirez de Fuente arrives in Hispaniola and is made the first Catholic bishop of the island.

1625

The first French settlers come ashore the northwest coast of Hispaniola and begin to settle there and on Tortuga, the adjacent island. They rename the colony "Saint-Domingue" and gradually extend French control. Meanwhile, almost all the original natives perish.

1665

French settlers establish the city of Port-de-Paix on the northwest coast of St-Domingue.

1670

Louis XIV of France authorizes the African slave trade in St-Domingue.

1685

The Black Code, *Code Noir*, which regulates and legalizes slavery in St-Domingue is enacted by the French Crown.

1697

The Treaty of Ryswick is signed in Europe. By this treaty, Spain recognizes French occupation of the western third of the island and agrees to cede it to the French Crown. The flourishing French colony of St-Domingue is officially born.

1743

François Dominique Toussaint Louverture is born on the plantation of Bréda located on the northern region of Saint-Domingue. He will later be known as the "Liberator of the Slaves" and the "Architect of Haitian Independence."

1749

November 26
     The city of Port-au-Prince is founded and officially declared to be the capital of the colony by the King of France. Its founder, Charles Brunier, Marquis of Larnage, Governor-General of Saint-Domingue from 1737 to 1746, relentlessly toiled to design and construct the city as the capital. It is named after the vessel *Prince*, which came ashore

at a gulf on the western region of Saint-Domingue. The natural and very convenient harbor was first called Port-du-Prince after the vessel.

1751-1757

Mackandal, a legendary maroon slave, organizes several rebellions in the northern region of St-Domingue.

1757

Henri Christophe is born on the British-held island of Grenada. He will be known as the great visionary of the Haitian civilization.

1758

Mackandal, the rebellious slave, is captured and executed in the public square of Cap-Français in the northern region of St-Domingue.

Jean-Jacques Dessalines, the Founder of the Haitian Nation, is born in the northern region of St-Domingue.

1776

Louis Boisrond-Tonnerre, the author of the Haitian Act of Independence, is born.

1778

A group of slave army volunteers leave St-Domingue for Savannah, Georgia, under the command of the French admiral, Count d'Estaing, to help in the United States War of Independence.

1789-1790

Ideas of the French Revolution, of the Declaration of Human Rights and of Liberty and Equality begin to spread in St-Domingue.

1791

February 25

Vincent Ogé and Jean-Baptiste Chavannes, two mulattoes who fought for equal political rights with the whites on behalf of the *Affranchis* (mulattoes and free blacks) in the colony, are executed. After unsuccessful attempts to obtain their claim through diplomatic means, they resort to force by leading several slaves to revolt and arming four hundred *Affranchis* against the colonial government. They are defeated by the colonial army and condemned to torture of wheels in the public square of Cap Français.

August 7

An important number of *Affranchis* (mulattoes and free blacks) gather at St. Louis of Mirebalais Church (Central Region) to discuss their political action. They demand equal political rights with the whites and create a committee of forty members: Council of the District Representatives, *Conseil des Représentants de la Commune*. The President of the committee is the mulatto Pinchinat.

August 14 - 15 (night)

The rebellious slave leader Boukman organizes the Bois-Caïman ceremony during which hundreds of slaves swear to die for their liberty.

August 20

Hundreds of *Affranchis* or freed people and three hundred slaves named "the Suisses" gather at the Diègue Habitation, located within a short distance from Port-au-Prince, to fight the white resistance and to win their political rights. The *Affranchis* win the battle called the Battle of Pernier. The slaves will later be abandoned by the *Affranchis*, and some of them deported and assassinated by the whites.

August 22

Slave leaders Boukman, Jean-François, Jeannot and Biassou conduct a major revolt in which Boukman is killed.

September 24

The Concordat of Damiens (Damiens' Agreement) through which the whites grant political rights to the *Affranchis* is signed.

End of November

The First Civil Commission arrives from France into the Colony. It is made up of three members: Roume, Mirbeck and Saint-Léger. The commissioners land at the city of Cap Français with the mission to evaluate the political situation and re-establish peace and order.

1792

September 18

The Second Civil Commission arrives in Cap-Français with the mission to execute the law of April 4, 1492 which grants political rights to all *Affranchis*. The Second Civil Commission is composed of Sonthonax, Polvérel and Ailhaud.

1793

April 12, 13

The authorities of the Second Civil Commission and the *Affranchis* lead an attack against the whites of the colony to force them to support the implementation of the Law of April 4, 1492 which grants to all *Affranchis* political equality with the whites of the colony. The armed forces of the Second Civil Commission win the attack.

Toussaint Louverture offers his services to the Spanish Crown.

June 20, 21

Galbaud, a white planter, revolts against the authority of the Second Civil Commission and is defeated by the colonial army.

Henri Christophe is promoted to the rank of captain of the French colonial armed forces. British troops land in St-Domingue.

End of June
> Toussaint Louverture captures the city of Dondon for Spain.

August 13
> Toussaint Louverture defeats the French general, Desfourneaux, at Ennery.

August 29
> Sonthonax, the head of the French Second Civil Commission, proclaims the abolition of slavery in the northern region of St-Domingue. This declaration is not officially approved by the French government.

December 6
> Toussaint Louverture seizes Gonaïves for Spain and later becomes Lieutenant-General of the colonial army of Spain.

1794

February 4
> The French National Convention officially declares the abolition of slavery in all the French colonies.

May
> Toussaint Louverture leaves the Spanish camp to join the French troops.

June 1
> After a weak resistance by Colonel Montbrun, Port-au-Prince falls to the English.

October 21
> Toussaint Louverture captures the cities of Saint-Michel and Saint-Raphaël for France.

1795

October 13
> Toussaint Louverture takes Dondon for France.

October 14

The Treaty of Bâle of July 22, 1795 is ratified in St-Domingue. Through this treaty, Spain departs from the coalition against the French and surrenders the eastern section of Hispaniola to France.

1796

March 30

The Villatte Revolt (*l'Affaire Villatte*). Toussaint Louverture rescues the French commander Laveaux from the mulatto Villatte, an insurrectionist of the city of Cap Français. To show his gratitude, Laveaux appoints Toussaint Louverture as the Lieutenant-Governor of Saint-Domingue.

May 11

The Third Civil Commission arrives in St-Domingue. The members are Sonthonax, Roume, Giraud, Leblanc, and Julien Raymond. The Commission was sent by the French government with the goal of establishing diplomatic relations between the colony and France.

1797

May 1

Sonthonax appoints Toussaint Louverture as Commander-in-Chief of the French armed forces of St-Domingue.

1798

April 20

General Hédouville, delegate of the French government, arrives in the city of Cap-Français with the mission of pruning the ambitions of Toussaint Louverture.

August 31

The British general, Maitland, signs negotiations with Toussaint Louverture to surrender the troops under his command and evacuate the Môle Saint-Nicolas.

1799

January 12

> During a meeting in Port-au-Prince between Toussaint Louverture and the other generals of the colony—Rigaud, Bauvais and Laplume—Toussaint Louverture is recognized as the commander, and Rigaud relinquishes control of the southern cities of Léogâne, Grand-Goâve, Petit-Goâve and Miragoâne.

1801

January 27

> Toussaint Louverture invades the Spanish section of the island of Hispaniola, victoriously enters Santo Domingo, and proclaims liberty for all slaves. He appoints a Central Assembly of ten members to issue a constitution that makes him Governor for Life.

July 8

> The Constitution of 1801, which bestows to Toussaint Louverture the title of Governor General for Life of St-Domingue, is promulgated.

1802

January 29

> Napoleon Bonaparte sends an expeditionary fleet to St-Domingue under the command of his brother-in-law, General Leclerc. The fleet anchors in Samana Bay with the mission to defeat the black generals and restore slavery.

February 1

> French vessels arrive off the harbor of Cap-Français.

February 4

> Henri Christophe sets Cap-Français on fire to resist against the French troops.

February 23

> Toussaint Louverture is defeated at the Battle of Ravine à Couleuvres by the army of Napoleon.

March 11

To resist French invasion at the Battle of La Crête-à-Pierrot, Dessalines gathers his troops. Then by swaying a lighted torch near the powder magazine he fiercely declares that he would blow up the fortress should the French troops invade it.

End of March

Toussaint Louverture is defeated by the army of Napoleon.

May 6

Toussaint Louverture arrives in the city of Cap to surrender to the French army and to negotiate his submission.

June 7

Toussaint Louverture is arrested through treachery by the French general, Leclerc. He is first embarked on the vessel *La Créole*, then sent to France on the vessel *Le Héros*. He is incarcerated in the jail of Fort de Joux, located in the apex of the icy Jura mountains of France.

October 13

Jean-Jacques Dessalines and Alexandre Pétion meet in the Haut-du-Cap to organize the independence war under the command of the appointed Commander-in-Chief Dessalines.

November 1-2 (night)

The French general, Leclerc, brother-in-law of Napoleon, dies of yellow fever in St-Domingue. His remains are sent back to France.

1803

April 7

Approaching his 60th birthday, Toussaint Louverture dies of ill treatment in France, in the Fort de Joux prison.

May 18

The Haitian flag is created at l'Arcahaie during a meeting between Dessalines and Pétion. They tear off the white middle section of the blue, white and red French flag and join the blue and red pieces symbolizing the unity of blacks and mulattoes. The flag is sewn by Catherine Flon.

November 18

The Battle of Vertières, the final battle for independence. Blacks and mulattoes led by Dessalines and Pétion defeat the army of Napoleon Bonaparte and win the war for independence.

November 19

Rochambeau, the French general succeeding Leclerc, signs a convention to surrender his troops and evacuate St-Domingue.

November 29

Dessalines arrives triumphantly in the city of Cap with his army. Christophe and Clerveaux issue a preliminary proclamation of independence. Rochambeau is prisoner of the British.

December 4

The French army cedes Môle Saint-Nicolas to the army of Dessalines. The fight for independence of the colony is officially terminated.

1804

January 1

Dessalines officially proclaims the independence of the colony in the city of Gonaïves and becomes Governor-General. To expunge the era of slavery in St-Domingue, he renames it with its original name: Haiti. Haiti, the second country to win independence in the American continent is the first Black Nation of the New World and the first Black Republic of the World.

September 22

Upon recommendations of his advisors, Dessalines proclaims himself Emperor of Haiti.

October 6

Dessalines is crowned Emperor in the city of Cap as Jacques I.

1805

May 20

Dessalines formulates the Imperial Constitution of 1805, which is the first constitution of Haiti as an independent country.

1806

October 17

Dessalines is assassinated at Pont-Rouge by disaffected leaders of his administration. He is remembered as the Father of the Haitian Nation.

December 27-28

In the old cathedral of Port-au-Prince, a new Constitution is promulgated by the Constituent Assembly, and Henri Christophe is appointed President of the Republic of Haiti for four years.

1807

January 1

Battle of Sibert. Henri Christophe provokes a civil war against Alexandre Pétion at Sibert. Subsequently, Haiti is divided into two states: the Northern State under the leadership of Henri Christophe and the Western and Southern States under the leadership of Alexandre Pétion.

February 17

In the north region of Haiti, Henri Christophe proclaims himself President of the State of Haiti. A state council of nine members, seven generals and two civilians, chosen by Henri Christophe, meets in the city of Cap-Haïtien and votes the Constitutional Act of Haiti. The first Haitian coins are minted in Cap-Haïtien, by the government of Henri Christophe.

March 9

Alexandre Pétion is elected President of the Republic of Haïti of the Western and Southern regions by the Constituent Assembly under the 1806 Constitution.

1809

Louis XVIII, King of France, sends a mission to Haiti to negotiate acknowledgment of Haiti's independence by France. One member, Dauxion-Lavaysse, meets with Pétion who defends the value of the independence for Haitians but agrees to a reasonable indemnity payable to the dispossessed French planters who fled to France after the independence.

1811

March 9

Alexandre Pétion is re-elected President of Haiti for four more years.

March 26

Henri Christophe proclaims himself King of the Kingdom of Haiti, as Henri I.

May 28

The Royal Constitution of Henri I in the Northern Region of Haiti is promulgated.

June 2

Henri Christophe is crowned King in Cap-Haïtien as Henri I.

1812

February 24

A special and advanced civil code named Henri Code is promulgated by Henri Christophe in the Northern State.

1814

November

Franco de Medina, a member of the mission sent by Louis XVIII, King of France, to negotiate the independence of Haiti, is delegated to Henri Christophe who strongly makes it clear that he will not negotiate.

1816

June 2

A new Republican Constitution is promulgated by Alexandre Pétion.

October 8

Another French mission sent by Louis XVIII of France arrives in the new Republic of Haiti to continue the negotiation of the recognition of independence by France. Pétion gives them the message that Haiti is independent and free, and there should not be any further negotiations. Christophe declines to meet them.

1818

March 29

Alexandre Pétion dies of fatigue, sadness, and of a persistent fever. He is the first President of Haiti and the Founder of the Republic of Haiti.

March 30

Jean-Pierre Boyer is appointed President for Life of Haiti. Born in 1775, he was the secretary of Alexandre Pétion, then was promoted to be the Chief of the Presidential Guard.

1820

October 8

After collapsing from a stroke in August, which left him paralyzed, King Henri Christophe commits suicide in his palace with a silver bullet, after being informed of the rebellion of his army. He is buried at the Citadel bearing his name. He is remembered as one of the heroes of the independence and the Haitian genius of all time.

October 26

Boyer is acclaimed in the northern city of Cap-Haïtien and promulgates the Republican Constitution.

1822

February 9

President Boyer arrives in Santo Domingo and unifies the island of Hispaniola (Haiti and Dominican Republic), which he will govern for 21 years.

1825

April 17

Charles X, King of France, brother of the deceased Louis XVIII, signs an ordinance in which he conditionally recognizes the independence of Haiti. He imposes on the Haitian government an indemnity of 150 million francs that Haiti should pay to France to compensate the French Planters expelled in 1804.

July 3

A squadron of fourteen ships of war headed by Baron Mackau, delegate of Charles X, arrives at the bay of La Gonâve. Mackau meets with Boyer and delivers the Ordinance of Charles X. It will take almost one hundred years for the Haitian government to liquidate this burdensome debt.

1831

September 22

President Boyer lays the base of Pétionville, a city dedicated to Alexandre Pétion and, a suburb of Port-au-Prince.

1838

The remaining debt of independence of 120 million francs is reduced to 60 million to be paid in equal installments to the French government.

1842

May 7

An earthquake shakes the northern region of Haiti and severely damages the Sans-Souci palace and the Citadel Henri Christophe.

1843

March 13
> President Boyer is deposed and forced to exile to Paris.

September 18 to December 31
> The Constitution of 1843 is formulated by the Constituent Assembly.

December 31
> Charles Hérard Aîné, also known as Rivière Hérard, is appointed President of the Republic of Haiti.

1844

February 28
> The Dominican Republic declares its independence from Haiti.

April 4
> The peasant farmers of the southern region of Haiti, the *Piquets*, led by Jean-Jacques Acaau, demand better distribution of the land and social justice. They revolt against the government.

May 3
> The *Piquets*, overthrow Rivière Hérard who is exiled.

> Philippe Guerrier, an octogenarian, is appointed President of the Republic of Haiti.

1845

April 15-16

> President Philippe Guerrier, dies in office.
> General Jean-Louis Pierrot is appointed President through a decree of the State Council.

1846

March 1

President Jean-Louis Pierrot is overthrown and succeeded by Jean Baptiste Riché who, like his two predecessors, is over eighty years of age.

1847

Thomas Madiou, a renowned Haitian historian, publishes the first volume of his History of Haiti.

February 27

President Riché dies after a short visit to the north of Haiti.

March 1

General Faustin Soulouque is elected President of Haiti. He was a slave who took part in the rebellion of 1791. He was freed by Rigaud in 1793, and later, appointed Commander of the Commune of Plaisance.

1852

April 18

President Faustin Soulouque is crowned Emperor as Faustin I.

1858

December

General Fabre Geffrard, Duke of Tabara, defeats Emperor Faustin I.

1859

January 13

Fabre Geffrard is elected President of Haiti after defeating the troops of the Emperor Faustin I. Born on September 19, 1806, he is the son of Nicolas Geffrard, the composer of the Haitian national Anthem, *La Dessalinienne*.

1860

March 28

An agreement is signed in Rome between the Vatican and the Republic of Haiti, which divides Haiti into five dioceses: Port-au-Prince, Gonaïves, Cap-Haïtien, Port-de-Paix and Les Cayes.

1862

December 15

Dupré Barbancourt finds the procedure to make the special Haitian rum that bears his name: Rum Barbancourt. The next day the rum made of sugarcane is sold at G.1.50 ($.30) a gallon.

1865

Beaubrun Ardouin publishes *Etudes sur l'Histoire d'Haïti*, an eleven volume work on the history of Haiti.

1867-1870

Fabre Geffrard resigns as the Chief Executive of Haiti and General Sylvain Salnave is elected President of Haiti.

The Constitution of 1867 is voted.

The State Council elects a provisional government to succeed to President Sylvain Salnave who was overthrown by a group of dissidents.

Nissage Saget is elected President for four years by the National Assembly.

Demesvar Delorme publishes *Les Théoriciens au Pouvoir*, a remarkable thesis in which he supports the idea that political power should belong to the intellectual elite.

1874

Nissage Saget relinquishes the Executive seat and retires in Saint-Marc. The Constituent Assembly elects General Michel Domingue who as President promulgates the Constitution of 1874, seven years after the former Constitution of 1867.

1875

January 20
President Michel Domingue signs a treaty of peace and friendship with the Dominican Republic.

1876-1879

President Michel Domingue is overthrown by disaffected members of the government and replaced by Boisrond Canal who, elected by the Constituent Assembly for four years, resigns as President of Haiti on July 17, 1879.

Lysius Félicité Salomon Jeune, a former Minister of Faustin I, is elected President of Haiti by the Constituent Assembly. He completes the payment of the Haitian independence debt to France. He also introduces a monetary reform in Haiti. During his government, Haiti is accepted in the Universal Union Postal and a submarine cable connects Haiti to the North-American continent.

1880

The Haitian Central Bank or the National Bank of Haiti is organized by President Salomon.

1882

February 5
Port-au-Prince and Haiti are dedicated to Our Lady of Perpetual Help during a mass celebrated by the Archbishop of Port-au-Prince, Jean-Marie Guilloux, in the chapel of St. Francis of Assisi of Bel Air.

1883

Oswald Durand, a noted Haitian poet, composes *Choucoune*, the famous poem set to music.

1884

Louis-Joseph Janvier publishes the striking *L'Egalité des Races*, Equality of Races, a thesis in which he vehemently defends the negro race.

1885

Anténor Firmin publishes his monumental 650 page essay on the Equality of the Human Races, and the merit of the Negro Race: *L'Egalité des Races Humaines*. This document is a response to the work of the French writer, Gobineau, *Essai sur l'Inégalité des Races Humaines*, "Essay on the Inequality of the Human Races."

1888-1889

President Salomon is overthrown. The Constituent Assembly installs a provisional government and later elects François Denys Légitime to the presidency. President Légitime keeps the presidential seat for eight months and is then overthrown and replaced by a provisional government.

The Constituent Assembly elects Florvil Hyppolite President of Haiti for seven years.

1893

Hannibal Price publishes *De la Réhabilitation de la Race Noire par la République d'Haïti*, "On the Rehabilitation of the Black Race by the Republic of Haiti." This is a work in defense of the black race and a response to Spencer Saint-John, the English diplomat who in 1884 published the offensive book on Haiti, "Hayti or the Black Republic."

1896

President Florvil Hyppolite dies of a heart attack during an expedition. General Tiresias Antoine Simon Sam is elected President for seven years.

1902

President Tiresias Antoine Simon Sam resigns and is succeeded by Nord Alexis as President of Haiti.

1904

January 1
>Haiti celebrates one hundred years of independence.

1908-1911

President Nord Alexis withdraws as Chief Executive and is replaced by Antoine Simon, appointed President by the Constituent Assembly. Two and a half years later, President Antoine Simon cedes the Presidential seat to Cincinnatus Leconte, a descendant of Dessalines.

1912

January 30
>The Haitian Federation of Soccer is created.

August 5
>The Haytian American Sugar Company (HASCO) is created as a corporate entity at Wilmington in the State of Delaware with a capital of five million dollars. Its objective was the production and sale of sugar and other related goods in Haiti and in the United States. The founders were Chs. Steinheim, John A. Christie and Franck Corpay. HASCO is one of the major Haitian industries with a high level of employment.

August 8

An explosion at three o'clock in the morning destroys the National Palace and kills President Cincinnatus Leconte and three hundred soldiers. The same day, the Constituent Assembly appoints General Tancrède Auguste President of Haiti.

1913-1915

President Tancrède Auguste dies during a visit to the northern region of Haiti. Two days later, Senator Michel Oreste is elected President of Haiti by the Constituent Assembly. He is later overthrown and followed by three presidents, Oreste Zamor, Davilmar Théodore and Vilbrun Guillaume Sam. Each holds power for a very short time and is overthrown.

1915

July 28

Three thousand U.S. Marines led by Admiral Caperton of the cruiser "George Washington" arrive in Port-au-Prince. Through this action, backed by U.S. President Woodrow Wilson, Haiti comes under the military occupation of the United States of America.

August 12

The Senator Sudre Dartiguenave is elected President by the Constituent Assembly for a term of seven years.

1919

April 12

The Haitian government undertakes a monetary reform with the National Bank of Haiti.

October 31-November 1

Charlemagne Péralte, the leader of the guerilla troop, Cacos, who stood against the United States occupation, is captured and executed.

1920

Léon Laleau publishes his first compilations of poems, *A Voix Basse.*

1921

January 24

President Dartiguenave addresses President Warren G. Harding, of the United-States, and sets forth the needs of the Haitian people.

April 12

President Harding responds to President Dartiguenave.

1922

April 10

Louis Borno is elected President of Haiti for four years by the State Council.

May 15

President Dartiguenave's term is ended.
Louis Borno is sworn in as President of Haiti.

December 28

The Agricultural School of Haiti, *Ecole Centrale d'Agriculture* in Damien is created to educate future Haitian agronomists.

1926

Louis Borno is re-elected President by the State Council, and makes a diplomatic trip to the United States.

Léon Laleau publishes his second compilation of poems, *La Flèche au Coeur.*

1928

Jean Price-Mars publishes his highly acclaimed novel, "So Spoke The Uncle," (*Ainsi Parla l'Oncle).*

Léon Laleau publishes two more compilations of poems, *Le Rayon des Jupes* and *Abréviations*.

1929

January 21

An agreement on the borders between Haiti and the Dominican Republic is signed.

1930

February 28

The Forbes Commission sent by President Hoover of the United States arrives in Haiti to investigate the political situation of the country.

April 21

Eugène Roy is designated as temporary President of the Republic by a state decree.

November 18

Senator Sténio Vincent is elected President of the Republic of Haiti for six years.

December 10

Fietta, the first Apostolic Nuncio of the Vatican to Haiti, arrives in Port-au-Prince.

1931

Jacques Roumain publishes his acclaimed novel, *Gouverneurs de la Rosée*.

August 5

The Haitian and United States of America governments agree on the concession of the Offices of Public Works, Health, Agriculture and Education to the Haitian government.

1932

December 15, 16, 17

Archbishop Joseph Legouaze commemorates the fiftieth anniversary of the dedication of Port-au-Prince to the Virgin Mary, Our Lady of Perpetual Help.

1933

August 7

The Haitian and United States governments sign an agreement on the withdrawal of U.S. troops from Haiti and the cessation of the U.S. occupation.

October 18

Presidents Vincent of Haiti and Trujillo of the Dominican Republic meet for diplomatic talks at Ouanaminthe, a city located in the northeastern region of Haiti, very close to the Frontier of Haiti and the Dominican Republic.

1934

July 5

President Franklin D. Roosevelt of the United States visits Cap-Haïtien.

August 14

The United States occupation of Haiti ends and the U.S. Marines leave Haiti.

August 21

The Haitian flag is unfurled at the Casernes Dessalines, where it was lowered in 1915, on the day of the United States occupation.

1935

May 16

A new constitution reinforces the authority of the Executive Branch of Government and warrants a new mandate to President Vincent for five years.

1938

May 18

Athletic festivities at the Champs-de-Mars take place in Port-au-Prince to celebrate the 135th anniversary of the Haitian flag.

1939-1940

The Haitian National Library, *Bibliothèque Nationale d'Haiti* is organized with the financial contribution of 116 people.

1941

April 14

Elie Lescot is elected President for a five-year term.

May 15

President Sténio Vincent's term is ended.
Elie Lescot takes office as President of Haiti.

1944

May 7

The Cathedral of Cap-Haïtien, on which restoration work took one hundred years, is consecrated.

May 14

The Art Center (*Centre d'Art*) of Haiti is founded. It exhibits the most important Haitian art works.

1946

President Lescot resigns. An Executive Military Committee is created before appointing Dumarsais Estimé as President of the Republic of Haiti.

1948

February 16

The *Régie du Tabac et des Allumettes*, a government-owned tobacco company is founded.

1949

December 8

Port-au-Prince celebrates two hundred years of its existence. The *Exposition du Bi-Centenaire,* Bicentennial Exposition is inaugurated.

1950

May 10

President Estimé relinquishes the Executive Seat and is replaced by a provisional government.

October 8

Presidential and legislative elections are held, and for the first time, the President of Haiti is elected directly by the people and by the Delegates and Senators. Colonel Paul E. Magloire wins the elections.

December 6

Paul Eugène Magloire is sworn in as President of Haiti.

1951

President Paul E. Magloire of Haiti meets with President Rafaël Leonidas Trujillo, President of the Dominican Republic, for diplomatic talks.

The Haitian Institute of Statistics *(Institut Haïtien de Statistique)* and the Haitian Institute of Farming and Industrial Credit *(Institut Haïtien de Crédit Agricole et Industriel)* are established by the government.

1953

May 31

The first Haitian bishop, Father Rémy Augustin is consecrated at the Cathedral of Port-au-Prince.

1954

January 1-4
> The 150th anniversary of Independence of Haiti is celebrated in Gonaïves and monuments for the Heroes of Independence are inaugurated in Port-au-Prince.

June 21-July 13
> President Magloire travels to Cuba, Puerto-Rico, Nicaragua and Panama.

1955

January 26-February 17
> President Magloire and his wife travel to the United States of America, Canada, and Jamaica.

March 3 to 5
> Richard Nixon, Vice President of the United States, and his wife, visit Haiti.

1956

President Paul E. Magloire relinquishes the Executive Seat to the President of the Supreme Court, Nemours Pierre-Louis, who becomes the Provisional President of Haiti.

1957

Franck Sylvain is elected President of Haiti and is later succeeded by an Executive Council of Government composed of thirteen members. Soon after Daniel Fignolé is elected President of Haiti and replaced by a Military Council of Government.

October 22
> Dr. François Duvalier is elected President of Haiti.

1964

The Duvalieriste Constitution establishing the Presidency for Life is voted by the National Assembly, and Dr. François Duvalier becomes President for Life of Haiti.

1968

October 28
> The first Haitian Archbishop, François Wolf Ligondé, is consecrated at the Cathedral of Port-au-Prince.

1971

February
> The National Assembly approves for a constitutional amendment that enables François Duvalier to name his son, Jean-Claude, as his successor.

April 21
> President for Life François Duvalier dies in Port-au-Prince.

April 22
> Jean-Claude Duvalier succeeds his father as President for Life.

1974

The National Soccer Team of Haiti for the first time participates in the World Soccer Cup game in Munich, Germany.

1977

August 15
> The U.S. Ambassador to the United Nations Commission arrives in Haiti. The commission meets with the Haitian government and discusses the improvement of civil rights in Haiti.

1980

May 27

President for Life Jean-Claude Duvalier weds Michèle Bennett.

1983

March

Pope Jean-Paul II arrives in Haiti. He is the first Pope to visit the Haitian territory.

August 27

The Constitution is amended under the Presidency of Jean-Claude Duvalier to create the title of State Minister and to allow the President to name his successor.

1985

June 6

Jean-Claude Duvalier amends the Constitution and allows the creation for a new post of Prime Minister.

July

A Referendum is held in which 99.48% of voters approve the proposition to allow political parties to participate in the government while recognizing the Presidency for Life of Jean-Claude Duvalier. This is followed by a constitutional amendment on the Presidency for Life.

November 28

Three young schoolboys are killed in Gonaïves during an anti-government demonstration. They are: Jean-Robert Cius, Daniel Israël, and Mackenson Michel.

1986

January 31

It is rumored in the capital that President Jean-Claude Duvalier had fled Haiti.

February 3

The President and members of the Cabinet visit the commercial and residential areas of the capital to convince the population that they are still in power.

February 7

Jean-Claude Duvalier flees Haiti for Talloires in France. The National Council of Government (CNG) (*Conseil National de Gouvernement*) is established. This interim Military-Civilian Government is presided by the Lieutenant General Henri Namphy as President, Colonels Williams Régala, Max Valles, Prosper Avril, and two civilians, Gérard Gourgue and Alix Cinéas, as members. The Legislative Chamber and the VSN body (*Volontaire Sécurité Nationale* - National Voluntary Security), the armed forces body of the Duvalier regime - are dissolved.

February 25

The original blue and red flag is unfurled at the National Palace replacing the black and red flag of the Duvalier regime.

Month of March

Daniel Fignolé, former President of Haiti, receives a warm welcome in Haiti. A second version of the CNG is formed with Henri Namphy, Williams Régala, and Jacques A. François.

March 20

A demonstration is conducted by more than two thousand students and public transportation drivers of the city of Carrefour against the CNG.

April 26

Fort-Dimanche is attacked by armed groups. Eight people are killed.

October 19

The CNG, which is governing Haiti under a decree without a constitution, invites the people to elect forty-one constituents to draw up the new constitution. The CNG appoints twenty more constituents to bring the total to sixty-one.

1987

March 10

The Constituent Assembly delivers the text of the Constitution to Henri Namphy, the President of the National Council of Government (*Conseil National de Gouvernement-CNG*). The text of the Constitution is written in French and Creole.

March 29

A referendum ratifies the new Constitution. Approximately 99.81% of people vote yes for a new constitution from the results of 215 voting places.

May 13

The National Council of Government (CNG) publishes a decree electing the members of the Provisional Electoral Council (*Conseil Electoral Provisoire - CEP*).

May 22

The CEP, Provisional Electoral Council (first version) proclaims itself independent from the CNG.

June 5

The CEP hands over the text of electoral law to the Minister of Justice.

July 17

The Haitian Armed Forces swears fidelity to the new 1987 Constitution during a ceremony at the Military Academy.

November 29

Election day. Disturbances occur at Ruelle Vaillant in Port-au-Prince. The elections are suspended, and the CEP is dissolved by General Henri Namphy.

December 10

General Namphy introduces a new electoral calendar and sets January 17, 1988, as the new election date. The CNG elects a new Provisional Electoral Council (CEP - *Conseil Electoral Provisoire*) second version.

1988

January 17

Election Day. Eleven candidates anxiously await the results.

January 24

Professor Leslie François Manigat wins the presidential elections with 50.29% of the votes according to the CEP.

February 7

Leslie François Manigat is inaugurated President of Haiti.

June 14

The transfer and retirement of some highly ranked officers of the army is announced by the Commander-in-Chief of the Army, Henri Namphy.

June 15

Through an announcement, newly-elected President Manigat orders the cancellation of measures of transfer and retirement of the highly ranked officials of the army as ordered by General Namphy the previous day.

June 19 (night)

A military coup against President Leslie Manigat by the army takes place.

Manigat is exiled. General Namphy immediately seizes power, appoints himself President of a Military Government, abolishes the 1987 Constitution and dissolves the Senate and Parliament.

June 20

Following the end of the Manigat administration, General Henri Namphy declares that he is the head of the Executive Power and that the government resolutions would be issued by decree.

September 17

> General Henri Namphy is ousted by a group of sergeants who replace him with General Prosper Avril as the new President of the Military Government.

1989

March 13

> The March 1987 Constitution is partially restored by General Prosper Avril.

1990

March 10

> General Prosper Avril resigns as President of the Military Government and Commander-in-Chief of the Army. Major General Herard Abraham replaces him for a voluntary period of only three days.

March 13

> Judge of the Supreme Court, Ertha Pascal Trouillot, is appointed Provisional President of Haiti. She is sworn in at the Justice Building. She is the first woman to hold this position in the history of Haiti.

March 26

> The Constitution of March 29, 1987 is re-adopted.

May 23-26

> Interim President Ertha Pascal Trouillot and a presidential delegation leave Haiti for a visit to the United States to renew Haitian-American relations.

August 7

> The United States Vice-President, Dan Quayle, visits Haiti on the invitation of the Provisional President Trouillot.

December 16

> Election Day. Jean-Bertrand Aristide, a Catholic priest, wins the presidential election with 67.5 percent of the votes. Marc Louis Bazin, the second most popular candidate, gets 14.2 percent of the votes.

1991

January 6 / 7 (night)

>An attempted coup-d'etat by Roger Lafontant, a member of the Duvalier group, fails. The 200-year old cathedral of Port-au-Prince is set on fire. The Archbishop's house and the residence of the Nuncio, the Vatican's Ambassador, are attacked by a mob.

February 7

>Jean-Bertrand Aristide is sworn in as President of Haiti for a five-year term in the presence of the National Assembly.

September 30

>A military coup against President Jean-Bertrand Aristide drives him out of Haiti. A provisional government is installed with Joseph C. Nerette, a judge of the Supreme Court, as President in accordance with the Article 149 of the Constitution. The Prime Minister appointed by the Parliament is Jean-Jacques Honorat.

October 8

>A commercial embargo against Haiti is approved by the thirty-four nations of the Organization of American States.

1992

June 4

>A new Prime Minister, Marc Louis Bazin, is elected by the Senate.

June 19

>A consent through which Joseph C. Nerette and Prime Minister Jean-Jacques Honorat retire from their functions is approved and signed at the "Villa d'Accueil" by the Provisional Government, the Ministries and the Army.

>The new elected Prime Minister, Marc Louis Bazin, officially takes office with the chief mission to continue the negotiations.

The Founding Fathers of Haiti

François Dominique Toussaint Louverture

The first hero of Haiti was born in 1743 on the Breda plantation located on the heights of Le Cap. His roots have been traced back to Africa, where his father was the son of Gaou Guinou, a king of the Aradas Tribe. As a child, he was so frail and delicate that he was not expected to live. Nevertheless, born with a natural strength of character, he hardened his body through severe and rigorous exercises such as riding and swimming. He distinguished himself so remarkably that he was made coachman, then a steward of all the livestock on the estate of his master, Bayon Libertat. As an adult, he learned to read and write with the help of his godfather, Pierre Baptiste, an old free negro. Toussaint Louverture acquired a passion for books and read the writings of famous authors such as the *Philosophical and Political History of the Indies* by a French priest, Abbé Raynald, from which he was struck by the prophecy of a black chief who would free all slaves. From that time on, Toussaint held the secret mission of breaking the chains that were holding him and his black brothers in slavery.

Determined to achieve his goal, Toussaint joined the camp of the insurgents in 1791. He fought first for the Crown of Spain, and then on the side of France. He earned the name "Louverture," which means "opening," for as a French soldier, he won several cities in St-Domingue for France by fighting against Spain and England. In 1801, he was proclaimed the Governor-for-Life of St-Domingue and declared the abolition of slavery in the colony. He administered St-Domingue with extraordinary skills and discipline, and was feared and respected by whites, mulattoes and blacks alike. He was a devout Catholic, who attempted to suppress voodoo and encourage Christian practices. In 1802, Napoleon Bonaparte sent an expeditionary fleet to restore slavery in the colony. Toussaint was defeated and arrested through treachery under the order of Napoleon who sought to restore slavery in St-Domingue. Toussaint was sent to France and jailed without judgment in the Fort de Joux prison, located in the icy mountains of that country. Incarcerated and separated from his family and friends, he died on April 7, 1803 of ill treatment, cold and humiliation.

He accomplished his greatest task of building the road to freedom for his slave brothers of St-Domingue and also by being the voice for all slaves in the American continent. He left a legacy of courage, human dignity, nobility and victory for all Haitians.

Jean-Jacques Dessalines

Born at the Cormiers Plantation north of Haiti in 1758, Dessalines was a slave on the plantation of Duclos who ran away to freedom at the age of 33. He was the principal lieutenant of Toussaint Louverture and became the General-in-Chief of the Revolution of St-Domingue after the deportation of Toussaint Louverture. He was a gifted soldier and distinguished himself during several combats, especially at the Battle of Crête-à-Pierrot. There he launched a splendid call to his soldiers and boosted their courage by leading them to blow up the fortress rather than give it up to the French. He led the indigenous army into victory over the French army of Napoleon Bonaparte in the Battle of Vertières on November 18, 1803.

On January 1, 1804, he proclaimed the independence of the colony, which he renamed Haiti. The same day he was acclaimed Governor-General-for-Life of Haiti, and on September 2, 1804 he was crowned Emperor under the name of Jacques I.

Dessalines was assassinated in a revolt on October 17, 1806 at Pont-Rouge. He is remembered as the Father of the Haitian Nation and the Founder of the Independence of Haiti.

Henri Christophe

Henri Christophe was born in 1757 on the island of Grenada. He was an adolescent when he arrived in Cap-Français in St-Domingue. In 1778, he fought as a volunteer in Savannah, Georgia, for the independence of the United States of America. He was only 21 years old. Henri Christophe, a lieutenant of Toussaint, who fought the army of Napoleon during the War of Independence, is very well known for his influence in the northern section of Haiti, where he built monuments, palaces and forts.

He proclaimed himself King of Haiti in 1811 and created an atmosphere of discipline, work and education in that region. He was feared and regarded as a man of steel. He carried an extraordinary vision of grandeur for the Haitian people, which can be seen in his accomplishments. Among his magnificent works are the Citadel, that carries his name, and the Sans-Souci palace, which, even in ruins, draws admiration.

Paralyzed by a stroke and faced with the weakening of his army, Henri Christophe took his life on October 8, 1820. He remains the most admired of Haitians for his genius and advanced vision of Haiti as a civilized and prosperous nation.

Alexandre Pétion

The "Founder of the Republic," Alexandre Pétion was born in Port-au-Prince in 1770, of a French father and a black mother. At 18 years of age, he became a soldier and was sent to France to study at the Military Academy of Paris. Jointly with Dessalines, he played a very important role in unifying blacks and mulattoes to fight together at the Independence War against the French army.

Pétion was elected President of the Republic of Haiti on March 9, 1806, elected again in 1811, and then in 1816 he was re-elected President for Life. He became the first President of Haiti. He designed the official flag and coat of arms of the second independent nation of the American continent. He also supported other countries of South America in their struggle to gain independence from Spain. After years of many hardships and challenges he confronted as a soldier and as president, Alexandre Pétion ill and tired died in Port-au-Prince on March 29, 1818.

Toussaint Louverture

Haiti: A Basic Reference Book

Jean-Jacques Dessalines

Haiti: A Basic Reference Book

King Henri Christophe

Haiti: A Basic Reference Book
Original Painting (MUSEUM or MUPANAH) haiti

PRIVATE COLLECTION of WILEY NICOLAS

Alexandre Pétion

Act of Independence of Haiti

Liberty or Death

Gonaïves, January 1, 1804, Year 1 of the Independence.

Indigenous Army:

Today, January 1, 1804, the General in Chief of the indigenous army, along with the generals of the army, convene to take measures that will lead to the happiness of the country.

After making the assembled generals acquainted with his true intentions to forever ensure a stable government for the inhabitants of Haiti, a subject of great concern to him, which he declared in a speech inclined to make known to the foreign powers the resolution to render the country independent, and to enjoy a freedom established through the blood of the people of this island; and after gathering thoughts, has requested that each of the assembled generals pronounce the oath to forever renounce allegiance to France, to die rather than live under its domination, and to fight until the last breath for independence.

The generals, imbued by these sacred principles after pledging by unanimous voice their adherence to the well manifested project of independence, have all sworn to posterity, to the entire universe, to forever renounce allegiance to France, and to die rather than live under its domination.

Declared at Gonaïves, this 1st day of January, 1804, and the first day of the Independence of Haiti.

Signers: Dessalines, General in Chief; Christophe, Pétion, Clerveaux, Geffrard, Vernet, Gabart, Major-Generals; P. Romain, E. Gérin, F. Capois, Daut, J.L. François, Férou, Cangé, L. Bazelais, Magloire Ambroise, J.J. Herne, Toussaint Brave, Yayou, Generals of Brigade; Bonnet, F. Papalier, Morelly, Chevalier, Marion, Warrant Officers; Magny, Roux, Chiefs of Brigade; Charéron, B. Loret, Qenez, Makajoux, Dupui, Carbonne, Diaquoi aîné, Raphaël, Mallet, Derenoncourt, Army Officers; and Boisrond Tonnerre, Secretary.

National Anthem of Haiti

La Dessalinienne
(Song of Dessalines)

Music by Nicolas Geffrard
Words by Justin Lhérisson

I

For our Country,
For our Ancestors,
Let's march in unity.
In our ranks no traitors,
We shall be the sole masters of our land.
Let's march in unity,
For our Country, for our Ancestors
Let's march in unity,
For our Country, for our Ancestors.

II

For our Founding Fathers,
For our Nation,
Let's happily plough,
When the field bears fruit
The soul is strengthened,
Let's happily plough
For our Founding Fathers, for our Nation
Let's happily plough,
For our Founding Fathers, for our Nation.

III

To our Country,
And to our Forefathers,
Let's be sons.
Free, strong and prosperous,

We will always be brothers.
Let's be sons,
To our Country,
And to our Forefathers,
Let's be sons,
To our Country,
And to our Forefathers.

IV

For our Founding Fathers,
For our Nation,
O God of the doughty knights!
Under your endless protection
Take our rights, our life.
O God of the doughty knights!
For our Founding Fathers,
For our Nation,
O God of the doughty knights!
For our Founding Fathers,
For our Nation.

V

For our Flag, for our Nation,
Dying is beautiful.
Our past is shouting to us:
"Harden your soul for battle."
Dying is beautiful,
For our Flag, for our Nation,
Dying is beautiful,
For our Flag, for our Nation.

Constitutions

1. Imperial Constitution of May 20, 1805 voted by Jean-Jacques Dessalines
2. Republican Constitution of December 27, 1806
3. Constitution of the State of Haiti of February 17, 1807 by Henri Christophe
4. Royal Constitution of May 28, 1811 voted by Henri I
5. Constitution of June 2, 1816 by Alexandre Pétion
6. Constitution of December 30, 1843 by President Rivière Hérard
7. Constitution of November 14, 1846 by President Jean-Baptiste Riché
8. Imperial Constitution of September 20, 1849 by Faustin I
9. Constitution of June 14, 1867 by President Sylvain Salnave
10. Constitution of August 6, 1874 by President Michel Domingue
11. Constitution of December 18, 1879 by President Lysius Salomon
12. Constitution of December 16, 1888 by President F.D. Légitime
13. Constitution of October 9, 1889 by President Florvil Hyppolite
14. Constitution of June 19, 1918 by President Sudre Dartiguenave
15. Constitution of July 15, 1932 by the National Assembly
16. Constitution of June 2, 1935, presidency of Sténio Vincent
17. Constitution of November 22, 1946 by Dumarsais Estimé
18. Constitution of November 25, 1950 by the Constituent Assembly
19. Constitution of December 19, 1957 by President François Duvalier
20. Constitution of May 25, 1964 by F. Duvalier President for Life
21. Constitution of August 27, 1983, presidency of J.C. Duvalier
22. Constitution of March 29, 1987, ratified through referendum

Total of 22 constitutions.

Rulers and Heads of Government of Haiti

Name	Title	Term	Outcome
Jean-Jacques Dessalines	Governor-General	Jan. 1, 1804 - Sept. 22, 1804	(assassinated)
Jacques I (Dessalines)	Emperor	Sept. 22, 1804 - Oct. 17, 1806	
Henri Christophe	President	Feb. 17, 1807- Mar. 26, 1811	
Henri I	King	Mar. 26, 1811- Oct. 8, 1820	(suicide)
Alexandre Pétion	President	Mar. 9, 1807 - Mar. 29, 1818	(died in office)
Jean-Pierre Boyer	President	Mar. 30, 1818 - Mar. 13, 1843	(ousted/exiled)
Executive Council	*Provisional Government*	*Mar. 14, 1843 - Dec. 30, 1843*	
Rivière Hérard	President	Dec. 31, 1843 - May 3, 1844	(ousted/exiled)
Philippe Guerrier	President	May 3, 1844 - April 15, 1845	(died in office)
Louis Pierrot	President	April 16, 1845 - Mar. 1, 1846	(overthrown)
Jean Baptiste Riché	President	Mar. 1, 1846 - Feb. 27, 1847	(died in office)
Faustin Soulouque	President	Mar. 1, 1847 - Aug. 25, 1849	
Faustin I	Emperor	Aug. 25, 1849 - Jan. 13, 1859	(overthrown)
Fabre Geffrard	President	Jan. 13, 1859 - Mar. 13, 1867	(resigned/exiled)

Name	Title	Term	Outcome
Sylvain Salnave	President	June 14, 1867 - Dec. 19, 1869	(executed)
Executive Council	*Provisional Government*	*Dec. 27, 1869 - Mar. 19, 1870*	
Nissage Saget	President	Mar. 19, 1870 - May 12, 1874	(resigned)
Michel Domingue	President	June 11, 1874 - April 15, 1876	(overthrown)
Boisrond - Canal	President	July 17, 1876 - July 17, 1879	(resigned)
Lysius Félicité Salomon	President	Oct. 23, 1879 - Aug. 10,1888	(ousted/exiled)
Executive Council	*Provisional Government*	*Aug. 18, 1888 - Dec.15, 1888*	
François Denys Légitime	President	Dec. 16, 1888- Aug. 22, 1889	(ousted/exiled)
Executive Council	*Provisional Government*	*Aug. 27, 1889 - Oct. 9, 1889*	
Florvil Hyppolite	President	Oct. 9, 1889 - Mar. 24, 1896	(died in office)
Tirésias Simon Sam	President	Mar. 31, 1896 - May 12, 1902	(resigned)
Executive Council	*Provisional Government*	*May 13, 1902 - Dec. 21, 1902*	
Nord Alexis	President	Dec. 21, 1902 - Dec. 2, 1908	(ousted/exiled)
Antoine Simon	President	Dec. 17, 1908 - Aug. 2, 1911	(ousted/exiled)
Cincinnatus Leconte	President	Aug. 14, 1911- Aug. 8, 1912	(Blown up in palace)
Tancrède Auguste	President	Aug. 8, 1912 - May 2, 1913	(died in office)
Michel Oreste	President	May 4, 1913 - Jan. 27, 1914	(overthrown)

Name	Title	Term	Outcome
Oreste Zamor	President	Feb. 8, 1914 - Oct. 29, 1914	(overthrown)
Davilmar Théodore	President	Nov. 7, 1914 - Feb. 22, 1915	(overthrown)
Vilbrun Guillaume Sam	President	Mar. 4, 1915 - July 27, 1915	(assassinated)
Sudre Dartiguenave	President	Aug. 12, 1915 - May 15, 1922	(end of term)
Louis Borno	President	May 15, 1922 - May 15, 1930	(end of term)
Louis Eugène Roy	President	May 15, 1930 - Nov. 18, 1930	(end of term)
Sténio Vincent	President	Nov. 18, 1930 - May 15, 1941	(end of term)
Elie Lescot	President	May 15, 1941 - Jan. 11, 1946	(resigned)
Executive Military Government	*Provisional Gov.*	*Jan. 11, 1946 - Aug. 16, 1946*	
Dumarsais Estimé	President	Aug. 16, 1946 - May 10, 1950	(resigned/exiled)
Junta	*Provisional Gov.*	*May 10, 1950 - Dec. 6, 1950*	
Paul Eugène Magloire	President	Dec. 6, 1950 - Dec. 6, 1956	(resigned)
Nemours Pierre-Louis	President	Dec. 12, 1956 - Feb. 3, 1957	(resigned)
Franck Sylvain	President	Feb. 7, 1957 - April 2, 1957	(resigned)
Executive Council of Government	*Provisional Gov.*	*April 6 1957 - May 25 1957*	
Daniel Fignolé	President	May 25, 1957 - June 14, 1957	(ousted/exiled)
Military Council of Government	*Provisional Gov.*	*June 14 1957 - Oct. 22, 1957*	
François Duvalier	President	Oct. 22, 1957 - April 21, 1971	(died in office)

Name	Title	Term	Outcome
Jean Claude Duvalier	President	April 22, 1971 - Feb. 7, 1986	(ousted/exiled)
CNG: National Council of Government	Provisional Government	Feb. 7, 1986 - Feb. 6, 1988	(overthrown)
Leslie François Manigat	President	Feb. 7, 1988 - June 19, 1988	(ousted/exiled)
Gen. Henri Namphy	Military. Pres.	June 20, 1988 - Sept. 17, 1988	(resigned/exiled)
Gen. Prosper Avril	Military. Pres.	Sept. 17, 1988 - Mar. 10, 1990	(end of term)
Gen. Hérard Abraham	Military. Pres.	Mar. 10, 1990 - Mar. 13, 1990	(end of term)
Ertha Pascal Trouillot	Provisional Pres.	Mar. 13, 1990- Feb. 6, 1991	(ousted/exiled)
Jean-Bertrand Aristide	President	Feb. 7, 1991- Sept. 30, 1991	(end of term)
Joseph C. Nerette	Provisional Pres.	Sept. 31, 1991 - June 19, 1992	(resigned)
Marc Louis Bazin	Prime Minister	June 19, 1992 - June 8, 1993	

PEOPLE AND PLACES 4

Population by Cities / 75

Historical Sites / 79

Holidays / 84

Population by Cities

(1989 estimates/ * including suburbs and rural sections)

Rank	City	Population
1	Port-au-Prince	750,693
2	Carrefour	240,061
3	Delmas	199,124
4	Jacmel	114,909
5	Petit-Goâve	110,684
6	Les Cayes	*109,662
7	Dessalines	109,116
8	Croix des Bouquets	106,818
9	St-Marc/Montrouis	*105,452
10	Léogâne/Trouin	101,798
11	Gonaïves	*97,441
12	Cap-Haïtien	92,021
13	Petite Rivière de l'Artibonite	89,327
14	St. Michel de l'Attalaye	85,283
15	Gros Morne	79,309
16	Bainet	75,472
17	Jean Rabel	74,393
18	Port-de-Paix	*71,795
19	Arcahaie	71,722
20	Pétionville	60,759
21	Mirebalais	60,165
22	Verrettes	59,751
23	Aquin/Fonds des Blancs	58,324
24	Miragôane	56,572
25	Grand-Goâve	54,425
26	Acul du Nord	49,746
27	Cornillon	49,047
28	Plaisance	47,823
29	Borgne	47,084
30	Hinche	46,938
31	Cabaret	45,730
32	St. Louis du Nord	43,855
33	Pilate	42,974

Rank	City	Population
34	St-Louis du Sud	42,928
35	Côtes-de-Fer	42,238
36	Ganthier	41,493
37	Marigot	41,378
38	Anse à Galets	38,666
39	Ouanaminthe	38,075
40	Cavaillon	37,704
41	Torbeck	36,784
42	Belladère	36,734
43	Lascahobas	36,438
44	Kenscoff/Thomassin	36,325
45	Anse à Veau	36,273
46	Petit Trou de Nippes	36,065
47	Limbé	35,825
48	Port Margot	34,751
49	Thomazeau	33,998
50	Maissade	33,597
51	Baradères	33,407
52	Grande Rivière du Nord	33,192
53	St Raphaël	33,113
54	Dondon	32,481
55	Pestel	32,307
56	Limonade	30,628
57	Camp Perrin	30,264
58	Belle-Anse/Mapou	29,299
59	Pointe-à-Raquettes	28,176
60	BoucanCarré	27,768
61	Jérémie	*27,673
62	Abricots	27,422
63	Dame Marie	26,569
64	L'Asile	26,167
65	Bassin Bleu	26,164
66	Thomassique	26,077
67	Ennery	25,610
68	Pl. du Nord/Robillard	25,513
69	Saut D'Eau	25,451
70	Port Salut	25,036
71	Roseau	25,006
72	Estère	24,450

Rank	City	Population
73	Cerca la Source	24,279
74	Cayes-Jacmel	23,728
75	La Tortue	23,713
76	Savonette	23,521
77	Thomonde	23,103
78	Les Anglais	22,973
79	St-Jean du Sud	22,751
80	Moron	22,435
81	Anse d'Hainault	21,924
82	Fonds Verrettes	21,810
83	Desdunes	21,738
84	Chardonnières	21,697
85	Trou du Nord	21,667
86	Tiburon	21,323
87	Petite Rivière de Nippes	20,960
88	Anse-Rouge	20,214
89	Corail	20,162
90	Anse à Foleur	20,116
91	Sainte Suzanne	19,906
92	Milot	19,447
93	Chantal	19,052
94	Marmelade	18,828
95	Terre-Neuve	18,510
96	Gressier	18,503
97	Bombardopolis	18,312
98	Fort Liberté	18,276
99	Môle St Nicolas	17,890
100	Pignon	17,524
101	Mombin Crochu	17,506
102	Bahon	16,887
103	Port-à-Piment	16,303
104	Cerca Cavajal	16,196
105	La Chapelle	16,190
106	Thiotte	15,557
107	Roche-à-Bateau	15,334
108	Chambellan	15,322
109	Coteaux	15,068
110	Quartier Morin	14,802
111	Terrier Rouge	14,736

Rank	City	Population
112	Grande Saline	14,686
113	Mont-Organisé	14,336
114	Ranquitte	14,169
115	Vallières	13,394
116	Arniquet	12,832
117	Irois	12,310
118	Anse-à-Pitre	11,761
119	Grand Gosier	11,660
120	Bas Limbé	11,412
121	Beaumont	11,274
122	Capotille	10,366
123	La Vallée	10,019
124	Baie de Henne	9,804
125	Ferrier	9,334
126	Chansolme	8,960
127	Carice	8,548
128	Bonbon	7,520
129	Ile à Vache	7,482
130	Maniche	7,131
131	La Victoire	5,058
132	Caracol	4,046
133	Perches	3,029

Historical Sites

The Citadel of Henri Christophe (Milot-Northern Haiti)
La Citadelle
This majestic and colossal fortress was built by Henri
Christophe, King of Haiti, to protect the country against
possible French invasion. This impressive monument is on the
UNESCO WORLD HERITAGE LIST. Two-hundred thousand
people worked on its construction which began in 1805. It was
inaugurated in 1813 and was still in progress in 1820 at the
time of the King Henri's death. Its area is 8,000 sq.m. It was
built at an altitude of approximately 900 meters, has a
structure of 12-foot thick walls, and a room that can hold
45,000 cannon balls. It was designed to accommodate 5,000
soldiers for three years in case of siege. This monument of
pride also serves as the tomb of its builder, King Henri I, who
died on October 8, 1820.

The Sans-Souci Palace (Milot, Northern Haiti)
Le Palais de Sans-Souci
The royal residence of the King Henri I, inaugurated in 1813
in the town of Milot, was designed to rival the Versailles
Palace of France. It was a rectangular building, 51 meters long
and 25 meters wide, made of brick, and marble floors. Though
in ruins today, since its destruction by the 1842 earthquake,
the Sans-Souci Palace still constitutes an imposing historical
monument.

Forts Jacques & Alexandre (Fermathe, Hills behind Port-au-Prince)
This fort, built by Pétion to defend Haiti against French
invasion, offers an excellent view of the Port-au-Prince harbor.

Vertières (Entrance of Cap-Haïtien, in Northern Haiti)
Monument to the heroes of independence. It was at this site
that Dessalines ultimately defeated the French army and won
the War of Independence on November 18, 1803.

Palace of 365 Doors (Petite Rivière de l'Artibonite)
Palace built by Henri Christophe, King of Haiti

The Crête-à-Pierrot (Petite Rivière de l'Artibonite)
This is the site of one of the remarkable battles for independence.

Heroes of Independence Square (Port-au-Prince)
La Place des Heros
Park with statues of Haiti's Founding Fathers, near the Presidential Palace.

Monument to the Unknown Maroon (Port-au-Prince)
Monument du Marron Inconnu
Bronze statue of the unknown maroon (fugitive slave) blowing the conch shell to call to a gathering. This monument was built in remembrance of the slaves in St-Domingue, who fought for the abolition of slavery.

City of Caracol (Northeast Region)
The place where Christopher Columbus' flagship, the Santa María, ran onto a coral reef and was destroyed on the night of Christmas, 1492.

Môle Saint-Nicolas (Northwest Region)
The site where Christopher Columbus first set foot on Hispaniola in 1492.

NATIONAL PALACE AND THE MONUMENT TO THE UNKNOWN MAROON.

SANS-SOUCI PALACE

Haiti: A Basic Reference Book

CITADEL HENRI CHRISTOPHE

Holidays

National and Legal Holidays

January 1	Independence Day
January 2	Forefathers Day (Jour des Aïeux)
May 1	Labor and Agriculture Day
May 18	Flag and University Day
October 17	Anniversary of Dessalines' Death
November 18	Battle of Vertières (Battle of Independence) and the Armed Forces Day
December 5	Discovery of Haiti Day

Roman Catholic Holidays Observed

August 15	Assumption Day
November 1	All Saints' Day
November 2	All Souls' Day
December 25	Christmas Day

Religious Holidays Which Change Every Year

Ash Wednesday	Forty days before Easter Sunday
Holy Thursday	The Thursday before Easter Sunday
Good Friday	The Friday before Easter Sunday
Easter Sunday	
Ascension Day	The sixth Thursday after Easter Sunday
Corpus Christi (Fête Dieu)	The fourth Thursday after Ascension Day

Other Celebrations

Mardi Gras	Tuesday before Ash Wednesday
Mother's Day	Last Sunday of May
Father's Day	Last Sunday of June
United Nations Day	October 24

Patron Saint Festivals

Celebrations pertaining to the Patron Saints of the cities. It is a highly respected custom in Haiti to celebrate a Patron Saint for each city or town. The festivals have a very important place in the lives of the residents and attract people from all over the country. Below is a list of some of the Patron Saint Festivals and the corresponding cities.

Date	Patron Saint	City
January 21	Our Lady of Altagrace	Delmas
February 11 or 18	St. Bernadette	Martissant
March 19	St. Joseph	Portail/Fort-Liberté
March 21	St. Benoît	Lascahobas
April 25	St. Marc	City of St-Marc
May 1 or 3	Sts. Philip and James, the Apostles	Jacmel
May 19	St. Yves	Miragoâne
June 24	St. John the Baptist	Arcahaie
June 27	Our Lady of Perpetual Help	Bel-Air
June 29	St. Peter	Pétionville
July 16	Our Lady of Mt. Carmel	Bizoton
July 22	St. Mary Magdalene	Sibert
July 25	St. James Major	Plaine du Nord, Fermathe
July 26	St. Ann	Morne à Tuf
August 11 or 12	St. Clare of Assisi	Marchand, Frères

Date	Patron Saint	City
August 15	Our Lady of Assumption	Port-au-Prince, Cayes, Cap-Haïtien, Ouanaminthe, Petit Goâve
August 25	St. Louis	Jérémie, Mirebalais, St Louis du Nord, St Louis du Sud
August 23 or 30	St. Rose of Lima	Léogâne, Pilate, Grande Rivière du Nord, Maniche
September 8	Our Lady of Nativity (The Birth of Our Blessed Mother)	Verrettes, Petit Trou de Nippes, Dame Marie
September 14	The Holy Cross	Croix des Missions, Fonds Verrettes
September 24	Our Lady of Mercy	Irois, Robillard
September 27	St. Vincent de Paul	Laboule
September 29	St. Michael	Boucan Carré, Roche à Bateau, Plaisance
October 6 or 7	Our Lady of the Rosary	Croix des Bouquets
November 4	St. Charles Borromeo	Gonaïves, Carrefour
December 8	Immaculate Conception	Hinche, Belladère, Port-de-Paix

LITERATURE AND ARTS 5

Haitian Literature / 88

Noted Haitian Artists / 107

Haitian Literature

Notable personalities of Haitian Literature and their works.

I.   **THE PIONEERS (1804-1836)**
       The early age of Haitian literature.

Juste Chanlatte [1766-1828] poet, playwright
       General Juste Chanlatte, Count of Rosiers, was born in
       Port-au-Prince. He studied in Paris and returned to his
       country during the reign of King Henri I of Haiti (1811-1820),
       to be a writer for the periodical *La Gazette du Cap*. After the
       death of Henri I, he offered his services to the Republican
       Party and became the editor of the *Télégraphe*, the official
       gazette of the government of President Boyer. He mainly
       wrote poetic songs:
              Ode à l'Indépendance (1821)
              Cantate à l'Indépendance (1821)
              La Triple Palme (1822)
              Le Naufrage de "l'Alexandre"

Hérard Dumesle [1784-1858] poet
       Dumesle was born in the city of Cayes on June 16, 1784. He
       took part in the insurrection against President Boyer, and
       became President of the Constituent Assembly, then Minister
       during the government of President Rivière Hérard. He was
       banished from Haitian territory in 1844 by the government of
       Guerrier. He died in Kingston, Jamaica, on June 22, 1858, after
       fourteen years of exile. His main work is *Macanda*, a historical
       poem.

Antoine Dupré [?-1816] poet, playwright
       Little is known about his life, but he is chronologically
       accepted as the first Haitian poet and writer. He was killed in
       a duel on January 13, 1816. He wrote historical, heroic poetry
       and plays.
              Hymne à la Liberté - poem
              Le Rêve d'un Haytien - poem

La Mort du Général Lamarre - drama
La Jeune Fille - comedy

François Romain Lhérisson [1798-1859] poet
>Lhérisson was born in Aquin in the Southern Region of Haiti in 1798. His knowledge was vast. He was an instructor of Latin, algebra, geometry and law in his native city of Aquin. He wrote poetic songs.
>*La Bergère Somnambule*

Jules Solime Milscent [1778- 1842] fabulist, poet
>Milscent was born at the Grande-Rivière du Nord in the Northern Region of Haiti of a French father and a free black mother. He studied in France. Back in his country, in 1817 he co-founded the periodical, ***L'Abeille Haytienne.*** In 1818, he was appointed by President Boyer as a Member of the Commission in charge of drafting the Haitian Civil Code. He served in several other government positions during his career. He died in the 1842 earthquake that destroyed the city of Cap-Haïtien. He is primarily known as a fabulist.
>>*L'Homme, la Guêpe et le Serpent*
>>*Le Cœur et l'Esprit*
>>*L'Homme et le Serpent*
>>*Le Chien et le Loup*
>>*L'Enfant et la Sauterelle*

Jean-Baptiste Romane [1807-1858] poet
>Little is known about his life, but he became a noted personality very early. At age eighteen, his first work, *Hymne à l'Indépendance* (Hymn to Independence), was sung at a national celebration upon the recognition of the Haitian independence by France. He was awarded a gold medallion by the French government for his poem, *Vers à la France.* He wrote poetic songs and hymns to the heroes of independence.
>>*Hymne à l'Indépendance* (1825)
>>*A l'Ozama*
>>*A l'Artibonite*
>>*Sur la Ville de Saint-Domingue*
>He also wrote a play:
>>*La Mort de Christophe* - drama

Boisrond-Tonnerre [1776-1806] prose-writer, historian

>   Louis Boisrond was born at Torbeck in the Southern Region of Haiti. As an infant, his cradle was struck by a thunderbolt without hurting him. Amazed by this event, his father decided to name him *Tonnerre* meaning thunder in French. He studied in France, and was chosen by Dessalines to write the Independence Act of Haiti in 1804. His major work is a memoir on the History of Haiti, a valuable historical document that traces events back to the Saint-Domingue revolution, the French expedition and the independence of the country.

>> *Mémoires pour Servir à l'Histoire d'Haïti* (1851)
>> *Acte d'Indépendance* - The Independence Act

Pompée Valentin Vastey [1735-1820] prose-writer

>   He was born of a French father and a Haitian mother. He became the secretary of King Henri I of Haiti and the private teacher of his son, Victor Henri. He wrote prose and essays.

>> *Le Système Colonial Dévoilé* (1814)
>> *Réflexions Adressées aux Haïtiens de l'Ouest et du Sud* (1815)
>> *Le Cri de la Patrie* (1815)
>> *Réflexions sur les Noirs et les Blancs* (1816)
>> *Réflexions Politiques sur quelques Ouvrages et Journaux Français Concernant Haïti* (1817)
>> *Essai sur les Causes de la Révolution et des Guerres Civiles en Haïti* (1819)
>> *Cri de la Conscience* (1819)

II.   BIRTH OF ROMANTIC LITERATURE (1836-1859)

Beaubrun Ardouin [1796-1865] historian

>   Raised during the revolutionary period in Saint-Domingue, he could not attend school regularly, so he became self-taught. He developed a passion for French literature and its writers, Voltaire, Montesquieu and J.J. Rousseau. He was elected Senator in 1832 and wrote a book on the geography of Haiti for schoolchildren, which is the first Haitian textbook. He is

mainly remembered for his valuable eleven volume work, "Studies on the History of Haiti," published in 1865.

> ***Etudes sur l'Histoire d'Haïti.*** (1865)
> *Instruction sur le Jury*
> *Géographie de l'Ile d'Haïti*

Céligni Ardouin [1806-1849] historian

Born in Petit-Trou-de-Nippes, brother of Beaubrun Ardouin, he developed a passion for politics. He was first Delegate in 1846, then Senator, and then Minister of the Interior in 1847. President Soulouque ordered his execution in 1849. He left a historical document on the history of Haiti, which was published by his brother Beaubrun.

> ***Essais sur l'Histoire d'Haïti*** (1865)

Coriolan Ardouin [1812-1836] poet

It is written that at his birth in Port-au-Prince on December 11, 1812, a black butterfly of bad omen landed on his cradle while his two-year old brother was dying in the other room. These events predicted the miseries that were to befall him. He became an orphan at fifteen, and thereafter lost his older sister. The woman he loved and married died five months after their wedding. Shortly after he died on July 12, 1836 at twenty-three years of age. He found solace in meditation, reading and writing. He attended a renowned institution in Haiti and began to write poetry at an early age. A talented writer, he left one compilation of poems entitled *Reliques d'un Poète Haïtien*, published posthumously in 1837.

Emeric Bergeaud [1818-1858] novelist

Born in Cayes, he was the Secretary of General Borgella. He participated in the insurrection against President Soulouque, after which he was exiled to Saint-Thomas. There he wrote the novel *Stella*, his main work.

Guy-Joseph Bonnet [1773-1843] historian

Major General of the Army of the Republic of Haiti, he published a historical book on Haiti - *Souvenirs Historiques* (1864)

Liautaud Ethéart [1826-1888] playwright
Born in Port-au-Prince, he was Secretary of State in 1879. He is honored for his theatrical works.
Miscellanées (1858)
La Fille de l'Empereur (1860)
Un Duel sous Blanchelande (1860)
Le Monde de Chez Nous (1857)

Pierre Faubert [1806-1868] poet, playwright
Son of a general of the Independence War, he was born in Cayes and studied in France. He became the Secretary of President Boyer and was chosen by President Geffrard as a negotiator for the Concordat between Haiti and the Vatican. He died at Vanves, near Paris, on July 31, 1868.
Poésies Fugitives - poems
Ogé ou le Préjugé de Couleur - drama

Général Alibée Féry [1818-1896] playwright, narrator, poet, storyteller
Born in Jérémie on May 28, 1818, he was self-taught and author of several Haitian stories. He was the first to tell the story of Bouqui and Malice, the two famous characters of Haitian tales.
Essais Littéraires - play
Fils du Chasseur - story
Les Bluettes - poems
Les Echantillons - stories
Les Esquisses - historical stories

Thomas Madiou [1814-1884] historian
He was born in Port-au-Prince on April 30, 1814. At age ten he was sent to France to study at the Collège Royal d'Angers. In 1833 at Rennes, France, he was awarded a Bachelor of Arts Degree in Letters, and for two years took classes at the Law School of Paris. He returned to Haiti to write the history of his country. He carried out several public functions as the Director of Le Moniteur — the official paper of the government — in 1849. His manuscript, *Histoire d'Haïti*, on the history of Haiti is a work of science and art seen as one of the most valuable documents in Haitian literature.

Emile Nau [1812-1860] historian
> Born in Port-au-Prince on February 26, 1812, he was the co-editor of two important magazines, the *Le Républicain* and the *L'Union.* At age thirty, he was appointed Delegate of Port-au-Prince during the government of President Boyer. His major work was a study on the history of the Caciques, the original inhabitants of Haiti.
>> ***Histoire des Caciques d'Haïti.*** (1854)

Ignace Nau [1808-1845] poet, storyteller
> Born in Port-au-Prince, he first studied at a renowned school, where he received a rigid military preparation. He completed his education at the Catholic University of New York. With his brothers and the Ardouin brothers, he founded a literary circle called "The School of 1836." He published a magazine, *Le Républicain,* which was censored by the government. *Le Républicain* reappeared as a literary and commercial magazine under the name of ***L'Union.*** Some of his writings include:
>> *Le Livre de Marie* - poem
>> *Pensées du Soir* - poem
>> *Le Lambi* - story
>> *Episode de la Révolution* - story
>> *Isalina* - story

Joseph Saint-Rémy [1815-1858] historian
> Born in Guadeloupe, very young he emigrated to Haiti and grew up in Cayes. He completed his education in France. His works are mainly on the history of Haiti.
>> *La Vie de Toussaint Louverture* (1850)
>> *Pétion et Haïti* (1854-1858)

III. GROWTH OF ROMANTIC LITERATURE
(1859 to the end of XIX century)

Massillon Coicou [1867-1908] poet, novelist, playwright
> He was born in Port-au-Prince on October 9, 1867 and was educated in Haiti at a Catholic school for boys. He was appointed to several diplomatic duties in France, where some of his works were published. He had a strong passion for

politics and publicly announced his intentions to overthrow the government of Nord Alexis. As a consequence, he was executed along with his two brothers on the orders of the President on the night of March 14 and 15, 1908.

The various themes of his poetry include nature, motherland, patriotism, love, race, God, melancholy and pain.

> *Poésies Nationales* (1892)
> *Complaintes d'Esclave* - poem
> *Vertières* - poem
> *Toussaint au Fort de Joux* (1896) - drama
> *Liberté* (1904) - drama
> *L'Alphabet* (1905) - drama
> *La Noire* (1905) - novel

Demesvar Delorme [1831-1901] theoretician, journalist, novelist, essayist. He was born in Cap-Haïtien on February 10, 1831. He loved to read and received a good education in Haiti. He engaged in politics, and in 1865 fought on the side of Salnave, who when elected President, appointed him Minister of External Relations, and later Minister of Public Education and Cults. In 1868 he was exiled, and he went to live in Paris, where he remained for ten years and published several of his works. He mainly wrote theoretical essays that are closely related to journalism.

> *Bulletin de la Révolution* (1865) - article
> *La Reconnaissance du Général Salnave* (1868) - article
> *La Démocratie et le Préjugé de Couleur aux Etats-Unis* -
>   article
> *Le Système Monroe* (1868) - article
> *Les Théoriciens au Pouvoir* (1870) - essay
> *Francesca* (1873) - novel
> *Le Damné* (2 vols, 1877) - novel
> *Réflexions Diverses sur Haïti* (1873) - essay
> *Les Paisibles* (1874) - article

Oswald Durand [1840-1906] poet

> Durand was born in Cap-Haïtien on September 17, 1840. First a teacher, he later engaged in politics and he was elected Delegate under the presidency of Salomon in 1885, a position to which he was re-elected six times. He was an active advisor

and a writer for several periodicals and newspapers, some of which he himself founded. He reached national fame and became one of the greatest writers. It is written that he is to Haiti what Shakespeare is to England and Dante to Italy. This assessment appears accurate because he skillfully depicted through his poetry all aspects of Haitian life: love, pain, patriotism, motherland and sadness. Among his most celebrated works is *Choucoune,* a poem set to music which praises the beauty of a Haitian woman and which has been acclaimed nationally and internationally. Durand also wrote a historic poem set to music, *Chant National,* which became as popular as the National Anthem. Oswald Durand died on April 22, 1906. Some of his most important works are:

> *Rires et Pleurs* (2 vols 1897)
> *Choucoune* (1883), *Chant National*
> *Ces Allemands* (June 14, 1872)
> *Pantoum Triste*
> *La Mort de nos Cocotiers*

Anténor Firmin [1850-1911] theoretician, commentator, novelist
Firmin was born of a modest family in Cap-Haïtien on October 18, 1850. He founded in Cap-Haïtien a political and literary publication, *Le Messager du Nord.* He engaged in teaching, politics and served in several diplomatic functions. He is mainly acclaimed in Haitian literature for his book on the equality of the human race through which he refutes the theory on the inferiority of the negro which the French writer Gobineau suggested in a book entitled, "Essay on the Inequality of Human Races." Firmin retorted by writing *De l'Égalité des Races Humaines,* "On the Equality of Human Races" in 1885, which strongly defended the negro race. He is till this day well known and acclaimed in Haiti for his political philosophy and accomplishments. He wrote essays, philosophical theories and commentaries.

> *De l'Egalité des Races Humaines* (1885)
> *Haïti et la France* (1891)
> *Une Défense* (1892)
> *Diplomate et Diplomatie* (1898)
> *M. Roosevelt, Président des Etats-Unis et la République d'Haïti* (1905)
> *Lettres de Saint -Thomas* (1910)

Louis-Joseph Janvier [1855-1911] theoretician, journalist, novelist
A native of Port-au-Prince, he was born on May 7, 1855. He started medical school in Haiti, then completed his education in France. In 1881 he was awarded a Doctorate in Medicine. He earned degrees in administration, economic, finance, diplomacy and also earned a license in law. In Paris he became very interested in journalism and wrote several articles such as: *The Republic of Haiti and Its Visitors, Haiti for the Haitians,* and *The Equality of Races.* He made his mark as a novelist by publishing novels about Haitian life. He came back to Haiti after twenty-eight years and then returned to Paris, where he died on March 24, 1911. He is honored for the following writings:

> *La République d'Haïti et ses Visiteurs* (1883) - article
> *L'Egalité des Races* (1884) - article
> *Haïti aux Haïtiens* (1884) - article
> *Les Affaires d'Haiti* (1885) - historical article
> *Les Constitutions d'Haïti* (1886) - constitutions of Haiti.
> *Le Vieux Piquet* (1888) - novel
> *Une Chercheuse* (1889) - novel

Solon Ménos [1859-1918] theoretician
He was born in L'Anse-à-Veau on March 9, 1859. After completing his secondary studies in Haiti, he went to France to study law and was awarded a Doctorate in Law at the age of twenty-two. He took part in politics. He published poems and a historical book on the conflict between Haiti and Germany, *L'Affaire Lüders.*

Hannibal Price [1841-1893] theoretician
A native of Jacmel, he was educated in his native town. He landed a diplomatic career starting out as a Counselor to the Provisional Government of 1875 after the fall of President Domingue. Then he was appointed Minister Plenipotentiary of Haiti to Washington from 1890 to 1893. During this mission he wrote his famous book, *De la Réhabilitation de la Race Noire par la République d'Haïti* (1893) "On the Rehabilitation of the Black Race by the Republic of Haiti." He died in Baltimore, Maryland, on January 1, 1893, at the age of fifty-two.

IV.   **GENERATION DE LA RONDE (1898-1915)**
Humano-Haïtienne literature. Haitian inspiration drawn from the universal world or the human family.

Fernand Hibbert [1873-1928] novelist
He was born in Miragoâne on October 3, 1873. He completed his education in Paris where he studied law and political science. On his return to Haiti in 1894, he performed several teaching, political and diplomatic functions. He earned national fame by publishing a rich collection of satiric, hilarious novels. He is one of the most widely read Haitian authors.
>   *Séna* (1905)
>   *Les Thazar* (1907)
>   *Romulus* (1908)
>   *Masques et Visages* (1910)
>   *Manuscrit de mon Ami* (1923)
>   *Simulacres* (1923)

Edmond Laforest [1876-1915] poet
Born in Jérémie on June 20, 1876 and educated in Haiti, he later taught French and mathematics. Among his writings we find, *Poèmes Mélancoliques* (1901), *Sonnets-Médaillons* (1909), *Cendres et Flammes*.

Léon Laleau [1892-1979] poet, novelist
Leon Laleau was born in Port-au-Prince on August 3, 1892 and obtained a degree in letters and sciences and a degree in law. He was appointed to various political and diplomatic posts as Minister of Foreign Affairs, Minister of National Education, Agriculture, and Public Works, Chief of Diplomatic Missions in Rome, London, Paris, Santiago, and Lima. He was also Special Mission Ambassador to Panama, Cuba, United Nations and the UNESCO. He is one of the members who signed the Accord on July 24, 1934 for the end of the United States occupation of Haiti. Acclaimed as one of the most brilliant writers of his time, he won many international awards, including the Edgar Allan Poe Prize in 1962. He was member of the Ronsard Academy and the Mediterranean Academy (Académie Méditerranéenne). He is recognized as a

poet, journalist, novelist, essayist, playwright, storyteller, and an outstanding literary figure.

A Voix Basse (1920) - poem
Le Rayon des Jupes (1928) - poem
La Flèche au Cœur (1926) - poem
Abréviations (1928) - poem
Musique Nègre (1931) - poem
Ondes Courtes (1933) - poem
Jusqu'au Bord (1916) - novel
La Danse des Vagues (1919) - novel
Le Choc (1932) - novel
La Pluie et le Beau Temps - play
Le Tremplin - play

Justin Lhérisson [1872-1907] novelist

He was born in Port-au-Prince on February 10, 1873. He earned a degree in law and devoted his career to practicing law, journalism and teaching. As a history teacher he published a textbook on the Spanish period. As a journalist, he was the founder of the periodical, *Le Soir*. As a poet, he wrote two compilations of poems, *Les Chants de l'Aurore* (1893) and *Passe-temps* (1893). He is acclaimed for his two notable novels — **La Famille des Pititecaille** (1905) and **Zoune Chez sa Ninnaine** (1906). Justin Lhérisson is praised for writing the text of the Haitian National Anthem, **La Dessalinienne.**

Frédéric Marcelin [1848-1917] novelist

Born in Port-au-Prince, he performed several political functions. In 1896 he published a book on Haiti and its National Bank, *Haïti et sa Banque Nationale,* and a book on the Finance and Commerce Department, *Le Département des Finances et du Commerce d'Haïti.* He is mainly known for his three bestselling novels: **Marilisse** (1903), **La Vengeance de Mama** (1902) and **Thémistocle Epaminondas Labasterre** (1901).

Charles Moravia [1875-1938] poet

Born in Jacmel on June 17, 1875, he became a teacher in his native city and became seriously involved in writing poetry. He founded the periodical, *La Plume* (1914-1915) and *Le Temps* in 1922. He was appointed Minister Plenipotentiary to Washington in 1919 and fiercely defended his country. He also became a Senator of the Republic during the government of President Vincent. He published poetry and drama.

Roses et Camélias (1903) - compilation of poems
La Crête à Pierrot (1903) - drama
Au Clair de Lune (1910) - drama
L'Amiral Killick (1943) - drama

Georges Sylvain [1866-1925] poet

Born in 1866 in Puerto-Plata, Dominican Republic, Georges Sylvain was first educated in his native city and then in Paris. After obtaining a degree in law in France he returned to Haiti in 1888, where he founded the law school of Haiti, the periodical *La Patrie*, and in 1922, the periodical *l'Union Patriotique*. He belonged to the famous literary circle, *La Ronde*. His accomplishments go even further since he was involved in several literary and diplomatic activities. He published a compilation of twenty-nine poems.

Confidences et Mélancolies, (1901).

Etzer Vilaire [1872-1951] poet

He was born in Jérémie on April 7, 1872. He attended law school and wrote poetry in his free time. He joined the literary circle *La Ronde* and published several of his poems. He is acclaimed in Haitian literature for his ability to colorfully express the soul of his time. His poetry celebrates nature, love for the motherland, melancholy, christianity, humanity, love and death.

Années Tendres (1907)
Nouveaux Poèmes (1910)
Dix Hommes Noirs (1901)
Page d'Amour (1897)

V.   LITERATURE OF THE TWENTIETH CENTURY

Stephen Alexis [1889-?] novelist

Born in Gonaïves in 1889, he completed his education in Haiti. He taught and exercised diplomatic and administrative functions. He was Ambassador to London and represented

Haiti at the United Nations. His novel *Le Négre Masqué* (1933) is highly acclaimed.

Jacques Stephen Alexis [1922-1961] novelist
Son of Stephen Alexis, he was born in Gonaïves on April 22, 1922. He started medical school in Haiti and completed it in Paris. He traveled throughout Europe and lived for a few years in Cuba. He wrote three novels that were edited in France, *Compère Général Soleil* (1955), *Les Arbres Musiciens* (1957), *L'Espace d'un Cillement* (1959), and a compilation of short stories: *Romancero aux Etoiles* (1960).

Dantès Bellegarde [1877-1966] historian, theoretician
Born in Port-au-Prince in 1877, he completed his education in Haiti and entered a political and diplomatic career. He was Minister Plenipotentiary in Paris in 1921, then transferred to Washington in 1930. He published several essays with a political and social capacity.
Histoire du Peuple Haïtien (1953)
La Résistance Haïtienne (1937)
Haïti et ses Problèmes (1943)
Pour une Haïti Heureuse (1928 and 1929)

Jean-Fernand Brierre [1909-1992] poetry
He was born in Jérémie on September 23, 1909. He performed several political and diplomatic functions. He is remembered as one of the most brilliant Haitian writers. His collection includes:
Les Aïeules (1954)
Images d'Or (1959)
Chansons Secrètes (1933)
Black Soul (1947)
La Source (1956)
Découverte (1960)
Aux Champs pour Occide (1960)

Carl Brouard [1902-1965] poet
He was born in Port-au-Prince on December 5, 1902 of an upper-class Haitian family. For several years he led a dissolute and incoherent life, but never stopped writing. He is one of the most acclaimed poets of the twentieth century. He is

described as a sensitive, delicate, brilliant and harmonious indigenous poet. *Ecrit sur du Ruban Rose* - compilation of poems

Edner Brutus (historian)
Timoléon Brutus started very early in a political, administrative and diplomatic career. He is mentioned in Haitian literature mainly for his historical work on the Revolution in Saint-Domingue.
> *Révolution dans Saint-Domingue* (1969)

Timoléon C. Brutus [1886-1971] historian
Father of Edner Brutus, he was an industrial and political figure. He wrote books on Toussaint Louverture and Dessalines. The two most important are: *Rançon du Génie ou la Leçon de Toussaint Louverture, 2 volumes* (1945) and *L'homme d'Airain* (1946).

Roussan Camille [1915-1961] poet
Born in Jacmel on August 27, 1915, he completed his education in his country. He engaged in journalism, and was appointed to several diplomatic functions. His poem *Assaut à la Nuit* (1940) was acclaimed nationally.

Christophe Charles [1951-] poet
Born in Port-au-Prince in 1951, he earned a degree in philosophy at the State University of Haiti. Among his noteworthy writings is the poem, *Désastre (1975).*

Marie Vieux Chauvet [1916-1973] novelist
Born and educated in Port-au-Prince, she is the author of four acclaimed novels. *Fille d'Haïti* (1954), *La Danse sur le Volcan* (1957), *Fonds des Nègres* (1961) and *Amour, Colère, Folie* (1969). She died in 1973 in the United States of America.

Jean-Baptiste Cinéas [1895-1958] novelist
Born in Cap-Haïtien, he obtained a degree in law, and was appointed Judge of the Supreme Court until his death in 1958. His works include the following novels:
> *Le Drame de la Terre* (1933)
> *La Vengeance de la Terre* (1940)

> *L'Héritage Sacré* (1945)
> *Le Choc en Retour* (1949)

Marie-Thérèse Colimon (novelist)
> She was awarded the prize France-Haïti for her first novel, *Fils de Misère* (1974), which reached national acclaim.

Georges Corvington Junior (historian)
> His seven-volume work on the history of Port-au-Prince, **Port-au-Prince au Cours des Ans (1743-1950)**, published from 1970 to 1992, has been highly acclaimed.

René Dépestre [1926-] poet
> Born in Jacmel on August 29, 1926, he developed an interest in communism as well as in poetry. He spent several years in Europe and published several of his poems in France.
> > *Etincelles* (1945)
> > *Gerbes de Sang* (1946)
> > *Végétations de Clarté* (1951)
> > *Traduit du Grand Large* (1952)
> > *Bonjour et Adieu à la Négritude*
> > *Hadriana dans Tous mes Rêves*

Dr. Jean Chrysostome Dorsainvil [1880-1942] theoretician, historian
> He was born in Port-au-Prince, where he enjoyed a highly successful career in teaching and was dedicated to writing books on science and on political and social aspects of Haitian culture. He also tried to scientifically explain voodoo.
> > *Vaudou et Névrose* (1913)
> > *Une Explication Philologique du Vaudou* (1924)
> > *Vaudou et Magie* (1937)
> > *Le Problème de l'Enseignement Primaire en Haïti* (1922)
> > *Quelques Vues Politiques et Morales* (1934)

Roger Dorsinville [1911-1992] poet, novelist
> Born in Port-au-Prince, he entered military school and was later Minister of Public Health and Ambassador to Venezuela. Some of his works are:
> > *Barrières* (1946),
> > *Pour Célébrer la Terre* (1954)

Le Grand Devoir (1962)
Toussaint Louverture (1965)

Franck Etienne [1936-] poet, playwright, novelist
Born in Saint-Marc, he pursued a teaching career and published several poems. He is one of the most acclaimed writers of the twentieth century. Some of his major works are:
Au Fil du Temps - compilation of poems
Ultravocal (1972) - novel
Pèlin Tèt - play in Creole
Dézafi - the first novel written in Creole
Mûr à Crever - novel
Les Affres d'un Défi - novel

Jean Fouchard [1912-1990] historian
Fouchard was born in Port-au-Prince on March 2, 1912 and earned a degree in law in his native city. He worked in journalism and founded the periodical *La Relève*. He exercised several political functions, one of which was Ambassador to Cuba. His noteworthy historical publications include:
Les Marrons de la Liberté (1972)
Les Marrons du Syllabaire (1953)
Langue et Littérature des Aborigènes d'Ayiti (1972)
Plaisirs de Saint-Domingue (1955)
Le Théâtre à Saint-Domingue (1955)
Artistes et Répertoires des Scènes de Saint-Domingue (1955)

Roger Gaillard [1923-] historian, novelist
Born in Port-au-Prince on April 10, 1923, he was awarded a degree in philosophy at the Sorbonne in France. His works are primarily literary studies and historical research. Gaillard is among the most renowned contemporary writers in Haiti. He wrote extensively on the United States occupation of Haiti.
L'Univers Romanesque de Jacques Roumain (1965)
La Destinée de Carl Brouard (1966)
Les Cent Jours de Rosalvo Bobo (1973)
Charlemagne Péralte le Caco (1982)
La Guérilla de Batraville (1983)
La Déroute de l'Intelligence (1992)

Gérard Mentor Laurent (historian)
> His writings on the history of Haiti include:
>> *Coup d'Oeil sur la Politique de Toussaint Louverture*
>> (1945)
>> *Six Etudes sur J. J. Dessalines* (1951)
>> *Pages d'Histoire d'Haïti* (1960)
>> *Haiti et l'Indépendance Américaine* (1976)
>> *Le Commissaire Sonthonax à Saint-Domingue*
>> (4 volumes 1965-1974)

Dr. Rulx Léon (historian, journalist)
> He is one of the most respected Haitian scholars. He wrote a documentary on the history of Haiti, *Propos d'Histoire d'Haïti* (1945/1974).

Alix Mathon [1908-?] novelist
> Lawyer, statesman, and journalist, he received the prize France-Haïti in 1972 for his novel on events that led to the United States occupation of July 1915, *La Fin des Baïonnettes* (1972). His other novels are:
>> *Le Drapeau en Berne (1974)*
>> *Témoignages sur les Evénements de 1957*
>> *La Reléve de Charlemagne*

Félix Morisseau-Leroy [1912-] poet, novelist
> He was born in Jacmel on March 13, 1912. He first studied in Haiti, then traveled to the United States to earn a master's degree in literature at the University of Columbia. He exhibited his literary skills in journalism, theatre, and poetry. He is an indigenous writer, as his writings are on Haiti and its roots. He also published several compilations of poems, among which are *Plénitudes* (1940) and *Diacoute* (1951), and a short story in verse, *Natif-natal.*

René Philoctète [1932-] poet
> Born in Jérémie in 1932, he published his first poem, *Saison des Hommes*, (1960). He also published *Les Tambours du Soleil* (1962) and *Ces Iles qui Marchent* (1969).

Pradel Pompilus (essayist)
He is the co-author of a three-volume study on the history of Haitian literature and is considered one of the most respected Haitian scholars.

Dr. Jean Price-Mars [1876-1968] theoretician, commentator
Born in 1876 at Grande Rivière du Nord, he entered a diplomatic career and completed his medical education. He wrote several bestselling books, among which is *Ainsi Parla l'Oncle* (1928) which was translated in English as "So spoke the Uncle." His other works include:
La Vocation de l'Elite (1919)
La République d'Haïti et la République Dominicaine (1953)
De Saint-Domingue à Haïti (1957)
Dr. Jean Price Mars is considered one of the greatest Haitian scholars.

Jacques Roumain [1907-1944] poet, novelist
A native of Port-au-Prince, he belonged to an upper class family. He is the grandson of Tancréde Auguste, President of Haiti from 1912 to 1913. Roumain studied in Haiti and in Europe. During the Second World War he conducted ethnographical research at Columbia University, and then founded the Office of Ethnology in Haiti. He contributed several poems and important novels and is well known and acclaimed for his famous work, *Gouverneurs de la Rosée* (1931). Some of his other novels are:
La Proie et l'Ombre (1930)
Les Fantoches (1931)
La Montagne Ensorcelée (1931)

Emile Roumer [1903-1988] poet
He was born in Jérémie on February 5, 1903, completed his secondary studies in France, and studied business in Manchester, England. The themes of his poetry are primarily nature, satiric attack and love.
Le Caïman Etoilé (1963)
Poèmes d'Haïti et de France (1925)
Poèmes en Vers (1947)
Rosaire Couronne Sonnets (1964)

Edris Saint-Amand [1918-] novelist
Born in Gonaïves on March 26, 1918, he published a notable novel titled *Bon Dieu Rit* (1952).

Laurore St Juste (historian)
He conducted research on the history of Haiti and is a very respected Haitian scholar.

Horace Pauléus Sannon [1870-1938] historian
Sanon was born in Cayes on April 7, 1870. He completed his secondary education in Haiti and pursued studies in social-political sciences in Paris. He is known for his research on the history of Haiti. He wrote *Essai Historique sur la Révolution de 1843* and *Histoire de Toussaint Louverture*.

Hénock Trouillot [1923-1988] historian, novelist
He is recognized for his notable historical and sociological books.
Historiographie d'Haïti (1954)
La Vengeance du Mapou (1967)
La Condition des Nègres Domestiques à Saint-Domingue (1955)
Economie et Finances de Saint-Domingue (1965)
Le Gouvernement du Roi Henri Christophe (1974)

Alain Turnier (historian)
Turnier is the author of several contemporary Haitian bestsellers:
Les Etats-Unis et le Marché Haïtien
Avec Mérisier Jeannis
Quand la Nation Demande des Comptes

Noted Haitian Artists

Gesner Abellard [1922-] painter, sculptor
Born in Port-au-Prince on February 11, 1922, he was educated in Haiti. A member of the Haitian Art Center, he received a Bronze Medal at the International Bicentennial Exposition of Port-au-Prince in 1949. His specialty is sculpture, but he also paints unusual birds and trees.

Gabriel Alix [1930-] painter
A native of Saint-Marc, and a member of the Haitian Art Center, he paints vases of flowers and religious life scenes.

Ralph Allen [1952-] painter
Born in Port-au-Prince, he was awarded a scholarship to the National Academy School of Fine Arts in New York. He exhibited his paintings at the Loeb Center in New York University, the National Academy of Design and the Audubon Society.

Jackson Ambroise [1952-] painter, landscapist
Born in Milot, he is a landscape and dream painter. His paintings are seen in Venezuela, France, Surinam, Guadeloupe and Martinique.

Montas Antoine [1926-] painter
Born in Léogane on December 13, 1926, he was educated in Haiti. He is a painter who likes strong color. He paints street scenes and palm trees and also rural marriages.

Gesner Armand [1936-] painter
Armand was born in Croix-des Bouquets on June 11, 1936. He studied in Haiti and France. He became Director of the Museum of Haitian Art at St. Pierre's College. His paintings were shown in Mexico, the United States, France, Spain, Jamaica, Martinique, Venezuela, Barbados, Dominican Republic, Guadeloupe and Israel.

Georges Auguste [1933-] painter
Born in Petit-Goâve, his style has been called the "Raw Art."

Castera Bazile [1923-1966] painter
Born in Jacmel on October 7, 1923, he worked on the murals of the Holy Trinity Cathedral of Port-au-Prince. In 1955, he won the Grand Prize of the Caribbean International Competition.

Rigaud Benoit [1911-1986] painter
A native of Port-au-Prince, he worked on the murals of the Holy Trinity Cathedral of Port-au-Prince. He painted folklore and voodoo scenes. He created the Nativity, which is one of the Holy Trinity Cathedral's masterpieces.

Wilson Bigaud [1931-] painter
Born in Port-au-Prince on January 29, 1931, he first worked with clay, then shifted to painting. He won the second prize for his canvas entitled "Paradise" at the International Exhibit in Washington in 1950. He painted on the walls of the Holy Trinity Episcopal Cathedral in Haiti.

Roland Blain [1934-] painter
A native of Port-au-Prince, he paints jungles, animals, exotic birds and landscapes.

Fabolon Blaise [1959-1985] painter
Born in Cap-Haïtien, he painted landscapes, historical scenes, folkloric and voodoo scenes.

Saint-Louis Blaise [1956-] painter
Born in Cap-Haïtien, he paints historical themes. His works have been shown in Paris.

Serge Moléon Blaise [1951-] painter
Hailing from Cap-Haïtien, he paints battles and historical scenes.

Gérald Bloncourt [1926-] painter
Born in Bainet, a small city in the Southern Region of Haiti, his specialty is in watercolor, etching, painted frescoes and

drawings. He is a Founding Member of the Haitian Art Center.

Ludovic Booz [1940-] painter, sculptor
Born in Aquin, his specialty is painting and sculpture. He carved the bronze bust of several presidents and had showings in France, Israel and Surinam.

Maurice Borno [1917 -1955] painter
Born in Port-au-Prince, he was educated in Haiti, New York and Paris. He was a Founding Member of the Haitian Art Center. He is considered as one of the pioneers of Haitian art.

Jn Baptiste Bottex [1918-1979] painter
From Port Margot in Northern Haiti, he was a Naïve painter. His interest was in biblical topics and daily scenes of Haitian life. His works were displayed at the Haitian Art Center.

Seymour Etienne Bottex [1926-] painter
A native of Port-Margot, Northern Haiti, he paints biblical and historical scenes. He exhibited in the United States, England, France and Italy.

Henry-Robert Brésil [1952-] painter
He hailed from Gonaïves. As a landscape painter he exhibited in the United States, Puerto Rico, France, Italy and Switzerland. He received recognition in the New York Times and The Miami Herald.

Murat Brierre [1938-1988] sculptor
Born in Port-au-Prince, he did voodoo and Christianity sculpture. His works are seen in the United States, Mexico, and Jamaica. His work is displayed at the National Pantheon of Haiti.

Bourmond Byron [1920-] painter
Originally from Jacmel, he paints Haitian life scenes and dream landscapes.

Jean Claude Castera [1939-] painter
> Born in Pétionville, he studied in San Juan, Puerto Rico. He paints libertines.

Dieudonné Cédor [1925-] painter
> Born in Anse-à-Veau, he exhibited in Guatemala (1951), Mexico (1952), Germany, Belgium, and Holland (1968), Miami (1969), and in Venezuela, Colombia and Panama. He painted the remarkable mural for the Haiti International Airport in 1967. He was awarded the Labor Department Exhibition Prize in Haiti in 1953 and the Grand Work Prize of the Office of Tourism, Haiti (1957). He is a renowned Haitian painter.

Ralf Chapoteau [1954-] painter
> Born in Gonaïves, his works were displayed in Guadeloupe and Santo Domingo.

Etienne Chavannes [1939-] painter
> Born in Cap-Haïtien, he likes to paint crowds, religious celebrations, funerals or sports events. He has a colorful descriptive style to which he adds humor, warmth and vivacity. His works were shown at the Brooklyn Museum in New York in 1978.

Villard Denis (Davertige) [1940-] painter
> From Port-au-Prince, he is known as a poet and painter. He has exhibited in Mexico, Spain, France, Canada.

Rose-Marie Desruisseaux [1933-1988] painter
> Born in Port-au-Prince, she had showings of her paintings in Senegal, Venezuela, Santo Domingo, the United States, Canada, and Martinique, and was awarded numerous prizes in Haiti.

Philippe Dodard [1954 -] graphic artist, painter
> Port-au-Prince was his birthplace. He worked as an advertising illustrator and received a scholarship to the International School in Bordeaux, France, to specialize in pedagogic drawing. He exhibited in Surinam, Brazil, France, and the United States.

Roland Dorcély [1930-] painter
> Born in Port-au-Prince, he had a showing of his work in the United States, France, Canada and Colombia. His paintings can be found in the private collections of The Museum of Modern Art in Paris and the New York Museum of Modern Art.

Nicolas Dreux [1956-] painter
> Born and raised in Port-au-Prince, he paints landscapes and seascapes. He held exhibitions in the West Indies.

Abner Dubic [1944-] painter
> Born in Léogane, he is a painter whose works were shown in Paris and sold in galleries in New York, Chicago and Paris.

G. Emmanuel Ducasse [1903-] painter
> Born in Port-au-Prince, he paints historical events.

Préfète Duffaut [1923-] painter
> Born in Jacmel, he is a Naïve painter who specializes in religious scenes. His works were shown in the United States and Europe.

Edouard Duval-Carrié [1954-] painter
> Born in Port-au-Prince, he studied at the University of Montreal and McGill University in Quebec. He was awarded a Bachelor of Arts degree from Loyola University in Montreal. His paintings have been purchased by the Detroit Museum and the Museum of Davenport in Iowa.

Franck Etienne [1936-] painter
> Born in Port-au-Prince, he is also known as a writer, poet and playwright. His paintings are colorful. He likes blue and red, and is classified as an Abstract painter.

Jacques Gabriel [1934-1988] painter
> A native of Port-au-Prince, he studied at the New School of Social Research in New York. He received a scholarship from the French Government to study in Paris. The Museum of Modern Art of the City of Paris acquired his drawings

entitled, *Transparencies*. His works were shown in the United States, France, Italy and Jamaica.

Marie José Nadal-Gardère [1931-] painter, metal sculptor
Port-au-Prince was her birthplace. She studied in France, then in Canada where she learned ceramics and metal sculpture. She is the owner of the Marassa Gallery in Pétionville, Haiti. She exhibited in the United States, Canada, Brazil, Spain, the Dominican Republic, France, Surinam, Martinique, Guadeloupe and Puerto-Rico. Her painting *Paysage Spatial* (Spatial Landscapes) is part of the collection of the Museum of Rennes, France.

Jean-Claude Garoute [1935-] painter, sculptor
Born in Jérémie, he is a sculptor and Abstract painter. He participated in numerous festivals around the world and is a co-founder of *Poto-Mitan*, the Museum of Ceramics in Haiti.

Max Gerbier [1951-] painter
Born in Milot, Northern Haiti, he paints landscapes and rural scenes of his native city. His paintings are found in France and the United States.

Jacques Enguerrand Gourgue [1930-] painter
A native of Port-au-Prince, he paints voodoo and rural scenes. He exhibited in Germany, Canada, Colombia, the Dominican Republic, Spain, the United States, Italy, Puerto Rico, Venezuela and Yugoslavia. He is viewed as one of the noted personalities in contemporary Haitian art.

Gérard Fombrun [1931-] sculptor
He studied architecture and sculpture in Haiti, France and Puerto Rico. He exhibited in Latin America and The Caribbean.

Alexandre Grégoire [1922-] painter
Born in Jacmel, his paintings are of pure Haitian naïve style. His themes are paradise, voodoo, historical events and daily Haitian life.

Georges P. Hector [1938-] painter

> Born in Petite Rivière de l'Artibonite, a small countryside town in Haiti, he specializes in outdoor landscape and murals. He exhibited in Senegal, Jamaica, Puerto Rico, the United States, and the Dominican Republic. He also became the General Secretary of the National Association of Haitian Artists (ANAH).

Edith Hollant [1938-] photographer, painter

> From Port-au-Prince, she specializes in photography and painting. She exhibited her works in New York.

Hector Hyppolite [1894-1948] painter

> Born in Saint-Marc, he produced 256 paintings in three years. His works are primarily voodoo scenes.

Harry Jacques (Arijac) [1937-] painter

> Hailing from Gonaïves, he studied architecture and painting. He exhibited in New York.

Eugène Jean [1950-] painter

> Born in Trou du Nord, he paints folkloric hilarious scenes and has had numerous exhibitions in the United States. He is a member of the Haitian Art Center.

Jean-Baptiste Jean [1953-] painter

> Born in Cap-Haïtien, and a member of the Haitian Art Center, his paintings were exhibited in the United States, the Dominican Republic, and France.

Néhémy Jean Paquot [1931-] painter, graphic artist, portraitist

> Born in Limbé, Northern Haiti, he worked as a graphic artist and studied portrait technique. He painted murals at the Haiti International Airport, and had showings in Europe and the United States.

Eric Jean-Louis [1957-] painter

> Born in Jérémie, he exhibited his paintings in the United States, Guadeloupe, Denmark, Curaçao, Switzerland and France. He was awarded several prizes in Haiti.

Henri Jean-Louis [1955-] painter
> A native of Jérémie, he is well known for his blue and green
> landscapes.

Jean-René Jérôme [1942-] painter, sculptor
> Born in Petit-Goâve, he taught at the School of Fine Arts in
> Port-au-Prince, and exhibited in Santo Domingo, Brazil,
> Canada, Senegal and Martinique. He does ceramics and
> sculpture.

Guy Joachim [1955-] painter
> Born in Cap-Haïtien, he paints historical themes and his
> works were exhibited in Germany, United States, Dominican
> Republic and France.

Antonio Joseph [1921-] sculptor, painter, serigrapher
> He was born in Barahona, Dominican Republic. While
> working as a professional tailor, he studied watercolor and
> sculpture in Haiti, and serigraphy in the United States. He
> travelled to France, Spain, Italy, Greece, Morocco, Germany
> and Switzerland in 1963. He received two Guggenheim
> Foundation Awards in 1953 and 1957. He became a member
> of the Administrative Council of the Museum of Haitian Art
> at St. Pierre's College in 1972, and taught drawing and
> serigraphy at the Art Center. He exhibited his works in the
> United States, Mexico, Jamaica, and Spain.

Gisou Lamothe [1935-] painter, clay sculptor
> Born in Port-au-Prince, she received a scholarship to Madrid
> and exhibited in Brazil, Venezuela, Spain, and the United
> States.

Lionel Laurenceau [1942-] painter
> He studied in Haiti and in France. He won the first prize at
> the New York World's Fair in 1966, and then established
> himself in Montreal, Canada. His paintings were shown in the
> United States, Canada, the Dominican Republic and Colombia.
> His inspiration is the human character.

Peterson Laurent [1888-1958] painter
> Born in Saint-Marc, he paints rural life scenes, U.S. battleships, vases of flowers, fish, baskets of fruits, and voodoo.

Luckner Lazare [1928-] painter, sculptor
> A native of Port-au-Prince, he studied painting and sculpture at the Haitian Art Center, and was granted a scholarship in 1951 to study in Paris. He exhibited at the French Institute in Mexico and the Zegri Gallery in New York. His works were also displayed in Puerto-Rico, Germany, Spain, France, Brazil, Cuba, the Virgin Islands, the United States and Canada. He is the founder of the *Brochette Gallery* (1956). Currently living in the United States, in 1976 he had an exhibition at the Paul Robeson Multimedia Center in Washington, D.C.

Jean-Claude Legagneur [1947-] painter
> His paintings were exhibited in the United States, Canada, France, Surinam and the West Indies.

Adam Léontus [1923-] painter
> He was born in Anse-à-Galets on the Haitian island of La Gonâve. A member of the Haitian Art Center, he paints birds and exotic fruits.

Georges Liautaud [1889-] sculptor
> Born in Croix-des-Bouquets, he is known as the leading sculptor and blacksmith in Haiti. He creates works of voodoo expression by using iron.

Frank Louissaint [1949-] painter
> Hailing from Aquin, he specializes in street scenes and rural life, and has developed a style called Hyper-realist.

Andrée Malbranche [1920-] painter
> Born in Port-au-Prince, she studied in Haiti. Her works were exhibited in Cuba in 1940 and in Mexico in 1941. She has been granted a special place in Haitian art.

Elzire Malbranche [1919-] painter
A native of Port-au-Prince, she is a member of the Haitian Art Center. She displayed her paintings in Brazil, the United States, Mexico and France.

Descollines Manès [1936-1985] painter, ceramic sculptor
Born in Petit-Trou-de-Nippes, he specialized in paintings and ceramics. He got his inspiration from the life scenes in Haiti and children on the streets.

Albert Mangonès [1917-] sculptor, painter
Born in Port-au-Prince, he studied at the Brussels Academy of Fine Arts and at Cornell University. He specializes in sculpture, drawing and painting. He became a Founding Member and Secretary General of The Haitian Art Center and built the Haitian monument *Marron Inconnu* "Unknown Maroon" (fugitive slave). He is the President and General Director of ISPAN, the Institute for the Preservation of Haitian National Heritage.

Michèle Manuel [1935-] painter
Born in Port-au-Prince, she studied in San Juan, Puerto Rico, then at the University of Rochester. Her paintings were shown in the United States and the Dominican Republic.

Ronald Mews [1945-] sculptor
Born in Port-au-Prince, he is celebrated as an excellent sculptor. He exhibited in the United States, Guadeloupe, the Dominican Republic, France and Surinam.

Pierre Monosiet [1922-1983] watercolor painter
Born in Port-au-Prince, he painted in watercolor and completed his education in Bad-Wurtemberg, Germany. He became Director of the Art Lovers' Gallery in Haiti in 1972, and the Curator of the Museum of Haitian Art at St. Pierre's College in Haiti. He was a consultant to the Haitian Art Center and was appointed to the Haitian National Commission for Cooperation in UNESCO.

Madsen Mompremier [1952-] painter
> A native of Gonaïves, his subjects are voodoo ceremonies. He exhibited his paintings in Italy, France, and the United States.

André Normil [1934-] painter
> Originating from Port-au-Prince, he paints voodoo, paradise scenes and holiday celebrations. He exhibited in England, Germany, Italy and France.

Charles Obas [1927-1968] painter
> Born in Plaisance, Northern Haiti, he painted scenes of rain and exhibited in the United States and South America.

Philomé Obin [1891-1986] painter
> Born in Limbé, he painted two murals for the Holy Trinity Cathedral in Port-au-Prince, and was highly acclaimed for his painting *Démocratie en Marche* "Democracy at Work." He strongly influenced Haitian art.

Sénèque Obin [1893-1977] painter
> Born in Cap-Haïtien and brother of the renowned Philomé Obin, he painted historical themes and used pure color and black.

Raymond Olivier [1943-] painter
> A native of Haiti, he won several first prizes for his paintings. He exhibited in Montreal, Spain, Switzerland, Tahiti, Miami, Paris and San Francisco.

Pierre Paillère [1904-1958] painter
> Born in Port-au-Prince, he painted in ink, pastels and oils, and displayed them at the Haitian Art Center.

Damien Paul [1941-] painter, sculptor
> Born in the Cul-de-Sac Plain, his inspiration is voodoo.

Gérard Paul [1943-] painter
> Born in Port-au-Prince, he paints voodoo scenes.

Salnave Philippe-Auguste [1908-1989] painter
>   Born in Saint-Marc, he was a lawyer by profession. He painted nature with animals and human beings. He was a member of the Haitian Art Center.

André Pierre [1914-] painter
>   Born in Port-au-Prince, he got his inspiration from voodoo scenes.

Emmanuel Pierre-Charles [1945-] graphic artist
>   Born in Port-au-Prince, he designs greeting cards and participates in several group exhibits. He also worked as a graphic artist and teacher. He was active in several arts associations in Haiti.

Vergniaud Pierre-Noel [1910-1982] graphic artist
>   Born in Port-au-Prince, he studied graphic art at Columbia University, and later studied in Buenos Aires and Paris. For six years, he worked for the American Museum of Natural History, producing entomological drawings. He was awarded the Prize for Excellence by the Washington Association of Industrial Artists for his drawing *Homage au Président John F. Kennedy*, "Tribute to President John F. Kennedy." He earned his international reputation in drawing stamps. He produced special editions for the Red Cross, the Third Inter-American Caribbean Congress, and the Pan-American Health Organization.

Max Pinchinat [1925-1985] plastic artist
>   From Port-au-Prince, he is a Plastic artist. In 1949, he won the Gold Medal at the International Exhibition in Port-au-Prince, He exhibited in France, United States, Mexico, South America, and Germany.

Louverture Poisson [1914-1985] painter
>   A native of Les Cayes, he became a member of the Haitian Art Center. His paintings were exhibited in Haiti and overseas.

Lucien Price [1915-1963] painter
Born in Port-au-Prince, he travelled to France and the United States, and shifted from a figurative to an abstract style. He used black and white in his paintings. He died in Port-au-Prince in 1963.

Georges Remponneau [1916-] painter, graphic artist
Growing up in Port-au-Prince, he studied industrial design in the United States. He specializes in drawing, painting, linoleum block illustrations for press and advertising. He is a Co-Founder and Treasurer of the Haitian Art Center. He received a medal for one of his works in New York City in 1939.

Camy Rocher [1956-1981] painter
Born in Baradères, Southern Haiti, he painted Voodoo scenes.

Alix Roy [1930-] painter
Born in Port-au-Prince, he completed his art and painting education in New York, and exhibited in the United States and Puerto Rico.

Robert Saint-Brice [1898-1973] painter
Born and raised in Pétionville, he primarily painted voodoo and religious scenes.

Lyonel Saint-Éloi [1950-] painter
A native of Port-au-Prince, he paints flowers and plants in grayish colors.

Fritz Saint-Jean [1954-] painter
Born in Port-au-Prince, he exhibited his paintings in Italy, Switzerland, France, England and the United States. He won a prize in Haiti.

Roosevelt Sanon [1952-] painter
Born in Jacmel, he exhibited his paintings in France, Switzerland and England.

Pétion Savain [1906-1973] painter
Hailing from Port-au-Prince, he studied at the Haitian School
of Agronomy and Law School. He won a Bronze Medal at the
New York World's Fair for his painting named *Market*. He
also studied at the Art Students' League in New York in 1941.
He used pink and purple semicircles and triangles as his
personal style.

Bernard Séjourné [1947-] painter, sculptor
Born in Port-au-Prince, he first studied in Haiti, then travelled
to the United States and enrolled at the Art Students' League
and at the American Art School in New York. He participated
in the Festival of Black Art in Dakar in 1966 and in the
Montreal Expo of 1967.

Jean-Louis Sénatus [1949-] painter
Born in Léogane, he exhibited his paintings in Martinique,
Guadeloupe, Denmark, France, Switzerland, Curaçao, the
United States, Italy and England.

Émilcar Similien (Simil) [1944-] painter, sculptor
Raised in Saint-Marc, he studied sculpture, casting, painting
and history of art. He became a professor at the Haitian Art
Center. He is an active member of the National Association of
Haitian Artists (ANAH), which was created in 1977.

Micius Stéphane [1912 -] painter
He was born in Bainet, a small town in Southern Haiti. He is
a Naïve painter and gets his inspirations from daily Haitian
scenes. He exhibited in Germany, the United States, England,
Italy, and France. He is one of the best contemporary Haitian
painters.

Hervé Télémaque [1937-] painter
Born in Port-au-Prince, he studied at the Art Students' League
in New York. He exhibited his paintings in Paris, London,
Rome, Milan, Turin, Barcelona, Washington, Zurich,
Copenhagen, Brussels and Havana.

Jean-Pierre Théard [1949-] painter
A native of Aquin, he studied architecture and exhibited in New York, Surinam and France. He has a special style named Fantastic Realism or *Réaliste Fantastique*.

Karoll Théard [1946-] portraitist
Growing up in Aquin, in Southern Haiti, he studied portrait technique in 1976 at the Art Students' League in New York and exhibited in Quebec, Canada. He specializes in portraits.

Sacha Thébaud [1934-] painter
He is the first Haitian artist to paint in beeswax. He had his works shown in Miami, Rio de Janeiro, St. Thomas, Madrid, Barcelona, San Juan, Montreal, New York and Sainte Croix.

Camille Torchon [1953 -] painter, landscapist
Born in Port-au-Prince, his favorite subjects are landscapes.

Luce Turnier [1924 -] painter
A native of Jacmel, a town in Southern Haiti, she received the French Government Scholarship in 1951, the Haitian Government Scholarship in 1952, and the Rockefeller Foundation Scholarship in 1967. She exhibited in Bonn, Bremen and Hamburg.

Fravrange Valcin (Valcin II) [1947 -] painter
Born in Jérémie, he is well known for his paintings, and is a member of the Haitian Art Center.

Gérard Valcin [1927 -1988] painter
Born in Port-au-Prince, he is one of the most admired Primitive painters. His inspirations are voodoo ceremonies, landscapes and rural life scenes.

Pierre-Joseph Valcin [1927 -] painter
Born in Port-au-Prince, he is a Naïve painter. He paints birds and flowers.

Louis Vassor [1887-1968] painter
Born in Port-de-Paix, he painted rural and historical themes.

Patrick Vilaire [1942 -] clay and ceramic sculptor, graphic artist
> Born in Port-au-Prince, he is a sculptor and graphic artist who works with ceramics and clay. He became a member of the International Ceramics Academy in 1964. He exhibited in Guyana, Senegal, the United States and Brazil.

Maurice Vital [1949 -] painter
> Born In Jacmel, he is inspired by voodoo and the ocean floors. He exhibited his paintings in the United States, France, Guadeloupe, Martinique, Denmark, Curaçao, Italy, Switzerland and England.

Bernard Wah [1939-1981] sculptor
> Born in Port-au-Prince, he studied in New York, and specialized in ceramics, sculpture and murals. His works were shown in the United States and Canada.

Hilda Williams [1924-] painter, sculptor
> Born in Port-au-Prince, she studied painting and sculpture. Her subjects are children. She participated in several exhibitions in Haiti.

LANGUAGE   6

Creole Expressions / 124

Creole - English Lexicon / 128

English - Creole Lexicon / 131

Selected Haitian Proverbs in Creole / 142

Creole Expressions

Bon jou.	Good morning.
Bon jou mézanmi.	Good morning, people (my friends).
Bon soua, tout moun.	Good evening, everybody.
Bon soua mésié, dam.	Good evening, Gentlemen and Ladies.
Ki jan ou yé?	How are you doing?
Pa pi mal. Mèsi.	Not bad. Thanks.
Pa pi mal. E ou minm?	Not bad. And you?
Ki jan moun yo yé?	How is everybody?
Ki jan fanmi ou Yé?	How is your family?
Ki jan ti moun yo yé?	How are the kids?
Ki jan kò-a yé?	How do you feel?
Ki jan santé-a yé?	How is your health?
Trè byin, mèsi.	Very well, thanks.
Bondié bon.	God is good.
Bondié.	God.
Bon.	Good.
Tan pri souplé.	Please.
Ou pa chita?	Why don't you sit?
Sa-k pasé?	What's up?
Nap boulé.	We are hanging in there.
Bam nouvél ou?	What's new with you?
Ki jan ou rélé?	What's your name?
Mouin rélé Diévé.	My name is Diévé.
Ki laj ou?	How old are you?
Mouin guin karant an.	I am forty years old.
Ki koté ou pralé?	Where are you going?
Koté ou pralé.	Where are you going?
M-pralé lakay mouin.	I am going home.
Ki koté ou rété?	Where do you live?
Mouin rété Kenscoff.	I live in Kenscoff.
Moun ki koté ou yé?	Where are you from?
Mouin cé moun Jacmel.	I am from Jacmel
Mouin cé abitan Kenscoff.	I am a peasant from Kenscoff.
Sa ou vlé?	What do you want?
Ki sa ou pédi?	What do you want?
Mouin vlé .	I want.
Map chèché travay.	I am looking for work.
Ki metié ou?	What's your profession?
Mézanmi!	Oh boy! really.
Ki moun ou yé?	Who are you?

Ki moun ki lá-a.?	Who is there?
Cé mouin qui lá-a.	It's me.
Eské ou grangou?	Are you hungry?
Oui mouin grangou anpil.	Yes, I am very hungry.
Anpil.	A lot, plenty.
E cé ké ou kap ban mouin?	Can you give me?
Oun tas dlo souplé.	A cup of water please.
Kèpòpòz.	Carefree.
Kaléwes.	Lazy.
Ou pa bwè Kafé?	Would you like a cup of coffee?
Télédjòl.	Grapevine. Word of mouth.
Véyé Zo ou.	Be careful.
M-ap vini kounyéa.	I am coming right away.
A Démin si dié vlé.	See you tomorrow.
Sé lavé min suyé até.	It is a waste of time.
Sé ransé yap ransé.	They are wasting time.
Mon compè.	My good old friend, buddy (male)
Ma comè.	My good friend (female)
Ou alé?	Are you leaving?
Di tout moun bon jou.	Say hello to everybody
M-alé. Na oué démin.	I am leaving. See you tomorrow.
admeton ke	let's assume
adouat agòch	left and right
bab pou bab	face to face
bay bouden	to do a bad job for
bay chenn	to bait, to harrass
bay kout ba	to play dirty trick
bay lebra	to give one's arm to.
bay lè	to make room, to get lost
gadé po ouè	to look and see, to wait and see
kont kò	to have more than meets the eye
lagé dé gidon dèyè	to pursue someone
maché di	to go around saying
ap malmennen	to treat roughly
ou poko la	that's not it
ralé kò	to get out of the way
gro lannuit	middle of the night
gro lajounen	middle of the day

LOVE EXPRESSIONS

Bèl fanm	Beautiful woman
Mouin rinmin ou	I love you.
Ma'p mouri pou ou.	I love you so much, i'll die for you.
Bèl négés.	Beautiful Haitian woman.
Bèl nèg.	Handsome man.
Mouin fou pou ou.	I am crazy about you.
Lanmou	Love
Ti chéri.	My darling.

FAMILY MEMBERS

Fanmi	Family
Papa	Father
Manman	Mother
Frè	Brother
Sè	Sister
Granmè	Grandmother
Grann	Grandmother
Granpè	Grandfather
Bèlmè	Mother-in-law
Bèlpè	Father-in-law
Granmoun	Grown ups (old person)
Fanmi mouin	My family
Pitit mouin	My child
Fanm	Woman, wife
Mari	Husband
Kouzin	Cousin
Tonton	Uncle (old man)

NATIONALITIES

Ayisyen	Haitian
Amérikin	American
Fransé	French

MONTHS (MOUA)

Janvié	January
Févriyé	February
Mas	March
Avril	April
Mé	May
Jin	June
Jiyè	July
Out	August
Séptanm	September
Octòb	October
Novanm	November
Désanm	December

DAYS (JOU)

Lindi	Monday
Madi	Tuesday
Mèkrédi	Wednesday
Jédi	Thursday
Vandrédi	Friday
Samdi	Saturday
Dimanch	Sunday

NUMBERS (NIMÉRO)

Zéro	Zero
Youn	One
Dé	Two
Toua	Three
Kat	Four
Sink	Five
Sis	Six
Set	Seven
Ouit	Eight
Nèf	Nine

Creole - English Lexicon

A

aba:	down with	akonpayé:	to accompany
abandonnen:	to abandon	akonpli:	to accomplish
abiman:	clothes	akouch:	to give birth
abitid:	habit	akouchman:	childbirth
abitué:	to be accustomed	anmoué:	help
		anvan:	before
abizé:	to abuse	apré:	after
abòdé:	to approach	aprémidi:	afternoon
aboli:	to abolish	avèg:	blind
abouti:	to arrive	avion:	airplane
absan:	absent	ayisyen:	Haitian
absoliman:	absolutely	Ayiti:	Haiti
achté:	to purchase		
adisyon:	addition		
adisyonnen:	to add	**B-C-D-E**	
admèton:	to assume		
administré:	to administer	bagay:	thing
adopté:	to adopt	baklé:	to botch
adouat agòch:	left and right	bay legen:	to give up
adrés:	address	bay:	give
advantist:	adventist	bon:	good
adié:	what a pity! oh! surprise	Bondié:	God
		bouat:	box
afè:	bargain or business	chak jou:	daily
		chapo:	hat
afeksyon:	affection	charmè:	bewitch
afòs:	because of, as a result of	chat:	cat
		chèz:	chair
afro:	afro	dapré:	according to
agòch	left	dat:	calendar date
agogo:	copiously	débaré:	to clear
agronòm:	agronomist	débodé:	audacious
ajans:	agency	deja:	already
ajisté:	to adjust	diné:	dinner
ak:	and	djòb:	job
akaryat:	bad-tempered	do:	back
akasan:	cornmeal porridge	dola:	dollar
		doloté:	to cuddle
akomodé:	to accommodate	éspoua:	hope

ésprè — on purpose
éspri — spirit
éstòmak — stomach

F-G-I

faché: — angry
fanmi: — family
fason: — behavior
fèt: — birthday
fi: — girl
garanti: — to assure
gason: — boy
gato: — cake
grangou: — hungry
grosomodo: — crude
grozotobré — important person
isit: — here
istwa: — history

J-K-L-M

jou: — day (date)
jounen: — the day
kabann: — bed
kado: — gift
kafé: — coffee
kapab: — to be able
kapital: — capital (city)
kat: — card
kay: — house
kinbé: — hold on
kòman: — how
kompayi: — company
konpliman: — congratulations
konplo: — conspiracy
konsa: — like that
konsanti: — consent
konsantman: — approval
konsolé: — to console
kont: — against
kontab: — accountant

kontak: — contact
kontra: — contract
labank: — bank
labib: — bible
lakay: — home
légliz: — church
liv: — book
lotbo: — abroad
machandé: — bargaining
mal: — bad
malfouti: — badly dressed
malgré: — although
manti: — lie
mari: — husband
mouin: — me
mouri: — die

N-O-P

nan: — in
noi: — black
Nouel: — Christmas
nuizib: — annoying
odians: — joke
oto: — car
oun lòt: — another
paback: — backwards
pami: — among, between
paské: — because
patou: — everywhere
péyi: — country
pitit fi: — daughter
pòt: — door
pozé: — ask
pyé: — leg

R-S-T-V-Z

rabaché: — botched
ranpli: — full
reklamasyon: — to claim
rélé: — to yell
sak: — bag

sal:	dirty
saldébin:	bathroom
si:	if
tabliye:	apron
tifi	young girl
tigason	young boy
timoun:	child
toujou:	always:
tout moun:	everyone
valiz:	handbag
vitès	speed
viv	to live
vivan	to be alive
vizib	visible
vizit	visit
vlé	to want
zaboka:	avocado
zanimo:	animals
zen:	gossip
zòrey:	ear
zouazo:	bird
zouti	tools

English - Creole Lexicon

A

abandon (to) :	abandonnen
able (to be):	kapab
abroad:	lòtbò
absent:	absan
absolutely:	absoliman
abuse (to):	abizé
accomodate (to):	akomodé
accompany(to):	akonpaye
accomplish(to):	akonpli
according to:	dapré
account:	kont
accountant:	kontab
accusation:	akizasyon
accustom (to):	abitué
add(to):	adisyonnen
addition:	adisyon
address:	adrès
adjust:	ajisté
administer (to):	administré
adopt (to):	adopté
adventist:	advantis
affection:	afeksyon
afro:	afro
after:	apré
afternoon:	aprémidi
against:	kont
agency:	ajans
agricultural:	agrikol
agriculture:	agrikilti
agronomist:	agronòm
airplane:	avion
alcoholic beverage:	grog
already:	deja
although:	malgré
always:	toujou
amen:	ensisoitil
among:	pami

ancestor:	zanset
and:	ak
angry:	faché
animals:	zanimo
annoying:	nuizib
another:	oun lòt
approach (to):	abodé
approval:	konsantman
approximately:	konsa
apron:	tabliye
arrive (to):	abouti
ask:	pozé
assure (to):	garanti
audacious:	débodé
audacious:	déchennen
avocado:	zaboka

B

back:	do
backwards:	pa bak
bad-tempered:	akaryat
bad:	mal
badly dressed:	malfouti
bag:	sak
bank:	labank
bargain:	afè
bargaining:	machandé
bark (to) :	japé
bathroom:	saldébin
beat up (to):	bay baton
beautiful:	bèl
because:	paské
bed:	kabann
before:	anvan
behaviour:	fason
belongings:	afè

better off:	miyò, pi bon	carry:	poté
between:	pami	castrate (to):	chatré
bewitch:	chamè	cat:	chat
bible:	labib	chair:	chèz
bird:	zouazo	change (to):	chanjé
birthday:	fèt	chapter:	chapit
bishop:	évek	charcoal :	chabon
black:	noi	charitable:	charitab
blacksmith:	machoket	charm:	cham
blind:	avèg	cheer (to):	rejoui
blister:	zanpoul	cheese:	fromaj
blue jeans:	abako	chest:	fal
boat:	chaloup	child:	timoun
book:	liv	childbirth:	akouchman
botch (to):	baklé	chocolate:	chokola
botched:	rabaché	christmas:	nouel
bouquet:	bouké flè	church:	légliz
bowl:	kui	claim (to):	reklamasyon
box:	bouat	clear (to):	débaré
boy:	gason	clothes:	abiman
bread:	pin	coals:	chabon difé
bring luck (to):	bay chans	coffee:	kafé
broom:	balè	company:	kompayi
buddy:	konpè	complain (to):	babye
bullet:	bal	condition:	éta
burden:	fado	congratulations:	konpliman
burst (to):	éklaté	consent (to):	maché
business:	afè	consent:	konsanti
butter:	bè	consequence:	konsekans
buy (to):	achté	console (to):	konsolé
		conspiracy:	konplo
		conspire (to):	konploté
C		constipated:	konstipé
		constipation:	konstipasyon
cake:	gato	consult (to):	konsilté
call:	rélé	contact:	kontak
camel:	chamo	continue (to):	kontinye
candle (white):	balenn	contract:	kontra
capital (city):	kapital	cope (to):	débouye
capricious:	kapris	copiously:	agogo
captain:	kapitenn	cornstarch:	farin mayi
car:	oto	cornmeal	
card:	kat	porridge:	akasan
cargo:	chajman	count (to):	konté
carpenter:	ébénis	country:	péyi

coward:	kapon	dress:	ròb
credulous:	égarè	drink:	bouè
crooked:	krochi	driver:	chòfè
crouch (to):	akoupi	drop off (to):	lagé
crude:	grosomodo	dry:	sèk
curse:	madichon		

D

E

daily:	chak jou	each:	chak
dance		ear:	zòrey
(social event):	bal	early:	bonè
date (calendar):	dat	easy:	fasil
daughter:	pitit fi	eat:	manjé
day:	jou, jounen	education:	édikasyon
decamp (to) :	dékanpé	effort:	jèfò
deceive (to):	bafoué	enjoyment:	jouisans
decipher (to):	déchifré	enlighten (to):	ékléré
declaration:	deklarasyon	enough:	asé, kont
declare (to):	déklaré	equal:	égal
dedicate (to):	dédié	erase (to):	éfasé
defend (to):	défann	escape (to):	chapé
deliver baby (to):	akouché	esteem (to):	estime
demand:	egzijans	even up (to):	égalizé
demolish (to):	déchalboré	evenly:	egalego
demon (small):	baka	event:	évenman
depressed:	afésé	every:	chak
devious:	entrigan	everyday:	touléjou,
die:	mouri		chak jou
dinner:	diné	everyone:	tout moun
dirty:	sal	everywhere:	patou
disadvantage:	enkonvenyan	exam:	egzamen
disconnect (to):	dékonnekté	exam:	konpozisyon
disheveled:	sankoutcha	example:	egzanp
disorder:	debanday	except:	sòf
dock (to) boat:	akosté	excite (to):	bay lafyev
doctor:	dòktè	exercise:	egzesis
dollar:	dola	exist (to):	egzisté
door:	pòt	explain (to):	espliké
double chin:	babin	explication:	esplikasyon
down with:	aba	extension:	ralonj
down:	anba	extinguish:	étenn
doze (to):	kabicha	exuberant:	débodé
dress (to):	abiyé	eyeglasses:	lunèt

F

factory:	faktori
family:	fanmi
farmer:	abitan
fatso:	patat si
field:	jaden
fifteen:	kinz
find (to):	join
fired (to):	déchouké
first:	prémié
fish:	pouasson
fit:	danblé
flour:	farin
follow:	suiv
food:	nouriti
foolishness:	égareman
for:	pou
forbid (to):	défann
foreign:	étranj
foreigner:	étranjé
forever:	toutan
forget:	bliyé
framework:	chapant
friend:	zanmi
frightful:	éfreyan
from there:	etan la
full:	ranpli
furious:	déchenen
furniture:	mèb
furthermore:	ansuit
future:	futu

G

garden:	jadin
gasoline:	gaz
gate:	bayé
gesture:	jès
get:	jouinn, trouvé
gift:	kado
girl:	fi
give birth (to):	akouché

give up (to):	bay legen
give:	bay
God:	Bondié
golden:	doré
goodbye:	bay bay
gossip:	zen
grapefruit :	chadek
grumble (to):	babye

H

habit:	abitid
Haiti:	Ayiti
Haitian:	ayisyen
hand:	min
handbag:	valiz
hangover:	mal makak
happiness:	kontantman
happy:	kontan
harrass (to):	baychenn
harvest (to):	rekolté
harvest:	rekolt
hat:	chapo
have:	gingnin
he:	li
heal (to):	géri
hear:	tandé
heat (to):	chofé
heat:	chalè
heel:	talon
help (to):	édé
help!	anmoué
here:	isit
history:	istwa
hold on:	kinbé
home:	lakay
honest:	debyen
honey:	siro miel
hook (to):	kroké
hook-and-eye:	agraf
hope:	espoua
hot:	cho

hope:	espoua	intelligent:	entelijan
hot:	cho	intention:	entansyon
hour:	lè	interest:	entéré
house:	kay	interested:	enterese
how:	kòman	interesting:	enteresan
how (many):	konbyen	intersection:	kafou
how long:	dépi ki lè	invasion:	envazyon
how much:	konbyen	invent (to):	envanté
hug:	anbrasé	invention:	envansyon
hungry:	grangou	invest (to):	envesti
hunt (to):	chasé	invisible:	envizib
hurt:	frapé	invite(to):	envité
husband:	mari	irresponsible :	dejoué
hypocrite:	ipokrit	irritate (to):	agasé
		irritating:	agasan

I

I(me):	mouin
idle:	envalib
if:	si
ignorance:	iyorans
ignore (to):	ignoré
immediately:	danblé
importance:	enpotans
important:	enpotan
impression:	enpresyon
imprudence:	enpridans
in:	nan
incompetent:	enkapab
indeed:	anvérité
independence:	endepandans
independent:	endepandan
informed:	enfomé
injure (to):	estopyé
injustice :	abi
innocent:	inosans
inside:	anndan
insolence:	ensolans
insolent:	ensolan
install (to):	enstalé
instruct (to):	enstui
instrument:	enstriman
insult (to):	jouré
intelligence:	entelijans

J

jaw:	machoué
jealous:	jalou
jealousy:	jalouzi
Jesus Christ:	Jézikri
Jesus:	Jézi
job:	djòb
joint (to):	join
joke:	odiàns
journey:	rout
joy:	joua
junk:	débri
just:	inosan

K

keep:	kinbé
key:	klé
kill:	touyé
killer:	ansasin
kind:	bon
king:	roua
kitchen:	kuizin
kneeling position:	ajenou
know:	konnin

L

label :	étiket
laboratory:	laboratoi
lampshade:	abajou
language (tongue):	lang
late:	ta
launch (to):	bay fil
launch:	chaloup
law:	loi
lawn:	gazon
lawyer:	avoka
left:	agòch
leg:	pyé
length:	longè
letter:	lèt
license:	patant
lie (down):	kouché
lie:	manti
life:	lavi
like that:	konsa
listen:	kouté
little (small):	piti, ti
live (to) :	abité
live:	viv
load (to):	chajé
load:	chay
long ago:	lontan
long time:	dat
look alike:	sanblé
look at:	gadé
look for (to):	chèché
lord:	ségnè
love (to be):	damou
love:	lamou

M

make a living (to):	chèché lavi
make fun of (to):	bay chalé
make up (to):	rékonsilye
make:	fabriké
makeshift bridle:	babouket

man:	nonm
mansion:	chato
many:	chay
marriage:	mariaj
marry:	marié
maybe:	pétèt
me:	mouin
meanwhile:	étan
medicine:	rémèd
meet:	rankontré
merchandise:	machandiz
milk:	lèt
Miss:	madmoizel
mock (to):	charé
money:	kòb, lajan
monkey:	makak
moon:	lalin
more:	ankò
more:	plis
morning:	matin
mother-in-law:	bèlmè
mountain:	mòn
mouse:	sourit
mouth:	bouch
Mrs.:	madan
much (very much):	bokou
much:	chay
mud:	labou
mumps:	mal mouton
music:	muzik
musician:	mizizyen
must:	doué
must:	fòk
my:	mouin
myself:	mouin-minm

N

nails:	zong
name:	non
national:	nasyonal

naturally:	natirelman	overflow (to):	débodé
near:	toupré	overseas:	lotbo dlo
neck:	Kou	oversleep (to):	domi tronpé
needle :	egui	overturn (to):	chaviré
neither:	nonplis		
never:	jamè		
new:	nouvo		**P**
news:	nouvél		
newspaper:	jounal	painting:	tablo
nice:	janti	pantry:	gadmanjé
night:	lannuit	paper bag:	saché
nine:	nèf	paper:	papyé
nobody:	pèsonn	part:	pyes
nod off (to):	bay kout tet	passion:	pasyon
none:	okinn	patience:	pasyans
not:	pa	pay:	péyé
nothing:	anyen	peace:	pè
nourish (to):	nouri	peddler (woman):	madansara
now:	kounyéa	pedestrian:	pyeton
nuisance:	nuizans	peel off (to):	dékalé
number:	niméro	pencil:	kréyon
nursery school:	jaden danfan	pharmacist:	famasyen
		pharmacy:	famasi
	O	pick a fight (to):	chèché kont
		picture:	imaj
obscenity:	jouman	pleasant:	agréyab
offended:	estomaké	please:	tanpri, souplé
office:	biro	plunder (to):	sakajé
oil:	luil	polite:	éduké
okra:	kalalou	ponder (to):	egzaminen
old:	ajé	poor:	pòv
oldest:	pi gran	pork:	kochon
on:	sou	porridge:	labouyi
one:	youn	post office:	lapòs
only:	sèl	post (to):	afiché
open:	ouvri	poster:	afich
opening:	ouveti	power:	puisans
orange:	zoranj	pregnant:	gro vant
other:	lot	presently:	koun yè-an
ourselves:	nou-menm	price:	pri
outdoors:	déyò	print (to):	enprimé
oven:	fou	prison:	prizon
over there:	laba	problem:	chay
over there:	laba-a	professor:	profésè
overactive:	about	prohibit (to):	défann

prune (to):	débranché	right (to the)	adouat
pull (to):	ralé	ring:	bag
pumpkin:	jouroumou	rip (to):	déchiré
punishment:	chatiman	river:	riviè
purchase:	acha	road:	rout
purpose (on):	espré	rob(to):	dévalizé
purpose:	bu	rock(to):	balansé
push:	pousé	room:	chanm
put on		rotten:	gaté
weight (to):	grosi	rudeness:	malonnekté
put on:	abiyé	rumpled:	dechifonnen
put:	mété		

Q-R

S

		sack (to):	sakajé
quality:	kalité	sacrifice:	sakrifis
quantity:	kantié	sad:	tris
quarrel:	kont	sail (to):	navigé
question:	késion	salt:	sèl
quick:	vit	sample:	echantiyon
quiet:	pozé	sandal:	sapat
quit:	kité	sandwich:	sandwich
railing:	balistrad	save (to):	ékonomizé
rain:	lapli	savings:	ékonomi
raincoat:	padsi	say:	di
rather:	pito	scald (to):	chodé
recess (school):	rékréyason	scatter:	gayé
recognize (to):	rekonet	school:	lékòl
recommendation:	rékomandasyon	scissors:	sizo
recovery:	gérizon	sea:	lanmè
register:	enskri	security guard:	gadyen
registration:	enskripsyon	see:	ouè
regret(to):	regret	seen:	te ouè
release (to):	lagé	selfish:	égois
relieve (to):	abréjé	sensitive:	sansib
remember:	sonjé	september:	séptanm
remove nails (to):	déklouré	serious:	sérié
remove stuffing		servants :	domestik
(to):	débouré	setback:	kontraryeté
rent:	loué	settlement:	règléman
resourceful:	débouyar	sexual relations:	afè
restless:	ajité	shadow:	lonbray
rice:	diri	shake hands (to):	bay lanmen
right now:	danblé	shark:	réken

shirt:	chémiz	stain:	tach
short:	kout	stairs:	eskalyé
shortchange (to):	bay bouden	standing:	débou
shove (to):	rabouré	start over (to):	rekomansé
show off (to):	bay jof	start:	kòmansé
sickness:	maladi	steal:	vòlé
sign (to):	siyen	stick:	baget
signature:	siyati	store:	magazin
silverware:	ajantri	story:	kont
since:	dépi, puiské	straighten out (to):	débarasé
singing:	chanté	street market:	maché
sister:	sè	street:	lari
sit (to):	chita	strong:	daplon
skillful:	abil	struggle (to):	débat
skin:	po	studies:	étid
slander (to):	bay moun non	study (to):	etidyé
		stupid:	ébété
slap:	sabo	subscription :	abonman
slate:	adouaz	suffocation:	étoufman
sleep (to):	domi	sugar:	sik
sleep:	somey	suitcase:	valiz
sleepy (to be):	endomi	summer:	été
smear (to):	badijonnen	sun:	soléy
smile:	souri	supplies:	provizion
so:	konsa	swallow (to):	valé
soap:	savon	sweep (to):	balé
socks:	choset	sweet potato:	patat
soldier:	solda	sweeten (to):	adousi
solid:	solid	swim:	najé
some:	inpé	syrup:	siro
someone:	you moun		
sometimes:	pafoua		
salmon:	somon	**T**	
son-in-law:	bofi		
sorrow:	chagren	table:	tab
sound:	son	take:	pran
spark:	étensel	tale:	kont
speak:	palé, kozé	tatters (in):	déchiré
speed:	rapidité	taxi:	taksi
speedy:	rapid	teacher:	profésè
spelling:	vokabilè	team:	ékip
spend money (to):	débouse	tear (to):	déchiré
sprinkle (to):	farinen	tear up (to):	déchèiyé
spry:	enganm	tell (to):	rakontée
spy:	espyon	temperature:	tanpératu

ten:	dis	traffic ticket:	kontravansyon
thanks:	mèsi	translate:	tradui
that:	sa	transport (to):	charye
the:	la	trap:	pyèj
their:	pa yo	trash:	fatra
theirs:	pou yo	tree:	pyeboua
them :	yo	trifle:	bagatel
there:	laba, la	troubled:	tèt chajé
therefore:	donk	troublemaker:	bagarè
these:	sa yo	try:	éséyé
thief:	vòlè	tumble down (to):	déboulinen
thigh:	kuis	turn:	tounin
thin:	mins	twelve:	douz
thing:	bagay	twin:	jimo, marassa
thirst:	souaf	two:	dé
thirteen:	trèz	typewriter:	machin-a-ékri
this:	sa-a		
thorn:	pikan		
those:	sa yo		
three:	toua		**U**
throat:	gagan		
throw away:	voyé	unbearable:	ensipotab
thumb:	gro pous	unbutton (to):	déboutonnen
thus:	konsa	uncomfortable:	jennen
time:	tan	uncontrollable:	déchennen
tired:	about	uncork (to):	débouché
today:	jodi-a	under:	anba
toe:	zotèy	understand:	konprann
together:	ansanm	unemployed:	chomè
toilet:	watè	unfair:	enjis
tolerant:	charitab	unhappy:	pa kontan
tolerate (to):	admet	unhook (to):	dékochté
tomato:	tomat	United States:	étazini
tomorrow:	démin	unkind:	malonnet
tongue:	lang	unload:	déchajé
too bad:	domaj	unscrupulous:	enkonsyan
too:	tou, osi	unseal (to):	dékachté
tool:	zouti	unstick (to):	dékolè
tooth :	dan	untidy:	débrayè
toothbrush:	bros-a-dan	unwind(to):	débobiné
toothpaste:	pat dantifris	upright:	débou
torch:	chandèl	uproot (to):	déchouké
total:	total	upset (to be):	kontraryé
touch:	manyen	upstart:	patékoué
toy:	jouet	us:	nou
		useful:	itil

useless:	initil	whipping :	kal
uselessness:	san itilité	white(man):	blan
		white (woman):	blanch
		why:	puokoua /
V-W			pouki
		wicked:	malfézan
vacation:	vakans	widen (to):	agrandi
vaccinate (to):	vaksinen	wife:	madanm
vaccine:	vaksen	wind:	van
vendor:	manchan	window:	fénèt
very:	trè	without:	san
violence:	déblozay	woman:	fanm
VIP:	zotobré	wonderful:	mèvéyé
visit:	vizité	word:	paròl
vomit (to):	bay djapot	work hard:	travay di
wait (to):	chitatann	work:	travay
walk:	mach	worker:	ouvriyé
war:	lagè	world:	lémonn
waste:	déchè,	would:	ta vlé
	gaspiyay	write:	ékri
wasted:	gaspiyé		
water:	dlo		
wave:	vag		
we:	nou	**Y-Z**	
Wednesday:	mèkrédi		
week:	sémèn	yard:	lacou
welcome:	akéyi	yawn (to):	bayé
well-behaved :	dosil	year:	ané
well:	byen	yearly:	chak ané
whale:	balènn	yell (to):	rélé
what:	kisa	yes:	oui
wheat flour:	farin frans	yesterday:	yè
when:	kilè	you:	ou
where:	kikoté	young:	jènn
whereas:	tandiské	yourself:	ou-menm
which:	ki	youth:	jènnes
while:	pandan,	zero:	zéro

Selected Haitian Proverbs in Creole

1. **A défò chien kabrit alé la chas.**
   Do the best with what you have.

2. **Afè kay moun cé mystè.**
   Other people's business is a mystery.

3. **A foce makak caressé pitite li, li tué li.**
   You may kill love with too much embrace.

4. **A foce poul nui niche li, li crazé zœ li.**
   By overdoing it, you end up destroying everything.

5. **Aidé tèt ou, pou Bondié kab aidé ou.**
   God helps those who help themselves.

6. **Allé pas di poté vini pou sa.**
   Looking for something does not necessarily mean you already get it.

7. **Ambition tué rat.**
   Too much ambition can kill you.

8. **Apparence conn trompé.**
   Appearances are deceptive.

9. **Apré plaisi cé déplaisi.**
   After good times come bad times.

10. **Attention pas capon.**
    Being careful is not being a coward.

11. **Avant chin mangé zo, li mesuré machoi li.**
    Before you do something, make sure you evaluate the risks.

12. **Avantaj béf cé nan kòn li li rété.**
    The strength of a cow lies on its horns.

13. **Anvan tiraj tout loterie bèl.**
    Before the drawing all lottery tickets are attractive.

14. **Avant ou voyé roche nan maché gadé si manman ou pas la.**
Before starting a fight, make sure you are not going to hit a loved one.

15. **Avek lé tan na oué anpil bagay.**
As time goes, events unfold.

16. **Babyé malfini, babyé manman poul.**
We always blame everybody around us.

17. **Bat fè a lè li chaud.**
Do it while you still have the time.

18. **Baton ki bat chin noi an bat chin blanc an tou.**
The lash that whips the black dog whips the white dog also. Fate does not discriminate.

19. **Bèf caca pou li sal savann min cé dèyè li, li sal.**
Trying to hurt someone, you end up hurting yourself.

20. **Bèf pa conn di savann mèci.**
Cows show no gratitude toward the valley.
We often take good things for granted.

21. **Bèf pa janm bouké pòté còne li.**
An ox never gets tired of carrying its own horns.

22. **Bèl figu pas empéché maladie.**
Good looks do not shield from misfortune.

23. **Bèl fleu san odeu.**
Flower rich in beauty yet poor in fragrance.
Attractive person lacking kindness, generosity, love, warmth, intelligence and any virtues.

24. **Bèl kay pa ezans.**
Having a beautiful house does not mean being well off.

25. **Bèt ak ké pa jambé difé.**
Animals with long tails do not jump fire.
Beware of what you do if you have offsprings.

26. **Bien pré pa la caille.**
Being close to the goal doesn't mean you have reached it.

27. **Boi pouri min paròl pa pouri**
     Wood rots, but words do not.

28. **Bon afè fait bon zanmi.**
     Honest transactions build honest friendship.

29. **Bondié di:"Tout ti moun yo, couché,"**
     Couleuvre di: "Moin a tè a déja."
     God says "You who are my children lie down." The snake replies
     "I am already on the ground."

30. **Bondié pi fò ké diable.**
     God is stronger than the devil.

31. **Bon francé pa lesprit.**
     Good education is not intelligence.

32. **Bouche manjé tout manjé li pa palé tout parol.**
     Although you may eat whatever you want, beware of what you say.

33. **Bouche gran moune senti; sak ladan'l cé vérité.**
     The mouth of grown-ups smell bad, but what they say may be the
     truth. Even if old advice is unpleasant, it might be helpful.

34. **Bourik fait pitite pou'l posé do li.**
     Offsprings are security for old age.

35. **Bourik travay choual galonnin.**
     The poor works while the rich plays.

36. **Causé mandé chaise.**
     You need to sit down to hear a good story.

37. **Cé graisse kochon ki kuit kochon.**
     It is the fat of the pork, that cooks the pork.

38. **Cé lesprit kò ki condui kò.**
     It's the spirit that leads the body.

39. **Cé nan chin maig ou oué puce.**
     It is easier to find faults in the poor and powerless.

40. **Cé nan chimin jinnin yo kimbé choual malin.**
     It takes a thief to catch a thief.

41. **Cé pain rassi ki fé bon soup.**
    Stale bread makes a better soup.

42. **Cé pa tout blésu ki guéri**
    Not all wounds heal.

43. **Cé pa tout pié bois ki gonmin.**
    Not all trees are the same.

44. **Cé pa tout victoi ki duré.**
    Not all victories last long.

45. **Cé pa tout zorey ki tandé.**
    Not all ears can hear well.

46. **Cé piment zouazo ki piqué.**
    It is the little things that hurt.

47. **Cé queue ki suiv kò.**
    The tail follows the body.

48. **Cé sak nan min ou ki pa ou.**
    Whatever you hold is yours.

49. **Cé tèt ki condui kò.**
    It is the thought that leads the action.

50. **Cé ti bouton ki minnin maling.**
    Little problems lead to big ones.

51. **Chaille sòti nan tèt, tombé nan zépòl.**
    The load falls from your head onto your shoulders. Going from bad to worse.

52. **Chak saint chak offrand.**
    To each saint his own offering.

53. **Chemin long pa tué moune.**
    A long road will not kill anybody.

54. **Choual kon longè còd li.**
    The horse knows the length of its rope.

55. **Connin tròp pa bon.**
    Knowing too much can be a problem.

56. **Consey pi fò pasè ouanga.**
    Good advice is better than any magic trick.

57. **Couté cé remèd kò.**
    Listening to advice can be a cure.

58. **Créole palé, créole comprenn.**
    If we speak the same language, we should understand each other.

59. **Dé gé pété pa joué zo.**
    Two blind persons do not play together.

60. **Dépi ou grangou ou pa oué.**
    When you are hungry you cannot see.

61. **Dé tèt, dè lesprit.**
    Two heads, twice the intelligence.
    Two heads are better than one.

62. **Dé trou menti pa fond.**
    Anything based on lies cannot be deep.

63. **Déveinn cé pian.**
    Bad luck is a disease.

64. **Dèyè mòn gin mòn**
    Behind mountains, there are more mountains. Problems line up.

65. **Dlò pa monté mòne.**
    Water does not climb hills.

66. **Evité malheu pi bon passé ranjé li.**
    Prevention is better than cure.

67. **Fait le fou pou pa payé patent.**
    Play the insane in order not to pay taxes.

68. **Fanm jalouse pa janm gras.**
    Jealousy makes one unattractive.

69. **Fi cé marchandise fragil.**
    Women are complex.

70. **Figu cé glass coeu.**
    The face is the window of the heart.

71. **Fòk ou pa tué poul lan pou ou pren zoeu li.**
You should not kill the hen just for its eggs.

72. **Gadé pa janm tròpe.**
One can never look too much.

73. **Gé ki hont cé li ki kriyé.**
Shame triggers tears.

74. **Ginyin joujou pou tout laj.**
There are games for every age.

75. **Ginyin moune ak moune.**
Not everybody is the same.

76. **Ginyin rémèd pou tout bagay excépté lan mò.**
There is a remedy for everything except for death.

77. **Grand lidé ti mémoi.**
Great ideas, little action.

78. **Grangou cé mizé, vent plein cé tracas.**
Hunger is misery, a full belly has worries.

79. **Grangou nan vent pa douce.**
Hunger is not sweet.

80. **Gro bounda pa vlé di la santé.**
Being hefty does not necessarily mean being healthy.

81. **Habitude cé vice**
Habits can become addiction .

82. **Jan chat maché cé pa konsa li kinbé rat.**
The way the cat walks is not the way it catches rats.

83. **Jouèt chat, cé cri sourit.**
Things that are pastimes for cats are tears for mice.
One man's loss is another man's gain.

84. **Kay voisin pa pa ou.**
Your neighbor's house is not yours.

85. **Kouri pou la pli, tombé nan la riviè.**
Running away from the rain, you fall in the river.

86. **La fimin pa soti san difé.**
There is no smoke without fire.

87. **Lajan caché duré lontan.**
Hidden money lasts longer.

88. **Lajan pa janm assez pou famnm.**
Money is never enough for a woman.

89. **Lajan rélé lajan.**
The more money you have the more you will get.

90. **Lamitié pa maché avek brui.**
Friendship does not work with noise.

91. **Lang cé oun bon baton.**
What one says can be hurtful.

92. **Lan mò pa kimbé kras.**
The ocean does not keep trash.

93. **Lan mò modé tout patout.**
Death strikes everywhere.

94. **Lanmou pas conn pantalon piécé.**
Love is blind.

95. **Lanmou viré tèt.**
Love makes fools.

96. **Lannée passé toujou pi bon.**
The old days are always the best.

97. **La riviè avèti pa tué cocobé.**
With a warning one can take action.

98. **Lennemi pa janm piti.**
Never underestimate your enemy

99. **Lesprit anpil bon min prudence pi bon.**
Being smart is good, but being careful is better.

100. **Leu bouch finmin mouch pa rentré.**
A closed mouth catches no flies.

101. **Leu maringouin ap volé ou pa konin kilés ki mal kilés ki femèl.**
When mosquitoes fly, you cannot tell the males from the females.

102. **Leu ou montré makak voyé roch, cé tèt ou li cassé.**
If you teach a monkey to throw rocks, it will throw rocks at you.

103. **Leu tèt pa travay cé pied ki travay.**
If your head is not working, your feet will be.

104. **Leu vant chat plein li di rat anmè.**
When a cat is full, it finds rats tasteless.

105. **Libèté pa license.**
Freedom is not anarchy.

106. **Makak pa joué ak tig.**
Monkeys do not play with tigers.

107. **Malhè pa gin klaxon.**
Misfortunes do not announce their arrival.
You cannot tell when misfortunes come.

108. **Mangé cuite pa gin mèt.**
What one creates benefits everyone who needs it.

109. **Marié bon, marié pa bon.**
Marriage has its good and bad side.

110. **Mauvé nouvèl toujou vré.**
Bad news is always true.

111. **Min anpil, chay pa lou.**
Many heads make work lighter.

112. **Moun ki manjé zoeu pa konnin doulè manman poul.**
Those who eat eggs do not know the pain of the hen.

113. **Mulate pòv cé nèg; nèg riche cé mulate.**
A poor mulatto is black and a rich black is a mulatto.

114. **Nan poin lajan nan poin fanm.**
No money, no woman.

115. **Nan poin kòb nan poin manjé.**
No money, no food.

116. **Nan poin rose san piquant.**
There is no rose without thorns.

117. **Nèg pa janm kontent sò yo.**
People are never happy with what they have.

118. **Ou pa discuté ak la vie, min ou subi li.**
You cannot argue with life, you just have to submit to it.

119. **Ou rékolté sa ou simin.**
You get what you work for.

120. **Ou toujou songé sa ou té vlé bliyé.**
You always remember what you want to forget.

121. **Pa janm konté zé nan vent poul.**
Never count the eggs that are not yet laid.

122. **Pa janm kouri nan dè chémin a la fois.**
Never try to take two roads at the same time.

123. **Pa janm lévè nèg nan domi pou ou bay li manjé.**
Do not wake up someone just to feed him/ her.

124. **Pa mété tout zé ou nan oun seul pagné.**
Do not put all your eggs in one basket.

125. **Papillon caressé lamp, li fait ronn li, et cé ladan li mouri.**
The moth flirts with the lamp, circles around it, and then is killed by it.

126. **Pa pren sa ki pa pou ou.**
Do not take what does not belong to you.

127. **Paròl nan koeu pa gaté zanmi.**
Words not said do not spoil friendship.

128. **Patience cé gagnan.**
Good things come to those who are patient.

129. **Pa voyé roche comblé lan mè.**
You cannot fill the ocean with rocks.

130. **Pié kout pren dévant.**
The slower your pace the earlier you should start.

131. **Piti pa chiche.**
A small gift is better than nothing.

132. **Piti pi bon pasé anyin.**
Just a little is better than nothing at all.

133. **Piti piti zouazo fè nich li.**
Step by step, the bird builds its nest.
Step by step, you'll build your dream.

134. **Pito ou prémié pasé ou dènié.**
It is better to be the first than the last.

135. **Pouasson pa oué dlò.**
Fish do not see the water.

136. **Poul ti taille pa janm fait coq kalité.**
A small hen cannot produce large chickens.

137. **Poul ki cacaillé cé li ki ponn.**
The hen that cackles is the one that has laid the egg.

138. **Priè avek criè pa empéché mouri.**
Prayers and tears cannot keep you from dying.

139. **Quand vent plin keu kontan.**
When you eat well, you are happy.

140. **Rat manjé kann, zandolit mouri inosan.**
The innocent always pays for the guilty.

141. **Ravét pa janm gin rézon dévan poul.**
The strongest always win.

142. **Rété trankil cé remèd kò.**
Being calm and quiet is a cure for the body.

143. **Sa Bondié ba ou, cé rété pranli.**
Take whatever God gives you.

144. **Sa Bondié kité pou ou lavalass**
     mét pasé li pap poté li alé.
     Whatever God has kept for you, no storm can wash away.

145. **Sa gé pa oué, coeu pa tounin.**
     What the eye does not see, the heart does not grieve over.

146. **Sa ki deyó guin tò.**
     The one who is absent is considered guilty.

147. **Sa ki pa guinyin pa pèdi anyin.**
     Those who have nothing lose nothing.

148. **Sa ki pa kapab kouri, maché.**
     If you cannot run, walk.

149. **Sa ki pa travay pa ka manjé.**
     If you don't work, you can't eat.

150. **Sa ki vlé paix préparé la gué.**
     If you want peace, you must prepare for war

151. **Sa mouin oué pou ou Antoine nan gonmyé pa oué li.**
     I can see you are heading for worse things than anyone can foresee.

152. **Sa ou pa konnin pi gran pasé ou.**
     What you do not know is greater than you can handle.

153. **Sa pov guinyin cé li li poté nan maché.**
     Your offering is contingent upon your wallet.

154. **Si ou bouè cé pou ou sou.**
     If you drink, you get drunk.

155. **Temps allé pap vini encò.**
     Past time will not come back.

156. **Ti moun cé richès.**
     Offsprings are gold.

157. **Ti moun konnin kouri min yo pa kon caché.**
     Children may know how to run, they do not know how to hide.

158. **Touléjou pa dimanch.**
     Everyday is not Sunday.

159. **Tout bagay ginyin temp yo.**
There is a time for everything.

160. **Tout bét nan lanmé manjé moune, min cé rékin ki poté mové non.**
Many animals of the ocean have hurt people, but the shark is the culprit.

161. **Tout campé pa vlé di fò.**
Not everybody who stands is strong.

162. **Tout chimin minnin Rome.**
All roads lead to Rome.

163. **Tout fanm koué yo bél.**
All women believe they are pretty.

164. **Tout maladi gin reméd.**
There is a cure for all illness.

165. **Tout manman pa minm.**
All mothers are not the same.

166. **Tout métié cé métié excépté volè.**
All jobs are valuable, except stealing.

167. **Tout métié nouri mèt li.**
All works bear fruits.

168. **Tout moun joinn soulié pou pié yo.**
There is a right person for everyone.

169. **Tout moun ki capon viv lontan.**
Cowards live longer.

170. **Tout prié gin amèn.**
All prayers can be answered.

171. **Tout rèv pa vérité.**
All dreams do not come true.

172. **Tout sa ki briyé pa lò.**
All that glitters is not gold.

173. **Tout sa ki ékri pa lévanjil.**
Everything that is written is not necessarily true.

174. **Tout sa ou pa rinmin cé li ou joinn.**
It is what you do not like which sometimes befalls on you.

175. **Tout sommeil cé mim.**
Sleep is the same for all.

176. **Tout voum cé do.**
All sound can be music.

177. **Travail fè mal.**
Working is not easy.

178. **Tro pressé pa di conn rout.**
Being in a hurry doesn't mean you know your way .

179. **Tròp lesprit, sot pa loin.**
Being too much of a genius can lead to madness.

180. **Tro pressé pa fait jou'l ouvri.**
Being in a hurry doesn't make the day go faster.

181. **Tro ri fait crié**
Laughing too much can make you cry.

182. **Vérité cé gé.**
You can only know what you see.

183. **Vérité offensé.**
Telling the truth hurts.

184. **Vérité rété nan fond puits.**
Truth lies at the bottom of a well.

185. **Vié chaudiè crevé bon pois.**
The old pot cooks beans better.
Old ways can be useful.

186. **Voisinaj cé fanmi.**
Neighbors are family.

187. **Vré couraj cé konin souffri.**
True courage is blaring suffering.

188. **Yo pa janm poté dlo nan pagné.**
You can never carry water in a basket.

189. **Yo pa janm pren mouch ak vinaig.**
You cannot catch flies with vinegar.

190. **Yo pa jugé moun sou mine yo.**
You cannot judge people by their appearances.

191. **Yo pa mété chat véyé mantég.**
Do not ask a cat to watch over the butter.
Do not expect the thief to watch over the prey.

192. **Yo rangé tout bagay excépté bonheu.**
You cannot buy happiness.

193. **Zafè mouton pa zafè cabrit.**
The sheep's business is not the goat's business.
What works for one does not work for another.

194. **Zandolite bail fanm li sel mésu main li.**
We evaluate others according to their assets.

195. **Zanmi fait penn.**
Friendship can hurt.

196. **Zéclè pa janm frapé mim koté.**
Lightning never strikes the same place twice.

197. **Zégui pa janm ouè gé pa li.**
It's hard to see one's own faults.

198. **Zorey pa doué pi long pasé tèt**
Ears cannot be longer than the head.
Do not try to do more than you can.

199. **Zorier cé bon conséyé.**
The night is a good counselor.

200. **Zouazo ki gin plim pa chanté**
Peacocks do not sing because they will draw too much attention.

ECONOMICS 7

Major Banks / 157

Currency and Exchange Rate / 159

Sample of Monthly Salaries in Haiti / 162

**Flows of Direct and
Fixed Investments in Haiti / 163**

- - -

Major Banks

GOVERNMENT BANKS

Banque de la République d'Haïti (BRH)
Bank of the Republic of Haiti (Central bank). Originally "Banque Nationale de la République d'Haïti" (BNRH), National Bank of the Republic of Haiti created on October 25, 1910. Reorganized under the law of August 17, 1979 into two banks: The Central Bank (BRH) and the National Bank of Credit (BNC).

Banque Populaire Haitienne (BPH)
Created on August 20, 1973
Headquarters in Port-au-Prince, with branches in other cities.

Banque Nationale de Crédit (BNC)
Created on August 17, 1979
National Bank of Credit
Provides all the services of a commercial bank.

FOREIGN COMMERCIAL BANKS

First National Bank of Boston
Since October 25, 1972

Banque Nationale de Paris, S.A.
National Bank of Paris
Since December 31, 1973

First National City Bank
Since July 1st, 1971

Bank of Nova Scotia
Since June 19, 1972

PRIVATE BANKS

Société Générale Haitienne de Banque S.A. (SOGEBANK)
      Created on January 27, 1986
      Provides the services of a commercial bank.

**Société Générale Haitienne de Banque
d'Epargne et de Logement S.A. (SOGEBEL)**
      Created on August 16, 1988
      Provides the services of a savings and loan institution plus
      offers real estate loans for residential and commercial
      properties.

Banque de L'Union Haitienne (BUH)
      Created on July 9, 1973
      Performs all the activities of a commercial bank.

DEVELOPMENT BANK

**Banque Nationale de Développement Agricole et Industriel
(BNDAI)**
      Created in January 11, 1984.
      Public autonomous government-owned bank.
      National Bank of Agricultural and Industrial Development.
      Provides long term lending for development of agricultural
      facilities and projects of development.

OTHER BANKS

Banque de Crédit Immobilier S.A. (BCI)
      Created on October 22, 1985
      Provides long term residential, commercial and industrial
      loans for construction, maintenance or renovation of
      properties.

Currency and Exchange Rate

The Haitian unit of currency is the Gourde which is divided into 100 centimes, and was fixed to the U.S. dollar at the exchange rate of U.S. $1=G.5 based on the April 12, 1919 Convention, signed between the Haitian Government and the National Bank of the Republic of Haiti, which was, at that time, almost the exclusive property of the National City Bank of New York. This rate has not remained in effect in the 1980s, when the gourde started to devaluate and a second exchange rate market developed. In the Haitian economy, the Gourde and the U.S. dollar are equally circulated and accepted as means of exchange.

TABLE
Five-year Average Exchange Rate Fluctuation

1985-1986--------15%-----G.5.75=U.S. $1
1986-1987--------10%-----G.5.50=U.S. $1
1987-1988--------19%-----G.5.95=U.S. $1
1988-1989--------28%-----G.6.40=U.S. $1
1989-1990--------44%-----G.7.20=U.S. $1

Source BNRH &
Librairie Au Service de la Culture - Economic Department

EXCHANGE RATE
Haitian Gourde (G.) against U.S. Dollar ($U.S.)

1990

	High		Low	
January	44%	(G. 7.20 = $1)	40%	(G. 7.00 = $1)
February	49%	(G. 7.45 = $1)	40%	(G. 7.00 = $1)
March	47%	(G. 7.35 = $1)	40%	(G. 7.00 = $1)
April	46%	(G. 7.30 ≚ $1)	40%	(G. 7.00 = $1)
May	47%	(G. 7.35 = $1)	40%	(G. 7.00 = $1)
June	50%	(G. 7.50 = $1)	40%	(G. 7.00 = $1)
July	50%	(G. 7.50 = $1)	40%	(G. 7.00 = $1)
August	45%	(G. 7.25 = $1)	40%	(G. 7.00 = $1)
September	50%	(G. 7.50 = $1)	45%	(G. 7.25 = $1)
October	64%	(G. 8.20 = $1)	50%	(G. 7.50 = $1)
November	65%	(G. 8.25 = $1)	60%	(G. 8.00 = $1)
December	65%	(G. 8.25 = $1)	45%	(G. 7.25 = $1)

Source: Librairie Au Service de la Culture - Economic Department

EXCHANGE RATE
Haitian Gourde (G.) against U.S. Dollar ($ U.S.)

1991

	High		Low	
January	53%	(G. 7.65 = $1)	50%	(G. 7.50 = $1)
February	55%	(G. 7.75 = $1)	52%	(G. 7.60 = $1)
March	60%	(G. 8.00 = $1)	52%	(G. 7.60 = $1)
April	52%	(G. 7.60 = $1)	47%	(G. 7.35 = $1)
May	52%	(G. 7.60 = $1)	42%	(G. 7.10 = $1)
June	52%	(G. 7.60 = $1)	50%	(G. 7.50 = $1)
July	50%	(G. 7.50 = $1)	45%	(G. 7.25 = $1)
August	49%	(G. 7.45 = $1)	45%	(G. 7.25 = $1)
September	51%	(G. 7.55 = $1)	45%	(G. 7.25 = $1)
October	61%	(G. 8.05 = $1)	51%	(G. 7.55 = $1)
November	72%	(G. 8.60 = $1)	55%	(G. 7.75 = $1)
December	70%	(G. 8.50 = $1)	65%	(G. 8.25 = $1)

Source: Librairie Au Service de la Culture - Economic Department

EXCHANGE RATE
Haitian Gourde (G.) against U.S. Dollar ($ U.S.)

1992

	High			**Low**	
January	70%	(G. 8.50 = $1)	60%	(G. 8.00 = $1)
February	78%	(G. 8.90 = $1)	60%	(G. 8.00 = $1)
March	79%	(G. 8.95 = $1)	76%	(G. 8.80 = $1)
April	87%	(G. 9.35 = $1)	77%	(G. 8.85 = $1)
May	92%	(G. 9.60 = $1)	80%	(G. 9.00 = $1)
June	105%	(G. 10.25 = $1)	89%	(G. 9.45 = $1)
July	99%	(G. 9.95 = $1)	96%	(G. 9.80 = $1)
August	100%	(G. 10.00 = $1)	98%	(G. 9.90 = $1)
September	108%	(G. 10.40 = $1)	98%	(G. 9.90 = $1)
October	113%	(G. 10.65 = $1)	100%	(G. 10.00 = $1)
November	126%	(G. 11.30 = $1)	113%	(G. 10.65 = $1)
December	130%	(G. 11.50 = $1)	113%	(G. 10.65 = $1)

Source: Librairie Au Service de la Culture - Economic Department

COMPUTATION RULE

If you are buying U.S. dollars at 40%, the exchange is 7.00 gourdes
for each U.S. dollar. For example, if you need U.S. $750.00 - multiply
750 by 7.00, that is, you have to exchange 5,250.00 gourdes to receive
U.S. $750.00.

Whether you are buying gourdes or selling U.S. dollars, the same rule
applies.

Sample of Monthly Salaries in Haiti

FACTORY OR INDUSTRY

TITLE	$ U.S. Based on U.S. $1= G.5 (Not taking into account fluctuating exchange rates).
General Manager	$1500 - 2500
Manager (of accounting, finance, production, marketing)	800 - 1500
High level professionals (Engineers: industrial, chemical, electronic, electrical, mechanical)	1,000 - 1600
Head Accountant	800 - 1200
Personnel Manager	800 - 1200
Head Secretary	500 - 800
Head Mechanic	300 - 1000
Head Electrician	300 - 600
Head Supervisor	300 - 800
Mechanic	200 - 400
Electrician	200 - 400
Bookkeeper	200 - 300
Typist/Office Clerk	150 - 300
Driver	150 - 200
Skilled worker	150 - 200
Security guard	100 - 180
Cleaning person	115 - 125
Maintenance person	100 - 125
Messenger clerk	90 - 125
Laborer	90 - 100

FLOWS OF DIRECT AND FIXED INVESTMENTS IN HAITI (U.S. Dollars)

Sector Reached	U.S.A.	France	Canada	Germany	Others	Total	Jobs Created
Agriculture (Cereals, vegetables, decorative flowers, citrus, forest products)	2,000,000	-	-	-	-	2,000,000	100
Industries based on natural mineral resources (clay, sand, marble)	150,000	350,000	-	650,000	-	1,150,000	65
Agro-Industries (poultry, beef, sugar, leather)	14,900,000	400,000	629,000	-	770,000	16,699,000	1,660
Domestic Industries (dairy, brewery, food products, pesticide)	1,300,000	628,000	-	-	1,500,000	3,428,000	510
Intermediary Industries (chemical products)	2,100,000	-	-	-	-	2,100,000	108
Other Industries (electro-technical, sports equipment, clothing)	23,033,592	300,000	240,000	964,000	300,000	24,837,592	13,081
Heavy Transportation and Public Works	-	14,600,000	2,000,000	-	-	16,600,000	708
Petroleum Companies	5,000,000	-	-	-	3,000,000	8,000,000	109
Hotels & Casinos	15,700,000	20,000,000	1,500,000	-	2,670,000	39,870,000	715
Airlines	2,600,000	1,000,000	50,000	-	100,000	3,750,000	191
Maritime Transport	700,000	-	-	-	-	700,000	30
Banks	2,825,112	1,088,777	2,099,651	-	500,000	6,513,540	406
Insurance Companies (Surety-bond)	1,990,000	660,000	30,000	-	15,000	2,695,000	100
TOTALS	72,298,704	39,026,777	6,548,651	1,614,000	8,855,000	128,343,132	17,783

Source: PROMINEX 1990

GOVERNMENT 8

Administrative Structure of the
Republic of Haiti / *165*

Foreigners and The Republic of Haiti / *171*

Constitution of The Republic of Haiti
March 29, 1987 - English Translation / *173*

Administrative Structure of The Republic of Haiti

The administrative structure of the Republic of Haiti as established in the Constitution of March 29, 1987, is composed of: the Three Branches of the State, the Permanent Electoral Council, the Public Forces, and the Independent Government Agencies.

I. BRANCHES OF THE STATE

The Haitian citizens delegate the exercise of national sovereignty to three (3) branches of authority: the Executive Branch, the Legislative Branch, and the Judicial Branch. The three branches constitute the essential foundation of the organization of the State, which is civil. Each branch is independent of the other two in the powers it exercises separately.

A. THE EXECUTIVE BRANCH

The Executive power is vested in the President of the Republic and the Government.

1. THE PRESIDENT OF THE REPUBLIC

The President of the Republic is the Head of State elected for five (5) years by direct universal adult suffrage of an absolute majority of votes.

The presidential term begins and ends on February 7th, following the date of the elections. The President of the Republic may in no case run for a third term.

2. THE GOVERNMENT

The Government is composed of the Prime Minister, the Ministers, and Secretaries of State.

a) The Prime Minister

The Prime Minister is the Head of the Government. He (she) is appointed by the President of the Republic and subject to parliamentary approval.

The Prime Minister appoints the members of his (her) office and goes before Parliament to obtain a vote of confidence on his declaration of general policy.

He (she) enforces the laws, and in concert with the President of the Republic is responsible for national defense.

b) The Ministries
The Ministers and Secretaries of State of each Ministry are appointed by the Prime Minister.

- Ministry of Interior and National Defense
- Ministry of Agriculture, Natural Resources and Rural Development
- Ministry of Commerce and Industry
- Ministry of Finance and Economy
- Ministry of Foreign Affairs and Cults
- Ministry of Planning and Foreign Aid
- Ministry of Information and Coordination
- Ministry of Justice
- Ministry of National Education, Youth and Sports
- Ministry of Public Health and Population
- Ministry of Public Works, Transportation and Communications
- Ministry of Social Affairs

B. LEGISLATIVE BRANCH
Legislative power is vested in two (2) Representative Houses that constitute the Legislature or Parliament: The House of Deputies and the Senate. They also constitute the National Assembly.

1. HOUSE OF DEPUTIES
The House of Deputies is a body composed of members elected for four years by direct suffrage by the citizens and is responsible for exercising on their behalf, in concert with the Senate, the function of the Legislative Branch. The Deputies may be reelected an indefinite number of times.

2. THE SENATE

The Senate is a body composed of members elected for six years by direct universal suffrage of the citizens and charged with exercising on their behalf, in concert with the House of Deputies, the duties of the Legislative Branch. Senators may be reelected an indefinite number of times.

3. THE NATIONAL ASSEMBLY

The National Assembly is made of the meeting in a single Assembly of the House of Deputies and the Senate. It is presided over by the President of the Senate, assisted by the President of the House of Deputies acting as Vice President. The Secretaries of the Senate and the House of Deputies are the Secretaries of the National Assembly.

C. THE JUDICIAL BRANCH

The Judicial Power is vested in the Supreme Court, namely *Cour de Cassation*, the Courts of Appeal, Courts of First Instance, Courts of Peace, and special courts whose number, composition, organization, operation and jurisdiction are set by law.

II. THE PERMANENT ELECTORAL COUNCIL

The Permanent Electoral Council is responsible for organizing and controlling with complete independence all electoral procedures throughout the territory of the Republic until the results of the election are announced. The Permanent Electoral Council consists of nine members appointed for a nine year nonrenewable period and chosen from a list of three names proposed by each Departmental Assembly. Three are chosen by the Executive Branch, three by the Supreme Court, and three by the National Assembly.

III. PUBLIC FORCES

The Public Forces are composed of two distinct bodies:
1. The Armed Forces of Haiti, and
2. The Police Force

A. THE ARMED FORCES OF HAITI

Commanded in practice by a general officer bearing the title COMMANDER-IN-CHIEF OF THE HAITIAN ARMED FORCES, the Armed Forces are comprised of the Land, Sea and Air Forces, and the Technical Services. They are set up to ensure the security and integrity of the territory of the Republic. The Commander-in-Chief of the Armed Forces is chosen from among the general officers on active service and has a renewable term set at three years.

B. THE POLICE FORCE

The Police Force is an armed body that operates under the Ministry of Justice and is established to ensure law, order and protection of the lives and property of citizens. Its organization and mode of operation are regulated by law. The Commander-in-Chief of the Police Forces is appointed, in accordance with the Constitution, for a three-year term, which is renewable.

IV. INDEPENDENT GOVERNMENT AGENCIES

The most important Government Agencies are:
-   **Banque de la République d'Haïti**
    Central Bank of Haiti.

-   **Electricité d'Haiti (EDH)**
    Power plant of Haiti.
    The autonomous industrial and commercial plant that provides electric service to the country, reorganized under the law of August 2, 1971.

-   **Télécommunications d'Haiti S.A.M. (TELECO)**
    Telecommunications of Haiti.
    Agency organized under the law of September 16, 1971 to oversee all telecommunications in the country.

-   **Office d'Assurance Véhicule Contre-Tiers (OAVCT)**
    This government agency has the monopoly to provide compulsory automobile insurance under the June 8, 1964 law.

- **Administration de l'Aéroport International de Port-au-Prince**
  Administration of the International Airport of Port-au-Prince. The law of January 22, 1962 created a public agency to build and administer the International Airport of Port-au-Prince.

- **Centrale Autonome Métropolitaine d'Eau Potable (CAMEP)**
  Agency providing water and sewer service to the Port-au-Prince population. Created under the decree of May 13, 1964.

- **Service National d'Eau Potable (SNEP)**
  Agency Providing Drinkable Water and Sewer Service to the whole country except Port-au-Prince. Created under the law of August 20, 1977.

- **Organisme de Développement de la Vallée de l'Artibonite (ODVA)**
  Agency for the Development of the Artibonite Valley.
  This agricultural agency created in 1949 was reorganized under the decree of March 24, 1971.

- **La Minoterie d'Haiti**
  The Flour-milling Company of Haiti.
  This autonomous government enterprise was created under the decree of March 20, 1969 to produce large amounts of flour for sale.

- **Le Ciment d'Haiti**
  The government run company that manufactures and sells cement in Haiti. Created under the contract of July 16, 1983.

- **Office National d'Assurance - Vieillesse (O.N.A.)**
  The National Pension Retirement Agency of Haiti created under the law of August 28, 1967. This agency oversees the collection of contributions and payment of pensions to all employees of profit organizations. The age of eligibility for retirement is 55.

- **Office Assurance Travail, Maladie et Maternité (OFATMA)**
  The National Agency for Workers' Compensation, Sickness and Maternity Insurance. Reorganized under the law of August 28, 1967.

- **Loterie de l'Etat Haitien (L.E.H)**
  Haitian National Lottery Agency.
  The agency overseeing the administration of lottery. Created under the law of March 21, 1958.

- **Presses Nationales d'Haïti**
  Government Printing and Publishing Agency.
  Reorganized under the decree of September 29, 1965

- **Les Magasins de L'Etat**
  The Government Retail Stores.
  The decree-law of December 21, 1944 organized the government retail stores and annexed them to the commercial department of the National Bank of the Republic of Haiti.

- **Société Nationale des Parcs Industriels (SONAPI)**
  National Association of Industrial Zones.
  The agency for government-owned Industrial Park Zones was created under the decree of October 22, 1981 making it an autonomous industrial and commercial organization.

- **Département de l'Agriculture, des Resources Naturelles et du Développement Rural (DARNDR)**
  Department of Agriculture, Natural Resources and Rural Development. Created in 1972.

- **Organisme de Développement du Nord (O.D.N.)**
  Agency for the Development of the Northern Region of Haiti. Created in 1976.

- **Organisme de Développement de la Plaine des Gonaïves (O.D.P.G.)**
  Agency for the Development of the Gonaïves Valley Created in 1972.

- **Organisme de Développement du Nord-Ouest (ODNO)**
  Agency for the Development of the Northwest Region of Haiti. Created in 1982.

- **Prominex-Haiti**
  Created under the decree of August 1986, this autonomous agency is responsible for attracting investments in Haiti and promoting exportation of Haitian products. It is administered by a council of seven members, three from the public sector and four from the private sector.

Foreigners and The Republic of Haiti

The conditions under which foreigners may be admitted into or remain in the country are established by law. While in the territory of the Republic, foreigners enjoy the same protection accorded to Haitians under the law. They enjoy civil, economic and social rights, subject to legal provisions on the right to own real property, to practice a profession, to engage in wholesale trade, serve as a commercial representative, and undertake in import and export operations.

The right to own real property is accorded to foreigners who reside in Haiti and to foreign companies for the needs of their sojourn in the country and for agricultural, commercial, industrial, religious, humanitarian or educational enterprises, within the limits and under the conditions prescribed by law. However, these foreigners may not own more than one dwelling in the same Arrondissement and may not be the owner of a building within the Haitian territory. They may, in no case, engage in renting real estate as a business. However, foreign companies engaged in real estate promotion are allowed to receive the benefits of a special status regulated by law. This right terminates five years after a foreigner ceases to reside in the country or after the operation of his or her companies have terminated.

Violators of the above provisions and their accomplices will be punished as provided for in the law. A foreigner may be expelled from the territory of the Republic if he or she becomes involved in the political life of the country or in cases determined by law.

The right to asylum for political refugees is recognized and Haitian nationality may be acquired by naturalization.

After five years of continuous residence in the Haitian territory, any foreigner may obtain Haitian nationality by naturalization, in conformity with the regulations established by law. Naturalized Haitians are allowed to exercise the right to vote but they must wait five years after the date of their naturalization to be eligible to hold public posts other than those reserved by the Constitution and by law for native-born Haitians.

Haitian nationality is lost by:

a) Naturalization in a foreign country;

b) Holding a political post in the service of a foreign government;

c) Continuous residence abroad of a naturalized Haitian without duly granted authorization by a competent official. Anyone who loses his/her nationality in this manner may not reacquire it.

A naturalized Haitian may recover his or her nationality by meeting all of the conditions and formalities imposed on aliens by the law. Dual Haitian and foreign nationality is not permitted.

Constitution of the Republic of Haiti March 29, 1987

Preamble

The Haitian people proclaim this constitution in order to:

- Ensure their inalienable and imprescriptible rights to life, liberty and the pursuit of happiness; in conformity with the Act of Independence of 1804 and the Universal Declaration of the Rights of Man of 1948.

- Constitute a socially just, economically free, and politically independent Haitian nation.

- Establish a strong and stable State, capable of protecting the country's values, traditions, sovereignty, independence and national vision.

- Implant democracy, which entails ideological pluralism and political rotation and affirm the inviolable rights of the Haitian people.

- Strengthen national unity by eliminating all discrimination between the urban and rural populations, by accepting the community of languages and culture and by recognizing the right to progress, information, education, health, employment and leisure for all citizens.

- Ensure the separation and the harmonious distribution of the powers of the State at the service of the fundamental interests and priorities of the Nation.

- To set up a system of government based on fundamental liberties, and the respect for human rights, social peace, economic equity, concerted action and participation of all the people in major decisions affecting the life of a nation, through effective decentralization.

TITLE I

The Republic of Haiti
Its Emblem and its Symbols

CHAPTER I

The Republic of Haiti

First Article:
Haiti is an indivisible, sovereign, independent, cooperative, free, democratic and social republic.

First Article-1:
The city of Port-au-Prince is the capital and the seat of government. This seat may be moved elsewhere for reasons of force majeure.

Article 2:
The national colors shall be blue and red.

Article 3:
The emblem of the Haitian Nation shall be a flag with the following description:

  a) Two (2) equal-sized horizontal bands: a blue one on top and a red one underneath;

  b) The coat of arms of the Republic shall be placed in the center on a white square;

  c) The coat of arms of the Republic are: a Palmette surmounted by the liberty cap, and under the palms a trophy with the legend:

Union Makes Strength

Article 4:
The national motto is: Liberty, Equality, Fraternity.

Article 4-1:
The national anthem shall be the "Dessalinienne."

Article 5:
All Haitians are united by a common language: Creole.
Creole and French are the official languages of the Republic.

Article 6:
The monetary unit shall be the gourde, which is divided into centimes.

Article 7:
The cult of the personality is categorically forbidden. Effigies and names of living personages may not appear on the currency, stamps, seals public buildings, streets or works of art.

Article 7-1:
Use of effigies of deceased persons must be approved by the Legislature.

CHAPTER II

Territory of the Haitian Republic

Article 8:
The territory of the Haitian Republic comprises:

a) The western part of the island of Haiti and the adjacent islands of La Gonâve, la Tortue, l'Ile à Vache, les Cayemittes, La Navase, la Grande Caye and the other islands of the Territorial Sea;

It is bounded on the east by the Dominican Republic, on the north by the Atlantic Ocean, on the south and west by the Caribbean Sea or Sea of the Antilles;

b) The territorial sea and the exclusive economic zone;

c) The air space over the land and sea of the Republic.

Article 8-1:
The territory of the Haitian Republic is inviolable and may not be alienated either in whole or in part by any treaty or convention.

Article 9:
The territory of the Republic is divided and subdivided into Departments, Arrondissements, Communes, suburban areas and Communal sections.

Article 9-1:
The law determines the number and boundaries of these divisions and subdivisions, and regulates their organization and operation.

TITLE II

Haitian Nationality

Article 10:
The regulations governing Haitian nationality shall be determined by law.

Article 11:
Any person born of a Haitian father or a Haitian mother who are themselves native-born Haitians and have never renounced their nationality possesses Haitian nationality at the time of birth.

Article 12:
Haitian nationality may be acquired by naturalization.

Article 12-1:
After five years of continuous residence in the territory of the Republic, any foreigner may obtain Haitian nationality by naturalization, in conformity with the regulations established by law.

Article 12-2:
Haitians by naturalization shall be allowed to exercise the right to vote but they must wait (5) years after the date of their naturalization to be eligible to hold public posts other than those reserved by the Constitution and by law for native-born Haitians.

Article 13:
Haitian nationality is lost by:
    a) Naturalization in a foreign country;

b) Holding a political post in the service of a foreign government;

c) Continuous residence abroad of a naturalized Haitian without duly granted authorization by a competent official. Anyone who loses his nationality in this manner may not reacquire it.

Article 14:
A naturalized Haitian may recover his Haitian nationality by meeting all of the conditions and formalities imposed on aliens by the law.

Article 15:
Dual Haitian and foreign nationality is in no case permitted.

TITLE III

Basic Rights and Duties of the Citizen

CHAPTER I

The Nature of Citizenship

Article 16:
Citizenship entails both civil and political rights.

Article 16-1:
The enjoyment, exercise, suspension and loss of these rights are regulated by law.

Article 16-2:
The age of majority is eighteen (18) years.

Article 17:
All Haitians, regardless of sex or marital status, who have attained twenty-one years of age may exercise their political and civil rights if they meet the other conditions prescribed by the Constitution and by law.

Article 18:
Haitians shall be equal before the law, subject to the special advantages conferred on native-born Haitians who have never renounced their nationality.

CHAPTER II

Basic Rights

SECTION A

Right to Life and Health

Article 19:
The State has the absolute obligation to guarantee the right to life, health, and respect of the human person for all citizens without distinction, in conformity with the Universal Declaration of the Rights of Man.

Article 20:
The death penalty is abolished in all cases.

Article 21:
The crime of high treason consists in bearing arms in a foreign army against the Republic, serving a foreign nation in a conflict with the Republic, in any official's stealing State property entrusted to his management, or any violation of the Constitution by those responsible for enforcing it.

Article 21-1:
The crime of high treason is punishable by forced labor for life without commutation of sentence.

Article 22:
The State recognizes the right of every citizen to decent housing, education, food and social security.

Article 23:
The State has the obligation to ensure for all citizens in all territorial divisions appropriate means to ensure protection, maintenance and restoration of their health by establishing hospitals, health centers and dispensaries.

SECTION B

Individual Liberty

Article 24:
Individual liberty is guaranteed and protected by the State.

Article 24-1:
No one may be prosecuted, arrested or detained except in the cases determined by law and in the manner it prescribes.

Article 24-2:
Except where the perpetrator of a crime is caught in the act, no one may be arrested or detained other than by written order of a legally competent official.

Article 24-3:
For such an order to be carried out, the following requirements must be met:

a) It must formally state the reason in Creole and in French for the arrest or detention and the provision of the law that provides for punishment of the act charged.

b) Legal notice must be given and a copy of the order must be left with the accused at the time of its execution;

c) The accused must be notified of his right to be assisted by counsel at all phases of the investigation of the case up to the final judgment;

d) Except where the perpetrator of a crime is caught in the act, no arrest by warrant and no search may take place between six (6) p.m. and six (6) a.m.

e) Responsibility for an offense is personal, and no one may be arrested in the place of another.

Article 25:
Any unnecessary force or restraint in the apprehension of a person or in keeping him under arrest, or any psychological pressure or physical brutality, especially during interrogation, is forbidden.

Article 25-1:
No one may be interrogated without his attorney or a witness of his choice being present.

Article 26:
No one may be kept under arrest more than forty-eight (48) hours unless he has appeared before a judge asked to rule on the legality of the arrest and the judge has confirmed the arrest by a well-founded decision;

Article 26-1:
In the case of a petty violation, the accused shall be referred to a justice of the peace, who shall then hand down a final decision.

In the case of more serious offenses or crimes, an appeal may be filed, without prior permission, simply by addressing a petition to the presiding judge of the competent civil court, who, on the basis of the oral statement of the prosecutor, shall rule on the legality of the arrest and detention, in a special session of the court, without postponement or rotation of judges, all other cases being suspended.

Article 26-2:
If the arrest is judged to be illegal, the judge shall order the immediate release of the arrested person and that order shall be enforceable immediately, regardless of any appeal to a higher court or the supreme court for an order forbidding enforcement of the judgment.

Article 27:
Any violation of the provisions on individual liberty are arbitrary acts. Injured parties may, without prior authorization, appeal to the competent courts, to bring suit against the authors and perpetrators

of these arbitrary acts, regardless of their rank or the body to which they belong.

Article 27-1:
Government officials and employees are directly liable under civil and administrative criminal law for acts carried out in violation of rights. In such cases, civil liability extends to the State as well.

SECTION C

Freedom of Expression

Article 28:
Every Haitian has the right to express his opinions freely on any matter by any means he chooses.

Article 28-1:
Journalists shall freely exercise their profession within the framework of the law. Such exercise may not be subject to any authorization or censorship, except in the case of war.

Article 28-2:
Journalists may not be compelled to reveal their sources. However, it is their duty to verify the authenticity and accuracy of information. It is also their obligation to respect the ethics of their profession.

Article 28-3:
All offenses involving the press and abuses of the right of expression come under the code of criminal law.

Article 29:
The right of petition is recognized. It is exercised personally by one or more citizens but never in the name of a body.

Article 29-1:
All petitions to the Legislative Branch must give rise to the regulatory procedure for ruling upon their purpose.

SECTION D

Freedom of Conscience

Article 30:
All religions and faiths shall be freely exercised. Everyone is entitled to profess his religion and practice his faith, provided the exercise of that right does not disturb law and order.

Article 30-1:
No one may be compelled to belong to a religious organization or to follow a religious teaching contrary to his convictions.

Article 30-2:
The law establishes the conditions for recognition and practice of religions and faiths.

SECTION E

Freedom of Assembly and Association

Article 31:
Freedom of unarmed assembly and association for political, economic, social, cultural or any other peaceful purposes is guaranteed.

Article 31-1:
Political parties and groups shall compete with each other in the exercise of suffrage. They may be established and may carry out their activities freely. They must respect the principles of national and democratic sovereignty. The law determines the conditions for their recognition and operation, and the advantages and privileges reserved to them.

Article 31-2:
The police authorities must be notified in advance of assemblies outdoors in public places.

Article 31-3:
No one may be compelled to join any association of any kind.

SECTION F

Education and Teaching

Article 32:
The State guarantees the right to education. It sees to the physical, intellectual, moral, professional, social and civic training of the population.

Article 32-1:
Education is the responsibility of the State and its territorial divisions. They must make schooling available to all, free of charge, and ensure that public and private sector teachers are properly trained.

Article 32-2:
The first responsibility of the State and its territorial divisions is education of the masses, which is the only way the country can be developed. The State shall encourage and facilitate private enterprise in this field.

Article 32-3:
Primary schooling is compulsory under penalties to be prescribed by law. Classroom facilities and teaching materials shall be provided by the State to elementary school students free of charge.

Article 32-4:
Agricultural, vocational cooperative and technical training is a fundamental responsibility of the State and its communes.

Article 32-5:
Preschool and maternal training, as well as informal education are encouraged.

Article 32-6:
Higher education shall be open to all, on an equal basis, according to merit only.

Article 32-7:
The State shall see to it that each territorial division, Communal Section, Commune or Department shall have the essential educational

establishments adapted to the needs of their development, without however prejudicing the priorities assigned to agricultural, vocational, cooperative and technical training, which must be widely disseminated.

Article 32-8:
The State guarantees that the handicapped and the gifted shall have the means to ensure their autonomy, education and independence.

Article 32-9:
The State and its territorial divisions have the duty to make all necessary provisions to intensify the literacy campaign for the masses. They encourage all private initiatives to that end.

Article 32-10:
Teachers are entitled to a fair salary.

Article 33:
There shall be freedom of education at all levels. This freedom shall be exercised under the control of the State.

Article 34:
Except where perpetrators of crimes are caught in the act, the premises of educational establishments are inviolable. No police forces may enter them except with the permission of the supervisors of those establishments.

Article 34-1:
This provision does not apply when an educational establishment is used for other purposes.

SECTION G

Freedom to Work

Article 35:
Freedom to work is guaranteed. Every citizen has the obligation to engage in work of his choice to meet his own and his family's needs, and to cooperate with the State in the establishment of a social security system.

Article 35-1:
Every employee of a private or public institution is entitled to a fair wage, to rest, to a paid annual vacation and to a bonus.

Article 35-2:
The State guarantees workers equal working conditions and wages regardless of their sex, beliefs, opinions and marital status.

Article 35-3:
Trade union freedom is guaranteed. Any worker in the public or private sector may join a union representing his particular occupation solely to protect his work interests.

Article 35-4:
Unions are essentially nonpolitical, nonprofit, and nondenominational. No one may be forced to join a union.

Article 35-5:
The right to strike is recognized under the limits set by law.

Article 35-6:
The minimum age for gainful employment is set by law. Special laws govern the work of minors and servants.

SECTION H

Property

Article 36:
Private property is recognized and guaranteed. The law specifies the manner of acquiring and enjoying it, and the limits placed upon it.

Article 36-1:
Expropriation for a public purpose may be effected only by payment or deposit ordered by a court in favor of the person entitled thereto, of fair compensation established in advance by an expert evaluation.

If the initial project is abandoned, the expropriation is canceled. The property may not be subject to any speculation and must be restored to its original owner without any reimbursement for the small holder. The expropriation measure is effective upon the inception of the project.

Article 36-2:
Nationalization and confiscation of goods, property and buildings for political reasons are forbidden.

No one may be deprived of his legitimate right of ownership other than by a final judgment by a court of ordinary law, except under an agrarian reform.

Article 36-3:
Ownership also entails obligations. Uses of property cannot be contrary to the general interest.

Article 36-4:
Landowners must cultivate, work, and protect their land, particularly against erosion. The penalty for failure to fulfill this obligation shall be prescribed by law.

Article 36-5:
The right to own property does not extend to the coasts, springs, rivers, water courses, mines and quarries. They are part of the State's public domain.

Article 36-6:
The law shall establish regulations governing freedom to prospect for and work mines, ore bearing earths, and quarries, ensuring an equal share of the profits of such exploitation to the owner of the land and to the Haitian State or its concessionaires.

Article 37:
The law shall set the conditions for land division and aggregation in terms of a territorial management plan and the well-being of the communities concerned, within the framework of agrarian reform.

Article 38:
Scientific, literary and artistic property is protected by law.

Article 39:
The inhabitants of the Communal Sections have the right of preemption for the exploitation of the State's land in the private domain located in their locality.

SECTION I

Right to Information

Article 40:
The State has the obligation to publicize in the oral, written and televised press in the Creole and French languages all laws, orders, decrees, international agreements, treaties, and conventions on everything affecting the national life, except for information concerning national security.

SECTION J

Right to Security

Article 41:
No person of Haitian nationality may be deported or forced to leave the national territory for any reason. No one may be deprived for political reasons of his legal capacity and his nationality.

Article 41-1:
No Haitian needs a visa to leave or return to the country.

Article 42:
No citizen, whether civilian or military, may be denied access to the courts open to him under the Constitution and the laws.

Article 42-1:
Military personnel accused of the crime of high treason against the country shall be tried in a court of ordinary law.

Article 42-2:
Military courts have jurisdiction only:

a) In the case of violation by military personnel of regulations in the Manual of Military Justice;

b) In the case of conflicts between members of the armed forces;

c) In the case of war.

Article 42-3:
Cases of conflicts between civilians and military personnel, abuses, violence and crimes perpetrated against a civilian by a member of the military in the performance of his duties are under the jurisdiction of courts of ordinary law.

Article 43:
No house search or seizure of papers may take place except under the terms of the law and in the manner prescribed by it.

Article 44:
Persons detained temporarily awaiting trial must be held separately from those who are serving sentence.

Article 44-1:
Prisons must be operated in accordance with standards reflecting respect for human dignity according to the law on this subject.

Article 45:
No penalty may be established except by law nor applied except in cases that the law determines.

Article 46:
No one may be compelled in cases of crimes, minor offenses, or petty violations to bear witness against himself or his relatives up to the fourth degree of consanguinity or the second degree of affinity.

Article 47:
No one may be compelled to take an oath except in the cases and in the manner provided for by law.

Article 48:
The State shall see to it that a Civil Pension Retirement Fund is established in the public and private sectors. The fund shall receive

contributions from employers and employees, in accordance with the criteria and in the manner established by law. The granting of a pension is a right and not a privilege.

Article 49:
Freedom and privacy of correspondence and any other forms of communication are inviolable. They may be limited only by a well-founded judicial ruling, according to the guarantees established by law.

Article 50:
Under the Constitution and the law, a jury is established in criminal cases for violent crimes and political offenses.

Article 51:
The law may not be made retroactive except in criminal cases when it favors the accused.

CHAPTER III

Duties of the Citizen

Article 52:
Citizenship entails civic duties. Every right is counterbalanced by a corresponding duty.

Article 52-1:
Civic duties are the citizen's moral, political, social and economic obligations as a whole to the State and the country. These obligations are:

a) To respect the Constitution and the national emblem;

b) To respect the laws;

c) To vote in elections without constraint;

d) To pay his taxes;

e)   To serve on a jury;

f)   To defend the country in the event of war;

g)   To educate and improve himself;

h)   To respect and protect the environment;

i)   To respect scrupulously the revenues and properties of the State;

j)   To respect the property of others;

k)   To work to maintain peace;

l)   To provide assistance to persons in danger;

m) To respect the rights and freedom of others.

Article 52-2:
Failure to abide by these provisions shall be punishable by law.

Article 52-3:
Compulsory civic service for both sexes is established.
The terms thereof shall be set by law.

TITLE IV

Aliens

Article 53:
The conditions under which aliens may be admitted to or remain in the country are established by law.

Article 54:
Aliens in the territory of the Republic shall enjoy the same protection accorded to Haitians, under the law.

Article 54-1:
Aliens enjoy civil, economic and social rights subject to legal provisions on the right to own real property, the practice of a profession, engaging in wholesale trade, serving as a commercial representative, and engaging in import and export operations.

Article 55:
The right to own real property is accorded to aliens resident in Haiti for the needs of their sojourn in the country.

Article 55-1:
However, aliens residing in Haiti may not own more than one dwelling in the same Arrondissement. They may in no case engage in the business of renting real estate. However, foreign companies engaged in real estate promotion shall receive the benefits of a special status regulated by law.

Article 55-2:
The right to own real property shall be accorded also to aliens residing in Haiti and to foreign companies for the needs of their agricultural, commercial, industrial, religious, humanitarian or educational enterprises, within the limits and under the conditions prescribed by law.

Article 55-3:
No alien may be the owner of a building bounded by the Haitian land border.

Article 55-4:
This right terminates five (5) years after an alien ceases to reside in the country or the operation of his companies have terminated, pursuant to the law establishing regulations to be followed for the transmission and liquidation of property owned by aliens.

Article 55-5:
Violators of the above provisions and their accomplices shall be punished as provided for in the law.

Article 56:
An alien may be expelled from the territory of the Republic if he becomes involved in the political life of the country, or in cases determined by law.

Article 57:
The right to asylum for political refugees is recognized.

TITLE V

National Sovereignty

Article 58:
National sovereignty is vested in all citizens.
Citizens directly exercise the prerogatives of sovereignty by:

   a) Electing the President of the Republic;

   b) Electing members of the Legislature;

   c) Electing members of all other bodies or all assemblies provided for by the Constitution and by law.

Article 59:
Citizens delegate the exercise of national sovereignty to three (3) branches of government:

   1) The Legislative Branch;

   2) The Executive Branch;

   3) The judicial Branch.

The principle of separation of the three (3) branches is embodied in the Constitution.

Article 59-1:
The three (3) branches constitute the essential foundation of the organization of the State, which is civil.

Article 60:
Each branch is independent of the other two (2) in the powers it exercises separately.

Article 60-1:
None of them may, for any reason, delegate their powers in all or in part, nor go beyond the bounds set for them by the Constitution and by law.

Article 60-2:
Each of the three (3) branches is entirely responsible for its own acts.

CHAPTER I

Territorial Divisions and Decentralization

Article 61:
The territorial divisions are the Communal Sections, the Communes and the Departments.

Article 61-1:
The law may create any other territorial division.

SECTION A

Communal Sections

Article 62:
The Communal Section is the smallest administrative territorial entity of the Republic.

Article 63:
Each Communal Section is administered by a council of three (3) members elected by universal suffrage for four (4) years. They may be re-elected an indefinite number of times.

Their mode of organization and operation is regulated by law.

Article 63-1:
The Administrative Council of the Communal Section is assisted in its work by an Assembly of the Communal Section.

Article 64:
The State is obligated to establish for each Communal Section the structures required for social, economic, civic and cultural training of its population.

Article 65:
Members of the Administrative Council of the Communal Section must:

    a) Be Haitians and be at least twenty-five (25) years of age;

    b) Have resided in the Communal Section for two (2) years before the elections and continue to reside there;

    c) Enjoy civil and political rights and never have been sentenced to death, personal restraint or penal servitude or the loss of civil rights.

SECTION B

Communes

Article 66:
Communes have administrative and financial autonomy.
Each Commune of the Republic is administered by a Council, known as the Municipal Council, of three (3) members elected by universal suffrage.

Article 66-1:
The President of the Council bears the title of Mayor. He is assisted by Deputy Mayors.

Article 67:
The Municipal Council is assisted in its work by a Municipal Assembly composed, among others of a representative of each of its Communal Sections.

Article 68:
The Municipal Council's term is four (4) years, and its members may be re-elected for an indefinite number of terms.

Article 69:
The mode of organization and operation of the Commune and the Municipal Council are regulated by law.

Article 70:
Members of a Municipal Council must:

a) Be Haitians;

b) Have attained twenty-five (25) years of age;

c) Enjoy civil and political rights;

d) Have never been sentenced to death, personal restraint or penal servitude or the loss of civil rights;

e) Have resided at least three (3) years in the Commune and undertake to reside there for the duration of their terms.

Article 71:
Each Municipal Council is assisted at its request by a Technical Council furnished by the Central Government.

Article 72:
The Municipal Council may be dissolved for negligence, embezzlement, or maladministration, legally determined by a court of competent jurisdiction.

If it is dissolved, the Departmental Council shall immediately fill the vacancy and call upon the Permanent Electoral Council to elect, in sixty (60) days starting from the date the Council is dissolved, a new Council and shall manage the affairs of the Commune for the remainder of the term. This procedure also applies to vacancies occurring for any other reason.

Article 73:
The Municipal Council manages its resources for the exclusive benefit of the Municipality and renders its accounts to the Municipal Assembly, which in turn reports to the Departmental Council.

Article 74:
The Municipal Council has priority in management of the State's real property in the private domain located within the limits of its Commune. They may not be subject to any transaction without the prior consent of the Municipal Assembly.

SECTION C

Arrondissements

Article 75:
The Arrondissement is an administrative division that may comprise several Communes. Its organization and operations are governed by law.

SECTION D

Departments

Article 76:
The Department is the largest territorial division. It comprises the Arrondissements.

Article 77:
The Department has legal personality and is autonomous.

Article 78:
Each Department is administered by a Council of three (3) members elected for four (4) years by the Departmental Assembly.

Article 79:
Members of the Departmental Council are not necessarily drawn from the Assembly, but they must:

a) Be Haitians and at least twenty-five (25) years of age;

b) Have resided in the Department three (3) years before the elections and undertake to remain there during their term;

c) Enjoy civil and political rights and have never been sentenced to death, personal restraint, or penal servitude or the loss of civil rights.

Article 80:
The Department Council is assisted in its work by a Departmental Assembly made up of:

One (1) representative from each Municipal Assembly.

Article 80-1:
The following may attend Assembly meetings in an advisory capacity:

a) Deputies and Senators of the Department;

b) One (1) representative of each socio-professional association or union;

c) The Departmental Delegate;

d) The Director of Public Services of the Department.

Article 81:
The Departmental Council draws up the Department's development plan in cooperation with the Central Government.

Article 82:
The organization and operations of the Departmental Council and the Departmental Assembly are regulated by law.

Article 83:
The Departmental Council manages its financial resources for the exclusive benefit of the Department and renders its accounts to the Departmental Assembly, which in turn reports to the Central Government.

Article 84:
The Departmental Council may be dissolved in the event of embezzlement or maladministration legally determined by a court of competent jurisdiction.

If it is dissolved, the Central Government appoints a Provisional Commission and calls upon the Permanent Electoral Council to elect a new Council for the remainder of the term within sixty (60) days of the dissolution.

SECTION E

Delegates and Vice Delegates

Article 85:
In each Departmental Capital, the Executive Branch appoints a Representative, who bears the title of Delegate. A Vice Delegate placed under the authority of the Delegate is also appointed in each Arrondissement Capital.

Article 86:
Delegates and Vice Delegates ensure coordination and control of public services and exercise no repressive police function.

Other duties of Delegates and Vice Delegates are determined by law.

SECTION F

Interdepartmental Council

Article 87:
The Executive is assisted by an Interdepartmental Council, the members of which are designated by the Departmental Assemblies on the basis of one (1) per Department.

Article 87-1:
This Representative chosen from among the members of the Departmental Assemblies serves as liaison between the Department and the Executive Branch.

Article 87-2:
The Interdepartmental Council, in concert with the Executive, studies and plans projects for decentralization and development of the country from the social, economic, commercial, agricultural and industrial standpoint.

Article 87-3:
It attends working meetings of the Council of Ministers, when they discuss subjects mentioned in the preceding paragraph, and has the right to vote.

Article 87-4:
Decentralization must be accompanied by decentralization of public services with delegation of power and industrial convergence for the benefit of the departments.

Article 87-5:
The law determines the organization and operation of the Interdepartmental Council, and the frequency of the meetings of the Council of Ministers, in which it participates.

CHAPTER II

The Legislative Branch

Article 88:
Legislative power shall be vested in two (2) representative Houses. One (1) House of Deputies and one (1) Senate, comprising the Legislature or Parliament.

SECTION A

The House of Deputies

Article 89:
The House of Deputies is a body composed of members elected by direct suffrage by the citizens and is responsible for exercising, on their behalf and in concert with the Senate, the functions of the Legislative Branch.

Article 90:
Each Municipal Authority comprises an electoral district and elects one (1) Deputy.

The law sets up to three (3) the number of Deputies at the level of large built-up areas.

Pending application of the above subparagraphs, the number of Deputies may not be fewer than seventy (70).

Article 90-1:
Deputies are elected by an absolute majority of votes cast in the Primary Assemblies, according to the conditions and in the manner prescribed by the Electoral Law.

Article 91:
To be elected a member of the House of Deputies, a person must:

1) Be a native Haitian and have never renounced his nationality;

2) Have attained twenty-five (25) years of age;

3) Enjoy civil and political rights and never have been sentenced to death, personal restraint or penal servitude or the loss of civil rights for any crime of ordinary law;

4) Have resided at least two (2) consecutive years prior to the date of the elections in the electoral district he is to represent;

5) Own at least on real property in the district and practice a profession or trade;

6) Have been relieved, if need be, of his responsibilities as a manager of public funds.

Article 92:
Deputies are elected for four (4) years and may be reelected an indefinite number of times.

Article 92-1:
They take office on the second Monday of January, and sit in two (2) annual meetings. The duration of their term comprises a legislative session.

Article 92-2:
The first session runs from the second Monday of January to the second Monday of May; the second session, from the second Monday of June to the second Monday of September.

Article 92-3:
The House of Deputies is completely replaced every four (4) years.

Article 93:
Beside the duties conferred upon it by the Constitution as a branch of the Legislature, the House of Deputies has the duty of arraigning the Chief of State, the Prime Minister, the Ministers and the Secretaries of State before the High Court of Justice, by a majority of two-thirds (2/3) of its members. The other powers of the House of Deputies are assigned by the Constitution and by law.

SECTION B

The Senate

Article 94:
The Senate is a body composed of members elected by direct suffrage of the citizens and charged with exercising on their behalf, in concert with the House of Deputies, the duties of the Legislative Branch.

Article 94-1:
The number of Senators is set at three (3) per Department.

Article 94-2:
A Senator of the Republic is elected by universal suffrage by an absolute majority of votes in the Primary Assemblies held in the geographic Departments, under the terms prescribed by the Electoral Law.

Article 95:
Senators are elected for six (6) years and may be reelected an indefinite number of times.

Article 95-1:
The Senate is permanently in session.

Article 95-2:
The Senate may however adjourn, but not during the Legislative Session. When it adjourns, it leaves a permanent Committee charged with handling current business. The committee may not make any decisions, except to convene the Senate.

In emergencies, the Executive may also convene the Senate before the end of the adjournment period.

Article 95-3:
One-third (1/3) of the Senate is replaced every two (2) years.

Article 96:
To be elected to the Senate, a person must:

1) Be a native-born Haitian and never have renounced his nationality;

2) Have attained thirty (30) years of age;

3) Enjoy civil and political rights and never have been sentenced to death, personal restraint or penal servitude or the loss of civil rights for a crime of ordinary law;

4) Have resided in the Department he will represent, at least four (4) consecutive years prior to the date of the elections;

5) Own at least on (1) real property in the Department and practice a profession or trade there;

6) Have been relieved, if need be, of his responsibilities as a manager of public funds.

Article 97:
In addition to the responsibilities incumbent upon it as a branch of the Legislature, the Senate shall have the following powers:

1) To propose to the Executive the list of Supreme Court (Cour de Cassation) justices according to the provisions of the Constitution;

2) Constitute itself as a High Court of Justice;

3) Exercise all other powers assigned to it by this Constitution and by law.

SECTION C

The National Assembly

Article 98:
The meeting in a single Assembly of the two (2) branches of the Legislature constitutes the National Assembly.

Article 98-1:
The National Assembly meets to open and close each session and in all cases provided for by the Constitution.

Article 98-2:
The powers of the National Assembly are limited and may not be extended to matters other than those especially assigned to it by the Constitution.

Article 98-3:
The Assembly's powers are:

1) To receive the constitutional oath of the President of the Republic;

2) To ratify any decision to declare war when all efforts at conciliation have failed;

3) To approve or reject international treaties and conventions;

4) To amend the Constitution according to the procedure indicated herein;

5) To ratify decisions of the Executive to move the seat of the Government in cases determined by the first article of this Constitution;

6) To decide on when a state of siege shall be declared, to order with the Executive that constitutional guarantees shall be suspended, and to decide on any request to renew that measure;

7) To contribute to selecting members of the Permanent Electoral Council, pursuant to Article 92 of this Constitution;

8) To receive at the opening of each session the report on the Government's activities.

Article 99:
The National Assembly is presided over by the President of the Senate, assisted by the President of the House of Deputies acting as Vice President. The Secretaries of the Senate and the House of Deputies are the Secretaries of the National Assembly.

Article 99-1:
In the event the President of the Senate is unable to discharge his duties, the National Assembly shall be presided over by the President of the House of Deputies, and the Vice President of the Senate shall then become Vice President of the National Assembly.

Article 99-2:
In the event the two (2) Presidents are unable to discharge their duties, the two (2) Vice Presidents shall replace them, respectively.

Article 100:
Sessions of the National Assembly are public. However, they may be held in closed session at the request of five (5) members, and the resumption of public sessions shall then be decided by an absolute majority.

Article 101:
In emergencies when the Legislature is not in session, the Executive Branch may call a special session of the National Assembly.

Article 102:
The National Assembly may not meet or take decisions and pass resolutions without a majority of each of the two (2) Houses being present.

Article 103:
The Legislature has its seat in Port-au-Prince. However, depending on the circumstances, this seat may be transferred elsewhere to the same place and at the same time as that of the Executive Branch.

SECTION D

Exercise of Legislative Power

Article 104:
A session of the Legislature dates from the opening of the two (2) Houses meeting as the National Assembly.

Article 105:
In the interval between regular sessions and in emergencies, the President of the Republic may call a special session of the Legislature.

Article 106:
The Chief of the Executive Branch reports on that measure by a message.

Article 107:

In the event the Legislature is convened in special session, it may not decide on any matter other than that for which it was called.

Article 107-1:

However, any Senator or Deputy may introduce a matter of general interest in an Assembly of which he is a member.

Article 108:

Each House checks and validates the credentials of its members and is the final judge of any disputes that may arise in this regard.

Article 109:

The members of each House shall take the following oath:

> "I swear to discharge my duties, to maintain and safeguard the rights of the people, and to be faithful to the Constitution."

Article 110:

Meetings of the two (2) Houses are public. Each House may meet in closed session at the request of five (5) members, and the decision to resume public meetings shall then be taken by a majority vote.

Article 111:

The Legislature makes the laws on all matters of public interest.

Article 111-1:

Laws may be initiated by each of the two (2) Houses as well as by the Executive Branch.

Article 111-2:

However, only the Executive Branch may initiate budget laws, laws concerning the assessment, percentage and manner of collecting taxes, and contributions, and laws designed to generate revenues or to increase revenues and expenditures of the Government. Bills introduced on these matters must be voted on first by the House of Deputies.

Article 111-3:

In the event of disagreement between the two (2) Houses regarding the laws mentioned in the preceding paragraph, each House shall appoint, by voting on a list of an equal number of members, a parliamentary committee that will make a final decision on the disagreement.

Article 111-4:

If a disagreement occurs with regard to any other law, a decision on it will be postponed until the following session. If, at that session, and even in the case of replacement of the Houses, no agreement is reached on the law when it is introduced again, each House shall appoint, by taking a vote on a list of an equal number of members, a parliamentary committee to decide on the final text that will be submitted to the two (2) Assemblies, beginning with the one that originally voted on the law. If these additional deliberations produce no result, the bill or proposed law will be withdrawn.

Article 111-5:

In the event of disagreement between the Legislature and the Executive Branch, the disagreement shall, at the request of one of the parties, be referred to the Conciliation Committee provided for in the Article 206 below.

Article 111-6:

If the Committee fails to reach a decision, it shall draw up a report of disagreement, which it shall remit to the two (2) high parties and inform the Supreme Court thereof.

Article 111-7:

Within two weeks of receipt of this report, the disagreement shall be referred to the Supreme Court. Sitting as a full court, the Court shall hand down its decision forthwith, setting all other matters aside. Its decision shall be final and is binding on the high parties. If, meanwhile, the high parties reach agreement, the terms of the agreement shall as a matter of course terminate the procedure under way.

Article 111-8:

In no case may the House of Deputies or the Senate be dissolved or adjourned, nor shall the terms of their members be extended.

Article 112:
Each House shall, in accordance with its regulations appoint its staff, establish discipline for them and determine the manner in which they shall perform their duties.

Article 112-1:
Each House may impose on its members for reprehensible conduct, by a two-thirds (2/3) majority vote, disciplinary penalties, except for expulsion.

Article 113:
Any member of the Legislature shall be disqualified as a Deputy or Senator, if, during his term, he has received a final sentence by a court of regular law, which renders him ineligible to serve.

Article 114:
Members of the Legislature are inviolable from the day they take oath up to the expiration of their term, subject to the provisions of Article 115 below.

Article 114-1:
They may at no time be prosecuted or attacked for the opinions and votes cast by them in the discharge of their duties.

Article 114-2:
No member of the Legislature shall be subject to civil imprisonment during his term of office.

Article 115:
No member of the Legislature may during his terms be arrested under ordinary law for a crime, a minor offense or a petty violation, except by authorization of the House of which he is a member, unless he is apprehended in the act of committing an offense punishable by death, personal restraint or penal servitude or the loss of civil rights. In that case, the matter is referred to the House of Deputies or the Senate without delay if the Legislature is in session, and if not, it shall be taken up at the next regular or special session.

Article 116:
Neither of the two (2) Houses may sit or take action without the presence of a majority of its members.

Article 117:
All acts of the Legislature must be approved by a majority of the members present, unless otherwise stipulated in this Constitution.

Article 118:
Each House has the right to investigate matters brought before it.

Article 119:
All bills must be voted on article by article.

Article 120:
Each House has the right to amend and to divide articles and amendments proposed. Amendments voted on by one House may be part of a bill only after it has been voted on by the other House in the same form and in identical terms. No bill shall become a law until it has been voted on in the same form by the two (2) Houses.

Article 120-1:
Any bill may be withdrawn from discussion so long as it has not been finally voted upon.

Article 121:
Any bill passed by the Legislature shall be immediately forwarded to the President of the Republic, who, before promulgating it, has the right to make objections to it in all or in part.

Article 121-1:
In such cases, the President of the Republic sends back the bill with his objections to the House where it was originally passed. If the bill is amended by that House, it is sent to the other House with the objections.

Article 121-2:
If the bill thus amended is voted on by the second House, it will be sent back to the President of the Republic for promulgation.

Article 121-3:
If the objections are rejected by the House that originally passed the bill, it shall be returned to the other House with the objections.

Article 121-4:
If the second House also votes to reject it, the bill is sent back to the President of the Republic, who must then promulgate it.

Article 121-5:
Rejection of the objection is voted on by either House by the majority stipulated in Article 117. In such cases, the votes of each House shall be taken by secret ballot.

Article 121-6:
If in either House the majority stipulated in the preceding paragraph is not obtained for the rejection, the objections are accepted.

Article 122:
The right of objection must be exercised within eight (8) full days starting with the date of the receipt of the bill by the President of the Republic.

Article 123:
If within the prescribed deadline, the President of the Republic has made no objection, the bill must be promulgated unless the session of the Legislature has ended before expiration of the deadline, in which case, the bill is deferred. At the opening of the following session, the bill thus deferred is sent to the President of the Republic to exercise his right of objection.

Article 124:
A bill rejected by one of the two (2) Houses may not be introduced again in the same session.

Article 125:
Bills and other acts of the Legislature and the National Assembly shall enter into force with their promulgation and their publication in the Official Gazette (Journal Officiel) of the Republic.

Article 125-1:
Bills shall be numbered and included in the printed and numbered bulletin entitled BULLETIN OF LAWS AND ACTS.

Article 126:
The bill is dated on the day of its final adoption by the two (2) Houses.

Article 127:
No one may submit petitions in person to the Legislature.

Article 128:
Only the Legislative Branch has the authority to interpret laws, which it does by passing a law.

Article 129:
Each member of the Legislature receives a monthly stipend from the time he takes oath.

Article 129-1:
Service as a member of the Legislature is incompatible with any other duty remunerated by the State, except that of teacher.

Article 129-2:
Every member of the two (2) Houses has the right to question and interpellate a member of the Government or the entire Government on events and acts of the Administration.

Article 129-3:
An interpellation request must be seconded by five (5) members of the body concerned. It becomes a vote of confidence or of censure when passed by a majority of that body.

Article 129-4:
When the interpellation request ends in a vote of censure on a question concerning a Government program or declaration of general policy, the Prime Minister must submit his Government's resignation to the President of the Republic.

Article 129-5:
The President must accept that resignation and appoint a new Prime Minister, pursuant to the provision of this Constitution.

Article 129-6:
The Legislature may not pass more than one vote of censure a year on a question concerning a Government program or declaration of general policy.

Article 130:
In the case of the death, resignation, disqualification, judicial interdiction, or acceptance of a duty incompatible with that of a member of the Legislature, the Deputy or Senator shall be replaced in his Electoral District for only the remainder of his term by a by-election called by the Primary Electoral Assembly to be conducted by the Permanent Electoral Council in the month the vacancy occurs.

Article 130-1:
The election shall take place within thirty (30) days after convocation of the Primary Assembly, pursuant to the Constitution.

Article 130-2:
The same procedure shall apply in the absence of an election or in the event that elections are declared null and void by the Permanent Electoral Council in one or more Electoral Districts.

Article 130-3:
However, if the vacancy occurs during the last regular session of the Legislature or after that session, a by-election may not be held.

SECTION E

Incompatibilities

Article 131:
The following may not be elected members of the Legislature:

1) Government concessionaires or contractors for the performance of public services;

2) Representatives or agents of Government contractors or concessionaires, or companies or corporations that have Government concessions or contracts;

3) Delegates, Vice Delegates, judges, and officers of the Public Prosecutor's Office whose duties have not terminated six (6) months before the date set for the elections;

4) Any person who comes under the other cases of ineligibility stipulated by this Constitution and by law.

Article 132:
Members of the Executive Branch and the Director Generals of Government departments may not be elected members of the Legislature unless they resign at least one (1) year before the date of the elections.

CHAPTER III

The Executive Branch

Article 133:
The Executive power is vested in:

a) The President of the Republic, who is the Head of State.

b) The Government, which is headed by a Prime Minister.

SECTION A

The President of the Republic

Article 134:
The President of the Republic is elected in direct universal suffrage by an absolute majority of votes. If that majority is not obtained in the first election, a second election is held.

Only the two (2) candidates who, if such be the case, after the withdrawal of more favored candidates, have received the largest number of votes in the first election may run in the second election.

Article 134-1:
The term of the President is five (5) years. This term begins and ends on the February 7 following the date of the elections.

Article 134-2:
Presidential elections shall take place the last sunday of November in the fifth year of the President's term.

Article 134-3:
The President of the Republic may not be re-elected. He may serve an additional term only after an interval of five (5) years. He may in no case run for a third term.

Article 135:
To be elected President of the Republic of Haiti, a candidate must:

a) Be a native-born Haitian and never have renounced Haitian nationality;

b) Have attained thirty-five (35) years of age by the election day;

c) Enjoy civil and political rights and never have been sentenced to death, personal restraint or penal servitude or the loss of civil rights for a crime of ordinary law;

d) Be the owner in Haiti of at least one real property and have his habitual residence in the country;

e) Have resided in the country for five (5) consecutive years before the date of the elections;

f) Have been relieved of his responsibilities if he has been handling public funds.

Article 135-1:
Before taking office, the President of the Republic shall take the following oath before the National Assembly: "I swear before God and the Nation faithfully to observe and enforce the Constitution and the laws of the Republic, to respect and cause to be respected the rights of the Haitian people, to work for the greatness of the country,

and to maintain the nation's independence and the integrity of its territory."

SECTION B

Duties of the President of the Republic

Article 136:
The President of the Republic, who is the Head of State, shall see to the respect for and enforcement of the Constitution and the stability of the institutions. He shall ensure the regular operations of the public authorities and the continuity of the State.

Article 137:
The President of the Republic shall choose a Prime Minister from among the members of the majority party of the Parliament. In the absence of such a majority, the President of the Republic shall choose his Prime Minister in consultation with the President of the Senate and the President of the House of Deputies.

In either case, the President's choice must be ratified by the Parliament.

Article 137-1:
The President of the Republic shall terminate the duties of the Prime Minister upon the latter's submission of the Government's resignation.

Article 138:
The President of the Republic is the guarantor of the nation's independence and the integrity of its territory.

Article 139:
He shall negotiate and sign all international treaties, conventions and agreements and submit them to the National Assembly for ratification.

Article 139-1:
He shall accredit ambassadors and special envoys to foreign powers, receive letters of accreditation from ambassadors of foreign powers and issue exequatur to consuls.

Article 140:
He declares war, and negotiates and signs peace treaties with the approval of the National Assembly.

Article 141:
With the approval of the Senate, the President appoints, by a decree issued in the Council of Ministers, the Commander-in-Chief of the armed forces, the Commander-in-Chief of the police, ambassadors and consul generals.

Article 142:
By a decree issued in the Council of Ministers, the President of the Republic appoints the directors general of the civil service, and delegates and vice delegates of Departments and Arrondissements.

He also appoints, with the approval of the Senate, Administrative Councils of Autonomous Agencies.

Article 143:
The President of the Republic is the nominal head of the armed forces, but he never commands them in person.

Article 144:
He has the seal of the Republic affixed to all laws and promulgates them within the deadline stipulated by the Constitution. Before the expiration of that deadline, he may avail himself of his right of objection.

Article 145:
He sees to the enforcement of judicial decisions, pursuant to the law.

Article 146:
The President of the Republic has the right to pardon and commute sentences in all res judicata cases, except for sentences handed down by the High Court of justice as stipulated in this Constitution.

Article 147:
He may grant amnesty only for political matters as stipulated by law.

Article 148:
If the President finds it temporarily impossible to discharge his duties, the Executive Authority shall be vested in the Council of Ministers under the Presidency of the Prime Minister, so long as the disability continues.

Article 149:
Should the Office of the President of the Republic become vacant for any reason, the President of the Supreme Court of the Republic, or in his absence, the Vice President of that Court, or in his absence, the judge with the highest seniority and so on by order of seniority, shall be invested temporarily with the duties of the President of the Republic by the National Assembly duly convened by the Prime Minister. The election of a new President for a new five (5) year term shall be held at least forty-five (45) and no more than ninety (90) days after the vacancy occurs, pursuant to the Constitution and the Electoral Law.

Article 149-1:
The acting President may in no case be a candidate in the next Presidential election.

Article 150:
The President of the Republic shall have no powers other than those accorded to him by the Constitution.

Article 151:
At the opening of each annual session of the Legislature, the President of the Republic shall deliver a message to the Legislature on the State of the Nation. This message may not be debated.

Article 152:
The President of the Republic shall receive a monthly salary from the Public Treasury upon taking the oath of office.

Article 153:
The President of the Republic shall have his official residence in the National Palace, in the capital city, unless the seat of the Executive Branch is moved.

Article 154:
The President of the Republic presides over the Council of Ministers.

SECTION C

The Government

Article 155:
The Government is composed of the Prime Minister, the Ministers and Secretaries of State. The Prime Minister is the head of the Government.

Article 156:
The Government conducts the policy of the Nation. It is responsible before Parliament under the terms stipulated by the Constitution.

Article 157:
To be appointed Prime Minister, a person must:

1) Be a native-born Haitian, and never have renounced Haitian nationality;

2) Have attained thirty (30) years of age;

3) Enjoy civil and political rights and never have been sentenced to death, personal restraint or penal servitude or the loss of civil rights;

4) Own real property in Haiti and practice a profession there;

5) Have resided in the country for five (5) consecutive years;

6) Have been relieved of his responsibilities if he has been handling public funds.

SECTION D

Powers of the Prime Minister

Article 158:
With the approval of the President, the Prime Minister shall choose the members of his cabinet of Ministers and shall go before Parliament to obtain a vote of confidence on his declaration of general policy. The vote shall be taken in open ballot, and an absolute majority of both Houses is required.

In the event of a vote of nonconfidence by one of the two (2) Houses, the procedure shall be repeated.

Article 159:
The Prime Minister enforces the laws. In the event of the President of the Republic's absence or temporary inability to perform his duties, or at his request, the Prime Minister presides over the Council of Ministers. He has the power to issue rules and regulations but he can never suspend or interpret laws, acts or decrees, nor refrain from enforcing them.

Article 159-1:
In concert with the President of the Republic, he is responsible for national defense.

Article 160:
The Prime Minister appoints and dismisses directly or by delegation Government officials, according to the provisions of the Constitution and the law on the general regulations for Government operations.

Article 161:
The Prime Minister and the Ministers may appear before the two (2) Houses to support bills and the objections of the President of the Republic and to reply to interpellation.

Article 162:
Acts of the Prime Minister are countersigned, if need be, by the Ministers responsible for enforcing them. The Prime Minister may be assigned a Ministerial portfolio.

Article 163:
The Prime Minister and the Ministers are jointly responsible for the acts of the President of the Republic and of their ministries that they countersign. They are also responsible for enforcement of the laws in the areas of their competence.

Article 164:
The duties of the Prime Minister and of a member of the Government are incompatible with membership in the Parliament. If such a case occurs, the member of Parliament must choose one duty or the other.

Article 165:
In the event of the Prime Minister's resignation, the Government remains in place until the appointment of a successor, in order to transact current business.

SECTION E

The Ministers and Secretaries of State

Article 166:
The President of the Republic presides over the Council of Ministers. The number of Ministers may be no fewer than ten (10).

When he deems it necessary, the Prime Minister may appoint Secretaries of State to the Ministers.

Article 167:
The number of Ministers is set by law.

Article 168:
Holding a ministerial post is incompatible with the exercise of all other public employment, except for higher education.

Article 169:
Ministers are responsible for the acts of the Prime Minister that they countersign. They are jointly responsible for enforcement of the laws.

Article 169-1:
In no case may an oral or written order of the President of the Republic or of the Prime Minister release Ministers from the responsibilities of their office.

Article 170:
The Prime Minister, the Ministers and the Secretaries of State receive monthly salaries established by the Budgetary law.

Article 171:
Ministers appoint certain categories of Government employees by delegation of the Prime Minister, according to the conditions set by the law on Government operations.

Article 172:
When one of the two (2) Houses during an interpellation calls into question the responsibility of a Minister by a vote of censure passed by an absolute majority of its members, the Executive shall recall the Minister.

CHAPTER IV

The Judiciary

Article 173:
The Judicial Power shall be vested in the Supreme Court (Cour de Cassation), the Courts of Appeal, Courts of First Instance, Courts of Peace and special courts, whose number, composition, organization, operation and jurisdiction are set by law.

Article 173-1:
Civil rights are exclusively the competence of the Courts.

Article 173-2:
No court and no jurisdiction in disputed matters may be established except by law. No special court may be established under any name whatever.

Article 174:
Judges of the Supreme Court and the Courts of Appeal are appointed for ten (10) years. Judges of the Courts of First Instance are appointed for seven (7) years. Their term begins at the time they take their oath of office.

Article 175:
Supreme Court justices are appointed by the President of the Republic from a list submitted by the Senate of three (3) persons per court seat. Judges of the Courts of Appeal and Courts of First Instance are appointed from a list submitted by the Departmental Assembly concerned; Justices of the Peace are appointed from a list drawn up by the Communal Assemblies.

Article 176:
The law regulates the conditions required for serving as a judge at any level. A school of the Magistrature shall be established.

Article 177:
Judges of the Supreme Court, the Courts of Appeal and the Courts of First Instance are appointed for life. They may be removed from office only because of a legally determined abuse of authority or be suspended following and indictment leveled against them. They may not be reassigned, without their consent, even in the case of a promotion. Their service may be terminated during their term of office only in the event of a duly determined permanent physical or mental incapacity.

Article 178:
The Supreme Court does not try cases on their merits. Nevertheless, in all cases other than those submitted to a jury, when a case between the same parties is tried upon second appeal, even with an incidental plea of defense, the Supreme Court, accepting the appeal, shall not remand the case to a lower court but shall rule on the merits, sitting as a full court.

Article 178-1:
However, in the case of appeals from temporary restraining orders or orders of examining magistrates, grants of appeal pronounced in connection with such orders or from final sentences of the Peace

Courts or decisions of special courts, the Supreme Court, admitting the appeal, shall pronounce a decision without remanding the case.

Article 179:
The duties of a judge are incompatible with any other salaried duties, except for education.

Article 180:
Court proceedings are public. However, they may take place in closed session in the interest of public order and good morals, at the decision of the Court.

Article 180-1:
Sentences may not be delivered in closed session in cases of political offenses or offenses involving the press.

Article 181:
All orders or judgments shall state the grounds for the decision and shall be handed down in a public hearing.

Article 181-1:
Orders or judgments are delivered and executed in the name of the Republic. They shall include writs of execution to officers of the Public Prosecutor's Office and agents of the police and armed forces. Acts of notaries shall be put in the same form when their compulsory execution is involved.

Article 182:
The Supreme Court rules on conflicts of jurisdiction, in the manner regulated by law.

Article 182-1:
The Supreme Court rules on both fact and law in all cases of decisions handed down by military courts.

Article 183:
When litigation is referred to it, the Supreme Court, sitting as a full Court, shall rule on the unconstitutionality of the laws.

Article 183-1:
The interpretation of a law given by the Houses of the Legislature shall be imposed for the purpose of that law without retroactively taking away any rights acquired by res judicata.

Article 183-2:
The Courts shall apply Government decrees and regulations only insofar as they are in conformity with the law.

Article 184:
The law determines the jurisdiction of the courts and tribunals, and regulates the manner of proceedings before them.

Article 184-1:
The law also provides for disciplinary penalties to be taken against judges and officers of the Public Prosecutor's Office, except for Supreme Court justices who are under the jurisdiction of the High Court of Justice for abuse of authority.

CHAPTER V

The High Court of Justice

Article 185:
The Senate may constitute itself as a High Court of Justice. The proceedings of this Court are presided over by the President of the Senate, assisted by the President and Vice President of the Supreme Court as Vice President and Secretary, respectively, except where the justices of the Supreme Court and officers of the Public Prosecutor's Office assigned to that court are involved in the accusation, in which case, the President of the Senate shall be assisted by two (2) Senators, one of whom shall be designated by the accused, and the Senators so appointed shall not be entitled to vote.

Article 186:
The House of Deputies, by a majority of two-thirds (2/3) of its members, shall indict:

a) The President of the Republic for the crime of high treason or any other crime or offense committed in the discharge of his duties;

b) The Prime Minister, the Ministers and the Secretaries of State for crimes of high treason and embezzlement or abuse of power or any other crimes or offenses committed in the discharge of their duties;

c) Members of the Permanent Electoral Council and the Superior Court of Auditors and the Court of Administrative Disputes for serious offenses committed in the discharge of their duties;

d) Supreme Court justices and officers of the Public Prosecutor's Office before the Court for abuse of authority;

e) The Protector of Citizens (Protecteur du Citoyen).

Article 187:
Members of the High Court of Justice serve on an individual basis, and on opening proceedings, take the following oath:

"I swear before God and before the Nation to judge with the impartiality and the firmness appropriate to an honest and free man, according to my conscience and my deep-seated conviction."

Article 188:
The High Court of Justice shall designate, by secret ballot and an absolute majority of votes, from among its members a Committee of Enquiry.

Article 188-1:
The decision in the form of a decree shall be handed down on the report of the Committee of Enquiry by a two-thirds (2/3) majority of the members of the High Court of Justice.

Article 189:
The High Court of Justice shall not sit unless a majority of two-thirds (2/3) of its members are present.

Article 189-1:
The Court may not impose any other penalties than dismissal, disqualification or deprivation of the right to exercise any public office for no less than five (5) years and no more than fifteen (15) years.

Article 189-2:
However, the convicted person may be brought before ordinary courts, in accordance with the law, if there is reason to impose other penalties or to rule on the institution of civil action.

Article 190:
Once a case is brought before the High Court of Justice, the Court must sit until it renders its verdict, regardless of the length of the sessions of the Legislature.

TITLE VI

Independent Institutions

CHAPTER I

The Permanent Electoral Council

Article 191:
The Permanent Electoral Council is responsible for organizing and controlling with complete independence all electoral procedures throughout the territory of the Republic until the results of the election are announced.

Article 191-1:
The Council also drafts the Electoral Bill that it submits to the Executive Branch for the necessary purposes.

Article 191-2:
The Council sees to it that the electoral lists are kept up-to-date.

Article 192:
The Permanent Electoral Council consists of nine (9) members chosen from a list of three (3) names proposed by each of the Departmental Assemblies:

> 3 are chosen by the Executive Branch;

> 3 are chosen by the Supreme Court;

> 3 are chosen by the National Assembly.

The above-mentioned organs see to it as far as possible that each of the Departments are represented.

Article 193:
Members of the Permanent Electoral Council must:

1) Be native-born Haitians;

2) Have attained forty (40) years of age;

3) Enjoy civil and political rights and never have been sentenced to death, personal constraint or penal servitude or the loss of civil rights;

4) Have been relieved of their responsibilities if they have been handling public funds;

5) Have resided in the country at least three (3) years before their nomination.

Article 194:
Members of the Permanent Electoral Council are appointed for a nine (9) year nonrenewable period. They may not be removed from office.

Article 194-1:
One-third of the members of the Permanent Electoral Council are replaced every three (3) years. The President is chosen from among its members.

Article 194-2:
Before taking office, the members of the Permanent Electoral Council take the following oath before the Supreme Court:

> "I swear to respect the Constitution and the provisions of the Electoral Law and to discharge my duties with dignity, independence, impartiality and patriotism."

Article 195:
In the event of a serious offense committed in the discharge of their duties, the members of the Permanent Electoral Council are liable for prosecution before the High Court of Justice.

Article 195-1:
The seat of the Permanent Electoral Council is in the capital. Its jurisdiction extends throughout the territory of the Republic.

Article 196:
Members of the Permanent Electoral Council may not hold any other public post, nor may they be a candidate for an elective post during their term.

In the event of dismissal, a member of the Council must wait three (3) years before he may run for an elective post.

Article 197:
The Permanent Electoral Council shall rule on all disputes arising either in elections or in the enforcement or the violation of the Electoral Law, subject to any legal prosecution undertaken against an offender or offenders before the courts of competent jurisdiction.

Article 198:
In the event of a vacancy caused by death, resignation or any other reason, the member shall be replaced following the procedure established in Article 192 for the remainder of his term, taking into account the branch of government that had designated the member to be replaced.

Article 199:
The law determines the rules for organization and operation of the Permanent Electoral Council.

CHAPTER II

The Superior Court of Auditors and Administrative Disputes

Article 200:
The Superior Court of Auditors and Administrative Disputes is an independent and autonomous financial and administrative court. It is responsible for administrative and jurisdictional control of Government receipts and expenditures, verification of the accounts of the Government enterprises and of the territorial divisions.

Article 200-1:
The Superior Court of Auditors and Administrative Disputes hears cases against the State and the territorial divisions, the Administration and Government officials, public services and citizens.

Article 200-2:
Its decisions are not subject to appeal, except to the Supreme Court.

Article 200-3:
The Supreme Court of Auditors and Administrative Disputes comprises two (2) sections:

1) The Financial Control Section;

2) The Administrative Disputes Section.

Article 200-4:
The Superior Court of Auditors and Administrative Disputes participates in drawing up the budget and is consulted on all matters concerning legislation on public finances and on all draft financial or commercial contracts, agreements and conventions to which the State is a party. It has the right to conduct audits in all Government agencies.

Article 200-5:
Members of the Superior Court of Auditors and Administrative Disputes must:

a) Be Haitians and never have renounced their nationality;

b) Have attained thirty-five (35) years of age;

c) Have been relieved of their responsibilities if they have been handling public funds;

d) Have a Bachelor of Law degree, be a certified public accountant or hold an advanced degree in government administration, economics or public finance;

e) Have five (5) years experience in public or private administration;

f) Enjoy civil and political rights.

Article 200-6:
Candidates for membership on the Court shall submit their applications directly to the Office of the Senate of the Republic. The Senate elects the ten (10) members of the Court, who select the Court's President and Vice President from among them.

Article 201:
Court members have a ten (10) year term and may not be removed.

Article 202:
Before taking office, the members of the Superior Court of Auditors and Administrative Disputes shall take the following oath before a section of the Supreme Court:

> "I swear to respect the Constitution and the laws of the Republic, to discharge my duties properly and loyally and to conduct myself at all times with dignity."

Article 203:
Members of the Superior Court of Auditors and Administrative Disputes are under the jurisdiction of the High Court of Justice for any serious offenses committed in the discharge of their duties.

Article 204:
The Superior Court of Auditors and Administrative Disputes shall submit each year to the Legislature within thirty (30) days following the opening of the first legislative session a complete report on the country's financial situation and on the efficacy of government expenditures.

Article 205:
The organization of the above-mentioned court, its membership regulations and its mode of operation are established by law.

CHAPTER III

The Conciliation Commission

Article 206:
The Conciliation Commission is responsible for settling disputes between the Executive Branch and the Legislature and the two (2) Houses of the Legislature. Its members are as follows:

a) The President of the Supreme Court - President;

b) The President of the Senate - Vice President:

c) The President of the House of Deputies - Member;

d) The President of the Permanent Electoral Council - Member;

e) The Vice President of the Permanent Electoral Council - Member;

f) Two (2) members designated by the President of the Republic - Members.

Article 206-1:
The mode of operation of the Conciliation Commission is determined by law.

CHAPTER IV

Protection of Citizens

Article 207:
An office known as the OFFICE OF CITIZEN PROTECTION is established to protect all individuals against any form of abuse by the Government.

Article 207-1:
The office is directed by a citizen bearing the title of PROTECTOR OF CITIZENS. He is chosen by consensus of the President of the Republic, the President of the Senate and the President of the House of Deputies. His term is seven (7) years and may not be renewed.

Article 207-2:
His intervention on behalf of any complainant is without charge, whatever the court having jurisdiction might be.

Article 207-3:
A law sets the conditions and regulations for the operation of the Office of Citizen Protection.

CHAPTER V

The University - The Academy - Culture

Article 208:
Higher education is free. It is provided by the University of the Haitian State (Université d'Etat d'Haïti), which is autonomous and by the superior public schools and the superior private schools accredited by the State.

Article 209:
The State must finance the operation and development of the Haitian State University and the public superior schools. Their organization and their location must be planned from the perspective of regional development.

Article 210:
The establishment of research centers must be encouraged.

Article 211:
Authorization for operation of universities and private superior schools is subject to the technical approval of the Council of the State University, to a majority of Haitian participation in the capital and faculty, and to the obligation to teach primarily in the official language of the country.

Article 211-1:
The University and the private and public superior schools provide academic and practical instruction adapted to the trends and requirements of national development.

Article 212:
An organic law regulates the establishment, location and operation of universities and public and private superior schools in the country.

Article 213:
A Haitian Academy shall be established to standardize the Creole language and enable it to develop scientifically and harmoniously.

Article 213-1:
Other academies may be established.

Article 214:
The title Academy Member is purely honorific.

Article 214-1:
The law shall determine the mode of organization and operation of academies.

Article 215:
Archaeological, historical, cultural, folkloric and architectural treasures in the country, which bear witness to the greatness of our past, are part of the national heritage. Consequently, monuments, ruins, sites of our ancestors' great feasts of arms, famous centers of our African beliefs, and all vestiges of the past are placed under the protection of the State.

Article 216:
The law determines special conditions for this protection in each sphere.

TITLE VII

Public Finance

Article 217:
The finances of the Republic are decentralized. Financial management is the responsibility of the Minister concerned. The Executive, assisted by an Interdepartmental Council, draws up the law that sets the portion and nature of public revenues allotted to the territorial divisions.

Article 218:
No Government levy may be established except by law. No charge or tax, whether imposed by a Department, a Municipality, or Communal Section, may be established without the consent of its territorial divisions.

Article 219:
No preferential tax treatment may be established. No tax exemption, increase, decrease or elimination may be established except by law.

Article 220:
No pension, bonus, allotment or subsidy charged to the Public Treasury may be authorized unless provided by law. Pensions paid by the State are indexed to the cost of living.

Article 221:
Subject to special provisions thereon, the holding of two or more salaried public offices at the same time is strictly forbidden, except posts in education.

Article 222:
Procedures for preparation of the budget and its execution are determined by law.

Article 223:
Enforcement of the law on the Budget and on Public Accounts is monitored by the Superior Court of Auditors and Administrative Disputes and by the Budget Office.

Article 224:
National monetary policy is set by the Central Bank jointly with the Minister of Economics and Finance.

Article 225:
An autonomous public agency with legal personality and financial autonomy performs the functions of a Central Bank. Its regulations are determined by law.

Article 226:
The Central Bank has exclusive authority to issue as legal tender throughout the territory of the Republic, paper money representing the monetary unit, and coins, according to the name, weight, description, amount and use set by law.

Article 227:
The budget of each Ministry is divided into chapters and sections, and must be voted upon article by article.

Article 227-1:
Amounts to be drawn on budget allocation may in no case exceed one-twelfth of the appropriations for a particular month, except in December, because of bonuses paid to all Government employees and officials.

Article 227-2:
General accounts of receipts and expenditures of the Republic shall be kept by the Minister of Finance according to an accounting method established by law.

Article 227-3:
The General accounts and budgets stipulated in the preceding article, accompanied by a report from the Superior Court of Auditors and Administrative Disputes must be submitted to the Legislative Houses by the Minister of Finance no later than fifteen (15) days after the opening of the legislative session. The same applies to the annual

balance sheet and statement of operations of the Central Bank, and to all other accounts of the Haitian State.

Article 227-4:
The Government fiscal year begins on October 1 of each year and ends on September 30 of the following year.

Article 228:
Each year the Legislature issues:

a) The statement of receipts and expenditures of the Government for the preceding year, or years;

b) The Government General Budget containing the rough estimates and the portion of funds allocated to each Ministry of the year.

Article 228-1:
However, no proposal or amendment may be introduced into the Budget when it is being voted upon, without provision of the ways and means therefore.

Article 228-2:
No increase or reduction may be made in the allocation of Government funds, except by amendment of the laws relating thereto.

Article 229:
The Legislative Houses may refrain from doing any legislative work until the above documents are submitted to it. They shall refuse to grant the Ministers discharge when the accounts submitted do not in themselves, or by supporting documents, provide the necessary data for verification and evaluation.

Article 230:
Examination and payment of the General Administration Accounts and all accounts of public funds are affected according to the method established by law.

Article 231:
If for any reason whatever the Legislative Houses do not act upon the budget for one or more Ministerial Departments before they adjourn,

the budget or budgets of the Departments concerned shall remain in force until a new budget is voted on and adopted.

Article 231-1:

In the event that, through fault of the Executive Branch, the Budget of the Republic has not been voted upon, the President of the Republic shall immediately call a special session of the Legislative Houses for the sole purpose of voting on the Government budget.

Article 232:

Autonomous agencies and enterprises and entities subsidized wholly or in part by the Public Treasury shall be governed by special budgets and salary and wage systems approved by the Executive Branch.

Article 233:

For the purpose of maintaining constant and careful supervision over Government expenditures, a fifteen-member Parliamentary Committee with nine (9) Deputies and six (6) Senators shall be elected by secret ballot at the beginning of each regular session, to report on the management Ministers, in order to enable the two (2) Assemblies to give them discharge.

This Committee may engage the services of specialists to assist it with its monitoring functions.

TITLE VIII

The Civil Service

Article 234:

The Haitian Civil Service is the instrument by which the State carries out its mission and achieves its objectives. To ensure its viability, it must be managed honestly and efficiently.

Article 235:

Government employees and officials shall be exclusively in the service of the State. It is their duty to abide faithfully by the norms and ethics determined by law for civil servants.

Article 236:
The law establishes the organization of the various Government structures and stipulates the conditions for their operation.

Article 236-1:
The law shall regulate the civil service on the basis of aptitude, merit and conduct. It shall guarantee security of employment.

Article 236-2:
The civil service is a career. No official may be hired except by competition or by meeting other conditions prescribed by the Constitution and by law, nor may he be dismissed except for causes specifically determined by law. Dismissals must in all cases be ruled upon by the Court of Administrative Disputes.

Article 237:
Career service officials are not members of any particular Government agency but are members of the civil service, which makes them available to the various Government agencies.

Article 238:
Officials indicated by law have the obligation to declare the status of their net worth to the Clerk of the Civil Court within thirty (30) days following their entry into service. The Government Auditor must take every step he deems necessary to verify the accuracy of the declaration.

Article 239:
Government employees and officials may form associations to defend their rights under the conditions established by law.

Article 240:
Holders of public office or positions, particularly Ministers and Secretaries of State, officers of the Public Prosecutor's Office, Delegates and Vice Delegates, ambassadors, private secretaries of the President of the Republic, members of the Cabinet of Ministers, the Director Generals of the Ministerial Department of autonomous agencies, and members of the Administrative Council are not eligible for the Government career service.

Article 241:

The law punishes violations committed against the treasury and unjust gain. Officials who have knowledge of such actions have the duty to report them to the competent authorities.

Article 242:

Unjust gain may be determined by all types of evidence, particularly presumption of a sharp disproportion between the official's means acquired after his entry into service and the accumulated amount of salaries and emoluments to which the post he has occupied entitles him.

Article 243:

Officials guilty of the above offenses are entitled to only the twenty-year statute of limitation. This limitation period begins to run with the termination of their duties or the causes that would have prevented any prosecution.

Article 244:

The State has the duty to avoid major salary disparities in the civil service.

TITLE XI

CHAPTER I

Economics and Agriculture

Article 245:

Economic freedom shall be guaranteed so long as it is not contrary to the public interest.

The State shall protect private enterprise and shall endeavor to see that it develops under the conditions necessary to increase the national wealth in such a way as to ensure the participation of the largest possible number of persons in the benefits of this wealth.

Article 246:

The State encourages in rural and urban areas the formation of cooperatives for production, processing of raw materials and the entrepreneurial spirit to promote the accumulation of national capital to ensure continuous development.

Article 247:
Agriculture, which is the main source of the Nation's wealth, is a guarantee of the well-being of the people and the socio-economic progress of the Nation.

Article 248:
A special agency to be known as THE NATIONAL INSTITUTE OF AGRARIAN REFORM shall be established to organize the revision of real property structures and to implement an agrarian reform to benefit those who actually work the land. This Institute shall draw up an agrarian policy geared to maximizing productivity by constructing infrastructure aimed at the protection and management of the land.

Article 248-1:
The law determines the minimum and maximum area of basic farm units.

Article 249:
The State has the obligation to establish the structures necessary to ensure maximum productivity of the land and domestic marketing of foodstuffs. Technical and financial management units shall be established to assist farmers at the level of each Communal Section.

Article 250:
No monopoly may be established to benefit the State and the territorial divisions except in the exclusive interest of society as a whole. Such a monopoly may not be granted to any private individual.

Article 251:
The import of foodstuffs and their byproducts that are produced in sufficient quantity in the national territory is forbidden, except in the event of force majeure.

Article 252:
The State may take charge of the operation of enterprises for the production of goods and services essential to the community in order to ensure continuity in the event the existence of these establishments

should be threatened. Such enterprises shall be grouped in a comprehensive management system.

CHAPTER II

The Environment

Article 253:
Since the environment is the natural framework of the life of the people, any practices that might disturb the ecological balance are strictly forbidden.

Article 254:
The State shall organize the enhancement of natural sites to ensure their protection and make them accessible to all.

Article 255:
To protect forest reserves and expand the plant coverage, the State encourages the development of local sources of energy: solar, wind and others.

Article 256:
Within the framework of protecting the environment and public education, the State has the obligation to proceed to establish and maintain botanical and zoological gardens at certain points in its territory.

Article 257:
The law specifies the conditions for protecting flora and fauna, and punishes violations thereof.

Article 258:
No one may introduce into the country wastes or residues of any kind from foreign sources.

TITLE X

The Family

Article 259:
The State protects the family, which is the foundation of society.

Article 260:
It must also protect all families regardless of whether they are constituted within the bonds of marriage. It must endeavor to aid and assist mothers, children and the aged.

Article 261:
The law ensures protection for all children. Any child is entitled to love, affection, understanding and moral and physical care from its father and mother.

Article 262:
A Family Code must be drawn up to ensure protection and respect for the rights of the family and to define procedures of the search for affiliation. Courts and other Government agencies charged with the protection of these rights must be accessible free of charge at the level of the smallest territorial division.

TITLE XI

The Armed Forces and the Police Force

Article 263:
The "Public Forces" (la Force Publique) are composed of two (2) distinct bodies:

a) The Armed Forces of Haiti; and

b) The Police Forces.

Article 263-1:
No other armed corps may exist in the national territory.

Article 263-2:
All members of the police and armed forces shall take an oath of allegiance and respect for the Constitution and the flag at the time of their enlistment.

CHAPTER I

The Armed Forces

Article 264:
The Armed Forces comprise the Land, Sea and Air Forces and the Technical Services.

The Haitian Armed Forces are set up to ensure the security and integrity of the territory of the Republic.

Article 264-1:
The Armed Forces are in practice commanded by a general officer bearing the title COMMANDER IN CHIEF OF THE HAITIAN ARMED FORCES.

Article 264-2:
The Commander in Chief of the Armed Forces, pursuant to the Constitution, is chosen from among the general officers on active service.

Article 264-3:
His term is set at three (3) years and is renewable.

Article 265:
The Armed Forces are apolitical. Their members may not be part of any political group or party, and they must observe the strictest neutrality.

Article 265-1:
Members of the Armed Forces exercise their right to vote, under the Constitution.

Article 266:
The duties of the Armed Forces are:

a) Defend the country in the event of war;

b) Protect the country against threats from abroad;

c) See to surveillance of the land, sea and air boundaries;

d) At the well-founded request of the Executive, they may lend assistance to the police when the latter are unable to handle a situation;

e) Assist the Nation in the event of a natural disaster;

f) In addition to their regular duties, the Armed Forces may be assigned to development work.

Article 267:
Military personnel on active duty may not be appointed to any Government post, except temporarily to perform a specialized service.

Article 267-1:
To be a candidate for an elective post, all military personnel on active duty must be placed on inactive service or on retirement one (1) year before publication of the electoral decree.

Article 267-2:
The military career is a profession. Its ranking, terms of enlistment, ranks, promotions, discharges, and retirement are determined by the regulations of the Haitian Armed Forces.

Article 267-3:
Military personnel are under the jurisdiction of a military court only for offenses and crimes committed in wartime or for violations of military discipline.

They may not be discharged, placed on inactive service, placed on half pay, or retired early except with their consent. If such consent is not given, the party concerned may lodge an appeal with the court of competent jurisdiction.

Article 267-4:
Military personnel retain for life the last rank obtained in the Haitian Armed Forces. They may be deprived of their rank only by a final judgment by a court of competent jurisdiction.

Article 267-5:
The State must award benefits to military personnel of all ranks, fully guaranteeing their physical security.

Article 268:
Within the framework of compulsory civilian national services for both sexes, provided for by Article 52-3 of the Constitution, the Armed Forces participate in organizing and supervising that service.

Military service is compulsory for all Haitians who have attained eighteen (18) years of age.

The law sets the method of recruitment, and the length and regulations for the performance of these services.

Article 268-1:
Every citizen has the right to armed self defense, within the bounds of his domicile, but has no right to bear arms without express well-founded authorization from the Chief of Police.

Article 268-2:
Possession of a firearm must be reported to the police.

Article 268-3:
The Armed Forces have a monopoly on the manufacture, import, export, use and possession of weapons of war and their munitions, as well as war material.

CHAPTER II

The Police Forces

Article 269:
The Police Force is an armed body. It operates under the Ministry of Justice.

Article 269-1:
It is established to ensure law and order and protect the life and property of citizens. Its organization and mode of operation are regulated by law.

Article 270:
The Commander in Chief of the Police Forces is appointed, in accordance with the Constitution, for a three (3) year term, which is renewable.

Article 271:
An Academy and a Police School have been established, whose organization and operations are set by law.

Article 272:
Specialized sections, particularly the Penitentiary Administration, the Firemen's Service, the Traffic Police, the Highway police, Criminal Investigations, the Narcotics Service and the Anti-Smuggling Service, have been established by the law governing the organization, operation and location of the Police Forces.

Article 273:
The police, as an auxiliary of the Justice System, investigate violations, offenses and crimes committed, in order to discover and arrest the perpetrators of them.

Article 274:
In the exercise of their duties, members of the "Public Forces" are subject to civil and penal liability in the manner and under the conditions stipulated by the Constitution and by law.

TITLE XII

General Provisions

Article 275:
National and legal holidays shall be celebrated by the Government and private and commercial enterprises.

Article 275-1:
The national holidays are:

1) Independence Day, January 1;

2) Forefathers' Day, January 2;

3) Agriculture and Labor Day, May 1;

4) Flag Day and University Day, May 18; and

5) Battle of Vertières Day, which is also ARMED FORCES DAY, November 18.

Article 275-2:
Legal holidays shall be determined by law.

Article 276:
The National Assembly may not ratify any international treaty, convention or agreement containing clauses contrary to this Constitution.

Article 276-1:
International treaties, conventions and agreements are ratified in the form of a decree.

Article 276-2:
Once international treaties or agreements are approved and ratified in the manner stipulated by the Constitution, they become part of the legislation of the country and abrogate any laws in conflict with them.

Article 277:
The Haitian State may join an Economic Community of States insofar as the association agreement stimulates the social and economic development of the Haitian Republic and does not contain any clause contrary to this Constitution.

Article 278:
No place or part of the territory may be declared in a state of siege except in the event of civil war or invasion by a foreign force.

Article 278-1:
The act of the President of the Republic declaring a state of siege must be countersigned by the Prime Minister and by all of the Ministers and contain an immediate convocation of the National Assembly to decide on the desirability of the measure.

Article 278-2:
The National Assembly decides with the Executive Branch as to what constitutional guarantees may be suspended in the parts of the territory placed under a state of siege.

Article 278-3:
The state of siege is lifted if it is not renewed by a vote of the National Assembly every fifteen (15) days after its entry into force.

Article 278-4:
The National Assembly shall be in session for the entire duration of the state of siege.

Article 279:
Thirty (30) days after his election, the President of the Republic must deposit with the Clerk of the Court of First Instance of his domicile a notarized inventory of all his movable and immovable goods, and he shall do the same at the end of his term.

Article 279-1:
The Prime Minister, the Ministers and Secretaries of State are subject to the same obligation within thirty (30) days of their installation and of the termination of their duties.

Article 280:
No general expenditures or compensation whatever shall be granted to members of the major organs of the State for any special duties that may be assigned to them.

Article 281:
In national elections, the State assumes responsibility, in proportion to the number of votes cast, for a portion of the expenses incurred in the election campaigns.

Article 281-1:
Only parties that obtain nationally ten percent (10%) of the votes cast, with a minimum of five percent (5%) of the votes cast in one Department, are eligible to receive these Government funds.

TITLE XIII

Amendments to the Constitution

Article 282:
On the recommendation, with reasons given to support it, of one of the two (2) Houses or of the Executive Branch, the Legislature may declare that the Constitution should be amended.

Article 282-1:
This declaration must be supported by two-thirds (2/3) of each of the two (2) Houses. It may be made only in the course of the last Regular Session of the Legislative period and shall be published immediately throughout the territory.

Article 283:
At the first session of the following legislature period, the Houses shall meet in a National Assembly and decide on the proposed amendment.

Article 284:
The National Assembly may not sit or deliberate on the amendment unless at least two-thirds (2/3) of the members of each of the two (2) Houses are present.

Article 284-1:
No decision of the National Assembly may be taken without a majority of two-thirds (2/3) of the votes cast.

Article 284-2:
The amendment passed may enter into effect only after installation of the next elected President. In no case may the President under the Government that approved the amendment benefit from any advantages deriving therefrom.

Article 284-3:
General elections to amend the Constitution by referendum are strictly forbidden.

Article 284-4:
No amendment to the Constitution may affect the democratic and republican nature of the State.

TITLE XIV

Temporary Provisions

Article 285:
The National Council of Government shall remain in operation up to February 7, 1988, the date of the investiture of the President of the Republic elected under this Constitution, in accordance with the electoral timetable.

Article 285-1:
The National Council of Government is authorized to issue in the Council of Ministers, pursuant to the Constitution, decrees having the force of law until the Deputies and Senators elected under this Constitution take up their duties.

Article 286:
Every Haitian who has adopted a foreign nationality during the twenty-nine (29) years prior to February 7, 1986 may, by a declaration made to the Ministry of Justice within two (2) years after publication

of the Constitution, recover his Haitian nationality with the advantages deriving therefrom, in accordance with the law.

Article 287:
In light of the situation of Haitians that have become expatriates voluntarily or involuntarily, the deadlines for residence stipulated in this Constitution are extended for a full year for the next elections.

Article 288:
When the next elections are held, the term of the three (3) Senators elected for each Department shall be established as follows:

a) The Senator who has received the largest number of votes shall have a term of six (6) years;

b) The Senator receiving the second largest number of votes shall have a term of four (4) years;

c) The Senator in third place shall be elected for two (2) years.

Following this, each elected Senator shall have a term of six (6) years.

Article 289:
Awaiting the establishment of the Permanent Electoral Council provided for in this Constitution, the National Council of Government shall set up a Provisional Electoral Council of nine (9) members, charged with drawing up and enforcing the Electoral Law to govern the next elections, who shall be designated as follows:

1) One for the Executive Branch, who is not an official;

2) One for the Episcopal Conference;

3) One for the Advisory Council;

4) One for the Supreme Court;

5) One for agencies defending human rights, who may not be a candidate in the elections;

6) One for the Council of the University;

7) One for the Journalists Association;

8) One for the Protestant religions;

9) One for the National Council of Cooperatives.

Article 289-1:
Within two weeks following ratification of this Constitution, the bodies or organizations concerned shall inform the Executive of the name of their representative.

Article 289-2:
If any of the above bodies or organizations does not appoint a member, the Executive shall fill the vacancy or vacancies.

Article 289-3:
The mission of the Provisional Electoral Council shall end when the President-elect takes office.

Article 290:
The members of the first Permanent Electoral Council shall divide among them by lot the terms of nine (9), six (6), and three (3) years, stipulated for replacement of the Council by thirds (1/3).

Article 291:
For ten (10) years following publications of this Constitution, and without prejudice to any criminal action or civil suit for damages, none of the following may be candidates for any public office:

a) Any person well known for having been by his excess zeal on the architects of the dictatorship and of its maintenance during the last twenty-nine (29) years;

b) Any accountant of public funds during the years of the dictatorship concerning whom there is presumptive evidence of unjustified gain;

c) Any person denounced by public outcry for having inflicted torture on political prisoners in connection with arrests and investigations or for having committed political assassinations.

Article 292:
The Provisional Electoral Council charged with receiving the registration of candidates, shall see to the strict enforcement of this provision.

Article 293:
All decrees expropriating real property in urban and rural areas of the Republic of the last two (2) Haitian governments for the benefit of the State or companies in the course of incorporation shall be annulled if the purpose for which such actions were taken has not been attained during the last 10 years.

Article 293-1:
Any individual who was the victim of confiscation of property or arbitrary dispossession for political reasons during the period from October 22, 1957 to February 7, 1986, may recover his property before the court of competent jurisdiction.

Article 294:
Sentences to death, personal restraint or penal service or the loss of civil rights for political reasons from 1957 to 1986 shall constitute no impediment to the exercise of civil and political rights.

Article 295:
Within six (6) months starting from the time the first President elected under the Constitution of 1987 takes office, the Executive Branch is authorized to proceed to carry out any reforms deemed necessary in the Government Administration in general and in the Judiciary.

TITLE XV

Final Provisions

Article 296:
All codes of law or Handbooks of Justice, all laws, all decree laws and all decrees and orders (Arrêtés) currently in force shall be maintained in all matters not contrary to this Constitution.

Article 297:

All laws, all decree laws, all decrees arbitrarily limiting the basic rights and liberties of citizens, in particular:

a) The decree law of September 5, 1935 on superstitious beliefs;

b) The law of August 2, 1977 establishing the Court of State Security (Tribunal de la Sureté de l'Etat);

c) The law of July 28, 1975 placing the lands of the Artibonite Valley in a special status;

d) The law of April 29, 1969 condemning all imported doctrines;

Are and shall remain repealed.

Article 298:

This Constitution shall be published within two weeks of its ratification by referendum. It shall enter into force as soon as it is published in the MONITEUR, the Official Gazette of the Republic.

Given at the Legislative Palace, in Port-au-Prince, the seat of the Constituent National Assembly, on March 10, 1987, in the One Hundred Eighty-Fourth Year of Independence.

Me Emile Jonassaint   Me Jean Supplice
President of   Vice President of
the Constituent Assembly   the Constituent Assembly

The Secretaries:

Mrs. Bathilde Barbancourt
Mr. Jacques Saint-Louis
Me. Raphaël Michel Adelson

The Members:

Mr. Daniel Anglade
Mr. Karl Auguste
Mr. Yvon Auguste
Mr. Richard Baker
Mr. Jean Adler Bassin
Me. Fresnel Bélizaire
Me. Rigaud Th. Bois
Me. Nyll Calixte
Me. Hugo Charles
Me. Clavaroche Cherenfant
Me. Alcan Dorméus
Me. Chantal Hudicourt Ewald
Me. Rotchild François
Mr. Rick Garnier
Me. Reynold Georges
Me. Antoine Gilles
Dr. Georges Greffin
Mr. Alexis C. Guerrier
Mr. Louis Dominald Guerrier
Mr. Apollon Israël
Me. Athanase Jean-Louis
Me. Wilbert Joseph
Mr. Julio Larosilière
Mr. Guy Latortue
Mr. Gérard M. Laurent
Mr. Lavelanet Lindor
Mr Jean Abraham Lubin

Me. Jean Léonidas Lucien
Me. François R. Magloire
Me. Jean Mainville
Mr. Volvick Mathieu
Me. Justin Mézile
Dr. Georges Michel
Me Barbantès Moussignac
Me. Justin Obas
Me. Ménès Ovide
Me. Thalès Paul
Mr. Franck Paulché
Mr. Pierre Th. Pierre
Mr. Gustave Pierre-Louis
Mr. Réginald Riboul
Me. Gérard Romulus
Dr. Louis Roy
Mr. Gary Sajous
Me. Gracia Saint-Louis
Mr. Eddy Saint-Pierre
Mr. Pierre Saint-Rémy
Mr. Benoit Sanon
Me. Michel Félix Sapini
Mr. Jacques Séide
Me. Marc Sémervil
Mr. Jean Edmond Tida
Mr. Ecclésiaste Valcin
Mr. Serge Villard

SELECTED BIBLIOGRAPHY ON HAITI 9

Special References / 257

I. French / 258

Agriculture
Anthropology
Art
Biography
Ecology
Economic Development
Economics - Finance
Education
Folklore
General Commentary
Geography
Geology
History
History - General
Indians of Haiti
Language
Law
Literature
Medicine and Health
Music and Dance
Nutrition
Politics and Government
Population
Religion
Rural - Urban Studies
Sports
Theater
U.S. Occupation of Haiti
Voodoo Studies
Women

II. English / 274

Agriculture
Anthropology
Art
Biography - Noted Figures
Economics
Education
General Commentary
Geology
Haiti - U.S. Relations
History
Industry and Trade
Language
Law
Literature
Music and Dance
Politics and Government
Religion
Rural - Urban Studies
U.S. Occupation of Haiti
Studies on Voodoo and Haitian Customs
Women

The following is a selective list of publications on Haitian subjects divided into two sections, French and English and by categories. It does not represent a complete bibliography, but serves the purpose of providing a good start for any researcher interested in Haitian topics. Many of these publications contain their own bibliographies which will lead to more resources. We have included a section called Special References where the reader can initiate a search for topics of interest. We believe that our Selected Bibliography will give you enough exposure to resources available on Haitian subjects.

SPECIAL REFERENCES

Bissainthe, Max. *Dictionnaire de Bibliographie Haïtienne*. Washington, D.C.: The Scarecrow Press, 1951. Dictionary of Haitian bibliography.

Duvivier, Ulrick. *Bibliographie Générale et Méthodique d'Haiti*. 2 vols. Port-au-Prince, Haiti: Imprimerie de l'Etat, 1941. General bibliography on Haiti.

Laguerre, Michel S. *The Complete Haitiana: A Bibliographic Guide to the Scholarly Literature, 1900-1980*. 2 vols. New York: Kraus International Publications, 1982. A comprehensive bibliography of publications by Haitians overseas and by foreigners on Haitian subjects.

Lowenthal, Ira, and Drexel Woodson. *Catalogue de la Collection Mangonès*. Yale University, 1974. Catalogue of the Mangonès Collection. A collection rich in documents and archival papers on the history of Haiti.

Lucien (Brother Jean Legendre). *The Catalogue of the Haitian Library of the Brothers of Christian Instruction, a Thesis*. Saint-Michael's College, 1958.

Manigat, Max. *Haitiana 1971-1975* (Bibliographie Haïtienne), Montreal: Collectif Paroles, 1980. Short bibliography of books published by Haitians overseas or by foreigners on Haitian subjects.

Ménier, Marie Antoinette. "Guide des Sources de l'Histoire d'Haïti (Ancienne Partie Française de l'île de Saint-Domingue) dans les Archives Françaises." *Conjonction*, N° 140, October - November 1978, Pp 119-135. A guide to the sources on the history of Haiti (former French region of the island of Saint-Domingue) in the French archives.

Monti, Laura V. *A Calendar of Rochambeau Papers at the University of Florida Libraries.* Gainesville: University of Florida Libraries, 1972.

Perusse, Roland I. *Historical Dictionary of Haiti.* Latin American Historical Dictionaries, No. 15. New Jersey: The Scarecrow Press, 1977.

Pratt, Frantz. *Haiti, Guide to the Periodical Literature in English, 1800 - 1990.* New York: Greenwood Press, 1991.

Saint-Juste, Laurore. *Documents sur Haïti dans les Archives et Bibliothèques de l'Europe.* 2 vols. Unpublished. Port-au-Prince. Documents on Haiti in European archives and libraries. Archival papers and documents on Haitian subjects found in Holland, Moscow, Vienna, and other European countries and cities.

_____. "Recherches Haïtiennes dans les Bibliothèques et Archives Américaines." *Conjonction*, N° 141-142, February 1979, Pp 65-73. Publications on Haiti in American libraries and archives.

I. FRENCH

Agriculture

Lespinasse, Raymonde. *Bibliographie Agricole Haitienne, 1950-1977.* Port-au-Prince: Institut Interaméricain des Sciences Agricoles de l'OEA. Représentation en Haiti, 1978.

Anthropology

Bureau National d'Ethnologie. *Bulletin du Bureau National d'Ethnologie.* No 1 & 2. Port-au-Prince, 1986.

Price-Mars, Jean. *La République d'Haïti et la République Dominicaine. Les Aspects Divers d'un Problème d'Histoire, de Géographie et d'Ethnologie. Depuis les Origines du Peuplement de l'Ile Antiléenne en 1492 jusqu'à l'Evolution des deux Etats qui en partagent la souveraineté en 1953.* Port-au-Prince, 1953. (Col. du Tricinquantenaire de l'Indépendance d'Haïti).

_____. *Ainsi Parla l'Oncle: Essais d'Ethnographie.* 3rd ed. Quebec, Canada: Editions Lémeac, 1973.

Romain, J.B. *Introduction à l'Anthropologie Physique des Haïtiens.* Port-au-Prince: Imprimerie Théodore, 1962.

_____. *L'Anthropologie Physique des Haïtiens.* Port-au-Prince: Imprimerie Séminaire Adventiste, 1971.

Art

Anquetil, Jacques. *Haïti, l'Artisanat Créateur.* Paris: Agence de Coopération Culturelle et Technique, 1982.

Desruisseau, Rose-Marie. *La Rencontre des Trois Mondes.* Port-au-Prince: Henri Deschamps, 1992.

Drot, Jean-Marie. *Journal de Voyage chez les Peintres de la Fête et du Vaudou en Haïti.* Genève: Skira, 1974.

Foubert, Alain. *Forgerons du Vodou.* France: Ulys Editions; Québec: CIDIHCA; Port-au-Prince: Henri Deschamps, 1990.

Lerebours, Michel Philippe. *Haïti et ses Peintres. De 1804 - 1980. Souffrances & Espoirs d'un Peuple.* 2 vols. Port-au-Prince: L'Imprimeur II, 1989.

Nadal, Marie-José, and Gérald Bloncourt. *La Peinture Haïtienne.* 2nd ed. Paris: Nathan, 1989.

Biography

Fouchard, Jean. *Toussaint Louverture: Biographie.* Port-au-Prince: Imprimerie Henri Deschamps, 1984.

Michel, Georges. *Charlemagne Péralte. Un Centenaire. (1885 - 1985)* Port-au-Prince: Le Natal, 1989.

Sannon, H. Pauléus. *Histoire de Toussaint-Louverture.*   3 vols. Port-au-Prince: Imprimerie Aug. A. Heraux, 1920-1933.

Scharon, Faine. *Toussaint L'Ouverture et la Révolution de St-Domingue.* 2 vols. Port-au-Prince: Imprimerie de l'Etat, 1957-1959.

Schoelcher, Victor. *Vie de Toussaint Louverture.* Paris: Paul Ollendorf, 1889.

Ecology

Barker, Henry D., and William S. Dardeau. *Flore d'Haiti.* Port-au-Prince: Imprimerie de l'Etat, 1930.

Jean-Louis, Victor Dulcine. *Documents pour la Flore Indigène D'Haiti.* Port-au-Prince, 1900.

Léon, Rulx. *Phytothérapie Haitienne - Nos Simples.* Port-au-Prince: Imprimerie de l'Etat, 1959.

Pierre-Noël, Arsène V. *Nomenclature Polyglotte des Plantes Haitiennes et Tropicales.* Port-au-Prince: Presses Nationales d'Haïti, 1971.

_____. and Timoléon Brutus. *Les Plantes et les Légumes d'Haïti qui Guérissent.* 2 vols. Port-au-Prince: Imprimerie de l'Etat, 1960. 2nd ed. Port-au-Prince: Presses Nationales d'Haïti, 1974.

R. P. Missionnaires du T. S. Redempteur. *Flore Médicinale d'Haiti.* Port-au-Prince: Monastère St. Gérard, 1943.

Economic Development

Anglade, Georges. *Cartes sur Table.* Port-au-Prince: Henri Deschamps, 1990.

Deshommes, Fritz. *Neo-Liberalisme.* Crise Economique et Alternative de Développement. Port-au-Prince: L'Imprimeur II, 1993.

Francisque, Edouard. *La Structure Economique et Sociale d'Haïti.* Port-au-Prince, Henri Deschamps, 1986.

Benoît, Joachim. *Les Racines du Sous-Développement en Haïti.* Port-au-Prince: Henri Deschamps, 1979.

Honorat, Jean-Jacques. *Haïti: l'Echec.* Economie et politiques d'un pays mis en lambeaux. Port-au-Prince: Le Natal, 1991.

Mathon, Alix. *Haïti, un Cas.* Port-au-Prince: Le Natal, 1985.

Organisation des Etats Américains. Bureau de Développement Régional. *Haïti: Mission d'Assistance Technique Intégrée.* 3 vols. Washington, D.C.: OEA, 1972.

Economics - Finance

Banque de la République D'Haïti. *Législation des Banques et des Institutions Financières.* Port-au-Prince: B.R.H., 1985.

Etienne, Eddy V. *Institutions Financières et Administratives en Haïti.* Port-au-Prince: Editions Etienne, 1988.

_____. *Monnaie & Banques.* Illustré des formulaires et monnaies utilisés en Haïti. Port-au-Prince: Henri Deschamps, 1992.

Marcelin, Frédéric. *La Banque Nationale d'Haïti- Une Page d'Histoire.* Paris: Kugelmann, 1890.

Moral, Paul. *L'Economie Haïtienne.* Port-au-Prince: Imprimerie de l'Etat, 1959.

Education

Antoine, Alphonse-Hugues. *La Pédagogie d'Aujourd'hui et l'Ecole de Demain.* Les Haïtiens et la Réforme de leurs Institutions. Un guide pédagogique, politique et gestion des affaires publiques. Montreal, 1989.

Pamphile, Léon D. *L'Education en Haïti sous l'Occupation Américaine (1915-1934).* Port-au-Prince: Editions Fardin, 1986.

Tardieux, Charles. *Education en Haïti.* Port-au-Prince: Henri Deschamps, 1990.

Trouillot, Hénock. *Les Limites du Créole dans Notre Enseignement.* Port-au-Prince: Imprimerie des Antilles, 1980.

Valdman, Albert. *Créole et Enseignement Primaire en Haïti.* Bloomington: Indiana University, 1980.

Folklore

Audain, J. J. *Recueil de Proverbes Créoles.* Port-au-Prince: J. Audain, 1877.

Bastien, Rémy. *Le Paysan Haïtien et sa Famille.* Paris: Editions Karthala, 1985.

Benoit, Max. *Cahier de Folklore et des Traditions Orales d'Haïti.* Port-au-Prince: Imprimerie des Antilles, 1980.

Hyppolite, Michelson Paul. *Civilisation Haitienne: Proverbes, Messages: Mesaj, Proveb.* 2 vols. Port-au-Prince: Editions Fardin, 1983.

Hoffmann, Léon-François. *Haïti: Couleurs, Croyances, Créole.* Montreal: Les Editions du CIDIHCA and Port-au-Prince: Henri Deschamps, 1990.

Labelle, Micheline. *Idéologie de Couleur et Classes Sociales en Haïti.* Montreal: Les Presses de l'Université de Montreal, 1978.

Moral, Paul. *Le Paysan Haïtien Etude sur la Vie Rurale en Haïti.* Paris: Maisonneuve et Larose, 1961.

Paul, Emmanuel C. *Notes sur le Folklore d'Haïti, Proverbes et Chansons.* Port-au-Prince: Imprimerie N. Telhomme, 1946.

_____. *Panorama du Folklore Haïtien. Présence Africaine en Haïti.* Port-au-Prince: Imprimerie de l'Etat, 1962.

Price-Mars, Jean. *Formation Ethnique, Folklore et Culture du Peuple Haïtien.* Port-au-Prince: Editions Virgile Valcin, 1929.

Romain, Jean-Baptiste. *Mœurs et Coutumes des Paysans Haïtiens.* Port-au-Prince: Imprimerie de l'Etat, 1959.

Théard, Gaston. *Contes Haïtiens.* Port-au-Prince: Cie Lithographique, 1949.

General Commentary

Charles, Christophe Philippe. *Manifeste Libéral-Démocrate.* Ecrits Politiques 1991-1992. Port-au-Prince: Editions Choucoune, No 14, Collection Essai, 1993.

Dorsinville, Roger. *Marche Arrière.* Outremont, Québec: Collectif Paroles, 1986.

Hurbon, Laënnec. *Comprendre Haïti, Essai sur l'Etat, la Nation, la Culture.* Paris: Editions Karthala, 1987.

Geography

Anglade, Georges. *L'Espace Haïtien.* Montreal: Les Presses de l'Université du Québec, 1974.

_____. *La Géographie et son Enseignement.* (Lettres ouvertes aux professeurs). Montreal: Les Presses de l'Université du Québec, 1976.

_____. *Mon Pays d'Haïti.* Port-au-Prince: Les Editions de l'Action Sociale, 1977.

_____. *Espace et Liberté en Haïti.* Montreal: Groupe d'Etudes et de Recherches Critiques d'Espace. 1982.

Rouzier, Séméxant. *Dictionnaire Géographique et Administratif Universel d'Haïti, Illustré, ou Guide Général en Haïti.* Paris: Imprimerie Ch. Blot (vols. I and II), 1892. Port-au-Prince: Imprimerie Auguste A. Héraux (Vols III and IV), 1927 and 1928.

Geology

Pierre-Louis, Fritz. *Géologie d'Haïti.* Port-au-Prince: Editions Caraïbes, 1980.

History

Ardouin, Beaubrun. *Etudes sur l'Histoire d'Haiti.* 2nd ed. Port-au-Prince: Imprimerie Dalencour, 1958.

Bellegarde, Dantès. *Haiti et son Peuple.* Paris: Nouvelles Editions Latines, 1953.

_____. *La Nation Haïtienne.* Paris: Gigord, 1938.

Dorsainvil, J. C. and Les Frères de L'Instruction Chrétienne. *Manuel d'Histoire D'Haïti.* Port-au-Prince: Henri Deschamps, 1924.

Fouchard, Jean. *Les Marrons du Syllabaire: Quelques Aspects du Problème de l'Instruction et de l'Education des Esclaves et Affranchis de Saint-Domingue.* Port-au-Prince: Imprimerie Henri Deschamps, 1988.

_____. *Plaisirs de Saint-Domingue.* Port-au-Prince: Deschamps, 1988.

_____. *Les Marrons de la Liberté.* Port-au-Prince: Deschamps, 1988.

_____. *Regards sur l'Histoire.* Port-au-Prince: Deschamps, 1988.

Hector, Michel, and Claude Moïse. *Colonisation et Esclavage en Haïti.* Port-au-Prince: Henri Deschamps, 1990.

Jean-Pierre, Jean Reynold. *Histoire D'Haïti. Période Nationale. Tome I. (Les Héros) 1804 - 1843.* Port-au-prince: Editions des Antilles, 1992.

Madiou, Thomas. *Histoire d'Haïti.* 8 vols. Port-au-Prince: Henri Deschamps, 1987-1991.

Saint-Méry, Moreau de. *Description Topographique, Physique, Civile, Politique et Historique de la Partie Française de l'Isle Saint-Domingue.*

3 vols. Paris: Société de l'Histoire des Colonies Françaises et Librairie Larose, 1958.

Pressoir, Catts, Ernst Trouillot, and Hénock Trouillot. *Historiographie d'Haiti*. Instituto Panamericano de Geografia y Historia, Publicacion num. 168. Mexico, 1953.

History - General

Corvington, Georges. *Port-au-Prince au Cours des Ans*. (1743 - 1950) 7 vols. Port-au-Prince: Deschamps, 1970 -1992.

Corvington, Georges. *La Cathédrale de Port-au-Prince: Histoire d'une Construction*. Port-au-Prince, Henri Deschamps, 1978.

Dominique, Rachel Beauvoir. *L'Ancienne Cathédrale de Port-au-Prince*. Port-au-Prince, 1991.

Dorsinville, Roger. *Toussaint L' Ouverture ou la Vocation de la Liberté*. Paris: Julliard, 1965.

Jolibois, Gérard. *L'Exécution des Frères Coicou*. Port-au-Prince: Imprimerie Le Natal, 1986.

Mangonès, Albert. *Les Monuments du Roi Christophe: La Citadelle, Le Palais Sans Souci, Le Site des Ramiers*. Port-au-Prince: Le Natal, 1980.

Oriol, Michèle. *Images de la Révolution à Saint-Domingue*. Port-au-Prince: Fondation pour la Recherche Iconographique et Documentaire and Editions Henri Deschamps, 1992.

Hugo, Victor. *Bug-Jargal ou la Révolution Haïtienne*. Fort-de-France: Désormaux, 1979.

Michel, Georges. *Les Chemins de Fer de l'Ile d'Haiti*. Port-au-Prince: Le Natal, 1989.

Indians of Haiti

Charles, Christophe Philippe. *Christophe Colomb, les Indiens et leurs Survivances en Haïti.* Port-au-Prince: L'Imprimeur II, Editions Christophe, 1992.

Fouchard, Jean. *Langue et Littérature des Aborigènes D'Ayiti.* Port-au-Prince: Deschamps, 1988.

Fombrun, Odette Roy. *L'Ayiti des Indiens.* Port-au-Prince: Editions Henri Deschamps, 1992.

Language

Archer, Marie-Thérèse. *Créolologie Haïtienne: Latinité du Créole d'Haïti:* Créole étudié dans son contexte ethnique, historique, linguistique, sociologique et Pédagogique. Port-au-Prince, Le Natal, 1987.

Bellegarde, Marie. *La Langue Française en Haïti.* Port-au-Prince: Imprimerie Chéraquit, 1925.

Bentolila, Alain. *Dictionnaire Elémentaire Créole Haïtien- Français (Ti Diksyonnè Kreyol - Fransé).* Port-au-Prince: Editions Caraïbes, 1976.

Déjean, Yves. *Comment Ecrire le Créole d'Haïti.* Montreal: Collectif Paroles, 1980.

Faine, Jules. *Dictionnaire Français - Créole.* Québec: Leméac Editions and Editions Caraïbes. 1974.

Lofficial, Frantz. *Créole / Français: Une Fausse Querelle?.* Montréal: Collectif Paroles, 1979.

Pompilus, Pradel. *La Langue Française en Haïti.* Université de Paris, Travaux et Mémoires de l'Institut de l'Amérique Latine. Ouvrage publié avec le concours du Centre National de la Recherche Scientifique. Paris: Imprimerie Protat Frères, 1961. Port-au-Prince: Fardin, 1981.

Law

Eugène, Grégoire. *Manuel de Droit Civil Haitien.* Vol.1. Programme de première année des Facultés et Ecoles Libres de Droit de l'Université d'Etat d'Haïti. Port-au-Prince, 1992.

Hector, Luc. D. *Code de Procédure Civile.* Port-au-Prince: Henri Deschamps, 1989.

Jean-Baptiste, Jacob. *Bulletin des Arrêts de la Cour de Cassation Rendus en Toutes Matieres. Années 1980 - 1981.* Port-au-Prince: Editions des Antilles, 1992.

Latortue, François. *Le Droit du Travail en Haïti.* Port-au-Prince: Editions des Antilles, 1992.

Pierre-Louis, Menan. *Code Pénal annoté.* Port-au-Prince: Editions Delta and La Gazette D'Haiti, 1989.

_____. *Code de Commerce Annoté.* Loi du 27 Mars 1826, modifiée par le Décret du 22 Decembre 1944. Port-au-Prince: Editions Fardin, 1987.

Trouillot, Ertha Pascal. *Code de Lois Usuelles.* 2 vols. Port-au-Prince: Deschamps, 1989-1990.

_____. *Statut Juridique de l'Haïtienne dans la Législation Sociale.* Port-au-Prince: Imprimerie des Antilles, 1973.

Vandal, Jean. *Code Pénal.* Port-au-Prince: Editions Fardin, 1988.

_____. *Code de Commerce.* Port-au-Prince: Imprimerie Henri Deschamps, 1989.

Literature

Bellegarde, Dantés. *Ecrivains Haïtiens.* 2nd ed. Port-au-Prince: Deschamps, 1950.

Berrou, Raphaël, and Pradel Pompilus. *Histoire de la Littérature Haïtienne Illustrée par les Textes.* 3 vols. Port-au-Prince: Editions Caraïbes, 1975-1978.

Charles, Christophe Philippe. *La Poésie Féminine Haïtienne.* (histoire et anthologie). Port-au-Prince: Editions Choucoune and Imprimerie Fardin, 1980.

_____. *Anthologie de la Nouvelle Poésie Haitienne.* Centres de Recherches Littéraires et Sociales. Port-au-Prince: Imprimeur II and Editions Choucoune, 1991.

Fleischmann, Ulrich. *Ecrivain et Société en Haïti.* Fonds St-Jacques, Ste-Marie, Martinique, Centre de Recherches Caraïbes. Québec: Université de Montréal, 1976.

Fouchard, Jean. *Regards sur la Littérature.* Port-au-Prince: Henri Deschamps, 1988.

Hoffmann, Léon-François. *Le Roman Haitien. Idéologie et Structure.* Québec: Naaman, 1982.

Laroche, Maximilien. *L'Avènement de la Littérature Haïtienne.* Québec: Groupe de Recherche sur les Littératures de la Caraïbe, Université Laval, 1987.

Price-Mars,Jean. *De Saint-Domingue à Haiti: Essai sur la Culture, les Arts et la Littérature.* Paris: Editions Présence Africaine, 1959.

Rey, Ghislaine. *Anthologie du Roman Haitien.* 2 vols. Québec: Naaman, 1982; Port-au-Prince: Editions du Soleil, 1982.

Medicine and Health

Bordes, Ary. *Evolution des Sciences de la Santé et de l'Hygiène Publique en Haïti. Vol.1. Fin de la Période Coloniale-1915.* Port-au-Prince: Centre D'Hygiène Familiale. 1980.

_____. *Haïti Médecine et Santé Publique sous l'Occupation Américaine 1915-1934.* Vol.2. Evolution des Sciences de la Santé et de l'Hygiène Publique en Haïti. Port-au-Prince: Henri Deschamps, 1992.

Delbeau, Jean-Claude. *Société, Culture et Médecine Populaire Traditionnelle.* Etude sur le Terrain d'un cas: Haiti. Port-au-Prince: Henri Deschamps, 1990.

Léon, Rulx. *Les Maladies en Haïti. Collection du Tricinquantenaire 1804-1954.* Port-au-Prince: Imprimerie de l'Etat, 1954.

Philippe, Jeanne. *Les Causes des Maladies Mentales en Haïti.* 2nd Ed. Port-au-Prince: Fardin, 1985.

_____. *Classes Sociales et Maladies Mentales en Haïti.* Revue de la Faculté d'Ethnologie de l'Université d'Etat d'Haïti et du Centre de Recherches en Sciences Humaines et Sociales (CRESHS).Port-au-Prince: Presses Nationales, 1975.

Pressoir, Catts. *La Médecine en Haïti.* Port-au-Prince: Imprimerie Modèle, 1927.

Music and Dance

Dumervé, Etienne, and Constantin Eugène Moïse. *Histoire de la Musique en Haïti.* Port-au-Prince: Imprimerie des Antilles, 1968.

Dunham, Katherine. *Les Danses D'Haïti.* Paris: Imprimerie Fasquelle, 1950.

Fouchard, Jean. *La Méringue, Danse Nationale D'Haïti.* Port-au-Prince: Henri Deschamps,1988.

Honorat, Michel Lamartiniére. *Les Danses Folkloriques Haitiennes.* Publication du Bureau d'Ethnologie de la République d'Haïti, series II, no. 2. Port-au-Prince: Imprimerie de l'Etat, 1955.

Nutrition

Beghin, Ivan, William Fougère, and Kendall W. King. *L'Alimentation et la Nutrition en Haïti.* Paris: Presses Universitaires de France, 1970.

Politics and Government

Coradin, Jean D. *Histoire Diplomatique d'Haïti, 1804 -1843.* Port-au-Prince: Edition des Antilles, 1988.

Delince, Kern. *Armée et Politique en Haïti.* Paris: L'Harmattan, 1979.

Désinor, Carlo A. *De Coup d'Etat en Coup d'Etat.* Port-au-Prince: L'Imprimeur II, 1988.

Diederich, Bernard and Al Burt. *Papa Doc et les Tontons Macoutes.* Paris: Albin Michel, 1971.

Etienne, Eddy V. *La Vraie Dimension de la Politique Extérieure des Premiers Gouvernements d'Haïti (1804-1843).* Québec: Editions Naaman, 1982.

Gaillard, Roger. *La République Exterminatrice. Première partie: Une Modernisation Manquée (1880 - 1896).* Port-au-Prince: Le Natal, 1984.

_____. *La Déroute de L'Intelligence. (Mai - Juillet 1902) La République Exterminatrice, Troisième partie.* Port-au-Prince: Le Natal, 1992.

Greene, Graham. *Les Comédiens.* Paris: Laffont, 1972.

Hurbon, Laennec. *Culture et Dictature en Haïti.* Paris: L'Harmattan, 1979.

Janvier, Louis-Joseph. *Les Constitutions d'Haïti.* Paris, 1886.

Marcelin, Frédéric. *Les Chambres Législatives d'Haïti (1892-1894).* Paris: Kugelmann, 1896.

Michel, Georges. *La Constitution de 1987: Souvenirs d'un Constituant.* Port-au-Prince: Le Natal, 1992.

Moïse, Claude. *Constitutions et Luttes de Pouvoir en Haïti.* 2 vols. (1804-1987) Québec: Editions du CIDIHCA, 1988 & 1990.

Nérée, Bob. *Duvalier Le Pouvoir sur les Autres. De Pére en Fils.* Port-au-Prince: Henri Deschamps, 1988.

Roy, Jean Claude H. *Entre la Lettre et L'Esprit de la Constitution de 87.* Port-au-Prince: Editions Henri Deschamps, 1992.

Saint-Méry, Moreau de, and Louis E Médéric. *Lois et Constitutions des Colonies Françaises de l'Amérique sous le Vent.* 6 vols. Paris, 1784-1790.

Turnier, Alain. *Quand la Nation Demande des Comptes.* 2nd ed. Port-au-Prince: Le Natal, 1992.

Population

Aristide, Achille. *Quelques Aspects du Problème de la Population en Haïti.* Port-au-Prince: Imprimerie de l'Etat, 1955.

Dewind, Josh, and David Kinley III. *Aide à la Migration: l'Impact de l'Assistance Internationale à Haïti.* Montreal: Les éditions du Cidihca, 1988.

Religion

Cabon, A. *Notes sur l'Histoire Religieuse d'Haïti.* Port-au-Prince: Petit Séminaire Collège Saint-Martial, 1933.

Guilloux, Mgr. *Le Concordat d' Haïti, ses Résultats.* Port-au-Prince: 1885.

Jan, Jean-Marie. *Port-au-Prince - Documents pour l'Histoire Religieuse.* Port-au-Prince: Editions Deschamps, 1956.

_____. *Histoire Religieuse du Cap.* Notes et Documents. Port-au-Prince: Henri Deschamps, 1949.

Leconte, J. B. V. *L'Eglise du Cap de 1680 à 1942.* Port-au-Prince: Imprimerie de L'Etat, 1942.

Pouplard, Jules. *Notice sur l'Histoire de l'Eglise de Port-au-Prince.* Port-au-Prince: Imprimerie de l'Abeille, 1905.

Rural - Urban Studies

Barthélémy, Gérard. *Le Pays en Dehors, Essai sur l'Univers Rural Haitien.* Port-au-Prince: Henri Deschamps; Montreal: CIDIHCA 1989.

Bernardin, Ernst A. *L'Espace Rural Haitien.* Bilan de 40 ans d'exécution des Programmes Nationaux et Internationaux de Développement (1950 - 1990). Port-au-Prince: Editions des Antilles, 1991.

Moral, Paul. *Le Paysan Haïtien. Etude sur la Vie Rurale en Haiti.* Paris: Maisonneuve et Larose, 1961 and Port-au-Prince: Editions Fardin, 1978.

Romain, J. B. *Développement Rural en Haiti et dans la Caraibe.* Port-au-Prince: Imprimerie M. Rodriguez, 1980.

Sports

Chauvel, Louis. *Le Football Haitien à Travers les Ages, 1900 - 1977.* Port-au-Prince: Henri Deschamps, [1977 or 1978].

Theatre

Cornevin, Robert. *Le Théâtre Haïtien des Origines à nos Jours.* Montreal: Leméac, 1973.

Fouchard, Jean. *Le Théâtre à Saint-Domingue.* Port-au-Prince: Henri Deschamps,1988.

_____. *Artistes et Répertoires des Scènes de Saint-Domingue.* Port-au-Prince: Henri Deschamps, 1988.

U.S. Occupation of Haiti

Bellegarde, Dantès. *L'Occupation Américaine d'Haïti, ses Conséquences Morales et Economiques.* Port-au-Prince: Chéraquit, 1929.

_____. *La Résistance Haïtienne.* Montreal, 1937.

Millet, Kethly. *Les Paysans Haïtiens et l'Occupation Américaine 1915-1930.* Montreal, 1978.

Voodoo Studies

Desquiron, Lilas. *Racines du Vodou*. Port-au-Prince: Henri Deschamps, 1990.

Dorsainvil, J.-C. *Vodou et Névrose, Etude Médico-Sociologique*. Port-au-Prince, 1931.

_____. *Vodou et Magie, Psychologie Haïtienne*. Port-au-Prince, 1937.

Hurbon, Louis. *Dieu dans le Vaudou Haïtien*. Paris: Payot, 1972.

Marcelin, Milo. *Mythologie Vodou*. Port-au-Prince, 1949.

Mars, Louis. *La Crise le Possession dans le Vodou*. Port-au-Prince. 1946.

Maximilien, Louis. *Le Vodou Haïtien*. Port-au-Prince: Imprimerie de L'Etat, 1945.

Métraux, Alfred. *Haïti: La Terre, les Hommes et les Dieux*. Neuchâtel: La Braconnière, 1957.

_____. *Le Vaudou Haïtien*. 6th ed. Paris: Gallimard, 1958.

Salgado, Antoine. *Le Phénomène des Zombis dans la Culture Haitienne*. Port-au-Prince: Imprimerie Des Antilles, 1982.

Trouillot, Hénock. *Introduction à une Histoire du Vaudou*. 2nd ed. Port-au-Prince: Fardin, 1983.

Women

Bouchereau, Madeleine. *Haiti et ses Femmes: une Etude d'Evolution Culturelle*. Ph.D. diss., Bryn Mawr College, 1941. Ann Arbor, MI: University Microfilms, 1941.

Ewald, Chantal Hudicourt. La Condition Juridique de la Femme Haïtienne. Port-au-Prince, 1979.

Fortunat, F. *Les Déterminants Proches de la Fécondité en Haïti*. Voorburg, Netherlands: International Statistical Institute, December 1984.

Neptune-Anglade, Mireille. *L'Autre Moitié du Développement: A Propos du Travail des Femmes en Haïti.* Pétion-Ville: Ed. des Alizés, 1986.

II. ENGLISH

Agriculture

Holly, Marc Aurèle. *Agriculture in Haiti.* New-York: Vantage Press, 1955.

Johnson, James L., and Jerry La Gra. *The Internal Agricultural Marketing System of Haiti: a Price Analysis.* Port-au-Prince, Inter-American Institute of Agricultural Sciences, Office in Haiti, 1975.

Anthropology

Price-Mars, Jean. *So Spoke The Uncle: Ethnographic Essays.* Trans. Magdaline W. Shannon. Washington, D.C.: Three Continents Press, 1983.

Rouse, Irving. *Prehistory in Haiti. A Study in Method.* Yale University Publications in Anthropology. No 21. Human Relations Area Files Press, 1964.

Art

Foubert, Alain. *Voodoo Blacksmiths.* France: Ulys Editions; Québec: CIDIHCA; Port-au-Prince: Henri Deschamps, 1990.

Nadal, Marie-José, and Gérald Bloncourt. *Haitian Arts.* 2nd ed. Paris: Nathan, 1989.

Rodman, Selden. *The Miracle of Haitian Art.* New York: Doubleday, 1974.

Stebich, Ute. *Haitian Art.* New York: The Brooklyn Museum, 1978.

Biography - Noted Figures

Beard, John Relly. *Toussaint L'Ouverture: A Biography and Autobiography.* Boston: James Redpath, 1863. Reprint by Books for Libraries Press, Freeport, N.Y., 1971.

Bellegarde-Smith, Patrick. *In the Shadow of Powers, Dantès Bellegarde in Haitian Social Thought.* New Jersey: Humanities Press, 1985.

Hoobler, Thomas & Dorothy. *Toussaint L'Ouverture.* World Leaders Past & Present. New York: Chelsea House Publishers, 1990.

Economics

The Economist Intelligence Unit. Cuba, *Dominican Republic, Haiti, Puerto Rico. Country Report.* Analysis of Economic and Political Trends Every Quarter. 1993.

World Bank. *Current economic position and prospects of Haiti.* Washington, 1976, 1978.

Education

Cook, Mercer. *Education in Haiti.* Washington, D.C.: Government Printing Office, 1948.

Dale, George A. *Education in the Republic of Haiti.* Washington, D.C.: U.S. Dept. of Health, Education and Welfare, Bulletin N° 20, 1959.

Moton, R.R. *Report of the United States Commission on Education in Haiti. October, 1930.* Washington, D.C.: U.S. Department of State, Government Printing Office, 1930.

Pamphile, Léon D. *Education in Haiti during the American Occupation 1915-1934.* Ann Harbor: University Microfilms International, 1980.

General Commentary

Antoine, Jacques C. *Jean Price-Mars and Haiti.* Washington, D.C.: Three Continents, 1981.

Bigelow, John. *The Wit and Wisdom of the Haitians*. New York: Scribner & Armstrong, 1877.

Bird, Mark B. *The Black Man; or Haytian Independence*. New York: Mark. B. Bird, 1869.

Craige, John Houston. *Black Bagdad. The Arabian Nights, Adventures of a Marine Captain in Haiti*. London: Stanley Paul & Co., 1931.

Foster, Charles R., and Albert Valdman. *Haiti-Today and Tomorrow. An Interdisciplinary Study*. Lanham: University Press of America, 1984.

Fowler, Carolyn. *A Knot in the Thread*. Washington, D.C.: Howard University Press, 1980.

Herskovits, Melville J. *Life in a Haitian Valley*. New York: Octagon Books, 1975.

Heinl, Robert D. and Nancy G. *Written in Blood: The Story of the Haitian People, 1492 - 1971*. Boston: Houghton Mifflin, 1978.

International Women's Association of Haiti, and The American Embassy Wives. *Guide to living in Haiti: A Directory for Port-au-Prince and Pétionville*. Port-au-Prince, 1978.

Laguerre, Michel S. *American Odyssey: Haitians in New York City*. New York: Cornell University Press, 1984.

Leyburn, James G. *The Haitian People*. New Haven: Yale University Press, 1941.

Lundahl, Mats. *Peasants and Poverty: A Study of Haiti*. London: Croom Helm and New York: St. Martin's Press, 1979.

Mackenzie, Charles. *Notes on Hayti, Made During a Residence in that Republic*. 2 vols. London: Henry Colburn and Richard Bentley, 1830.

Nicholls, David. *Haiti in the Caribbean Context*. Basingstoke, England: Macmillan, 1985.

Paquin, Lyonel. *The Haitians: Class and Color Politics.* Brooklyn: Lyonel Paquin, 1983.

Prince, Rod. *Haiti: Family Business.* London: Latin American Bureau, 1985.

Rodman, Selden. *Haiti: The Black Republic.* 5th ed. Old Greenwich: The Devin-Adair Company, 1980.

Spitzer, Daniel Charles. *A Contemporary Political and Socio-Economic History of Haiti and the Dominican Republic.* Ph.D. Dissertation. Ann Arbor: University of Michigan, 1972.

Weil, Thomas E. *Area Handbook for Haïti.* Washington, D.C.: U.S. Government Printing Office for Foreign Area Studies, American University, 1973.

Geology

Goddard, E. N., L. S. Gardner, and W. S. Burbank. *Manganese Deposits of the Republic of Haiti.* United States Department of the Interior. Washington, D.C.: U.S. Government Printing Office, 1947.

Haiti - U.S. Relations

Logan, Rayford W. *The Diplomatic Relations of the United States with Haiti, 1776-1891.* Chapel Hill: University of North Carolina, 1941.

MacCorkle, William A. *The Monroe Doctrine. In its Relation to the Republic of Haiti.* New York: The Neale Publishing Company, 1915.

Montague, Ludwell Lee. *Haiti and the United States, 1714-1938.* Durham, N.C.: Duke University Press, 1940.

U.S. Congress. *U.S. Foreign Assistance for Haïti - Report of Senator Edward W. Brooke.* Washington, D.C., 1974.

History

Crouse, N. M. *The French Struggle for the West Indies, 1665-1713.* New York: Columbia University Press, 1943.

Edwards, Brian. *An Historical Survey of the French Colony in the Island of St. Domingo: 1789 to 1794.* London: Printed for J. Stock Dale, 1797.

Fick, Carolyn E. *The Making of Haiti. The Saint-Domingue Revolution from Below.* Knoxville: The University of Tennessee Press, 1990.

James, Cyrill Lionel Robert. *The Black Jacobins: Toussaint L'Ouverture and the San Domingo Revolution.* 2d ed. New York: Vintage Books, 1989.

Ott, Thomas O. *The Haitian Revolution, 1789 - 1804.* Knoxville: The University of Tennessee Press, 1973.

Industry and Trade

Warren, David. *Report on Study of HAMPCO (Haitian-American Meat and Provisions Company).* Port-au-Prince: US AID/ Haiti, May 9, 1973.

Language

Jeanty, Edner. *Diksyonè Kréyòl. Dictionary Creole-English/ Anglé - Kréyòl.* Port-au-Prince: La Presse Evangélique, 1989.

_____. *Speak Creole in No Time.* Port-au-Prince: La Presse Evangélique, [?].

Targète, Jean. *Advanced Grammar of Haitian Creole.* Port-au-Prince: Fardin, 1979.

Valdman, Albert. *Haitian Creole-English-French Dictionary.* Bloomington: Indiana University, Creole Institute, 1981.

_____. *Basic Course in Haitian Creole.* Bloomington: Indiana University, 1980.

Law

Organization of American States, General Secretariat. *A Statement of the Laws of Haiti, in Matters Affecting Business.* Washington, D.C. [?]

Literature

Dash, J. Michael. *Literature and Ideology in Haiti 1915 - 1961.* London: The Macmillan Presses, 1981.

Music and Dance

Bowman, Laura, and Antoine Leroy. *The Voice of Haiti; Original Native Ceremonial Songs, Voodoo Chants, Drumbeats, Stories of Traditions of the Haitian People.* New York: Clarence Williams Music Publishing Co., 1938.

Cale, John G. *French Secular Music in Saint-Domingue. (1750-1795) Viewed as a Factor in America's Musical Growth.* Ph. D. dissertation, Louisiana State University, 1971.

Hutson, Alaveta E. *Folk Dances of Haiti.* Master's Thesis. New York: New York University, 1946.

Thomas, Jerry C. *Theory of Haitian Meringue.* Port-au-Prince, 1957.

Politics and Government

Abbott, Elizabeth. *HAITI The Duvaliers and Their Legacy.* New York: McGraw-Hill Book Company, 1988.

Bellegarde-Smith, Patrick. *Haiti the Breached Citadel.* Boulder: Westview Press, 1990.

Brinkerhoff, Derick W., and Jean-Claude Garcia-Zamor. *Politics, Projects and People: Institutional Development in Haiti.* New York: Praeger, 1986.

Diederich, Bernard, and Al Burt. *Papa Doc and The Tontons Macoutes: The Truth About Haiti Today.* New York: McGraw-Hill, 1969.

Ferguson, James. *Papa Doc Baby Doc: Haiti and the Duvaliers.* London: Basil Blackwell, 1987.

Forbes, W. Cameron. *Report of the President's Commission for the Study and Review of Conditions in the Republic of Haiti.* Washington, D.C.: Government Print Office, 1930.

Greene, Graham. *The Comedians.* Aylesbury: Penguin Books, 1984. First edition by The Bodley Head, 1966.

Nicholls, David. *From Dessalines to Duvalier: Race, Colour and National Independence in Haiti.* Warwick University Caribbean Studies. London: Macmillan, 1988.

Plummer, Brenda. *Haiti and the Great Powers, 1902 -1915.* Baton Rouge: Louisiana State University Press, 1988.

Weinstein, Brian, and Aaron Segal. *HAITI, Political Failures, Cultural Successes.* New York: Praeger Publishers, 1984.

Religion

Bastien, R. and H. Courlander. *Religion and Politics in Haiti.* Washington, D.C: ICR Studies 1, Institute for Cross Cultural Research, 1966.

Rural - Urban Studies

Ahlers, Théodore H. *Haitian Rural-Urban Migration: A Case Study of Four Small Towns.* Port-au-Prince, Inter-American Institute of Agricultural Sciences, Representation in Haiti, 1978.

Laguerre, Michel S. *Urban Life in the Caribbean: A Study of a Haitian Urban Community.* Cambridge, Mass.: Schenkman Publishing, 1982.

Lundahl, Mats. Peasants and Poverty: A Study of Haiti. London: Croom Helm, 1979.

Wood, Harold A. *Northern Haïti: Land, Land Use, and Settlement.* A Geographical Investigation of the Département du Nord. Toronto: University of Toronto Press, 1963.

U.S. Occupation of Haiti

Balch, Emily Greene. *Occupied Haiti.* New York: Negro Universities Press, 1969.

Healey, David F. *Gunboat Diplomacy in The Wilson Era: The U.S. Navy in Haiti, 1915-1916.* Madison: University of Wisconsin Press, 1976.

Millspaugh, Arthur. *Haiti under American Control 1915-1930.* Boston: World Peace Foundation, 1931.

Schmidt, Hans. *The United States Occupation of Haiti, 1915-1934.* New Jersey: Rutgers University Press, 1971.

Studies on Voodoo and Haitian Customs

Dunham, Katherine. *Island Possessed.* New York: Doubleday, 1969.

Huxley, Francis. *The Invisibles: Voodoo Gods in Haiti.* New York: McGraw-Hill, 1966.

Hurston, Zora. *Voodoo Gods.* London: J.M. Dent, 1939.

Women

World Fertility Survey. *The Haiti Fertility Survey, 1977: A Summary of Findings.* Voorburg, Netherlands: International Statistical Institute; London: World Fertility Survey, September 1981.

APPENDICES

APPENDIX 1 / *283*
Acte de l'Indépendance d'Haiti
Liberté ou La Mort

APPENDIX 2 / *284*
L'Hymne National de la République d'Haïti
La Dessalinienne

APPENDIX 3 / *285*
Constitution de la République d'Haïti
29 Mars 1987

Appendix 1

Acte de L'Indépendance
Liberté ou la Mort

Gonaïves, le 1er janvier 1804, an 1er de l'Indépendance.

Armée Indigène:

Aujourd'hui, 1er janvier 1804, le Général en Chef de l'armée indigène, accompagné des généraux de l'armée, convoqués à l'effet de prendre les mesures qui doivent tendre au bonheur du pays;

Après avoir fait connaître aux généraux assemblés, ses véritables intentions, d'assurer à jamais aux indigènes d'Haïti, un gouvernement stable, objet de sa plus vive sollicitude; ce qu'il a fait par un discours qui tend à faire connaître aux puissances étrangères, la résolution de rendre le pays indépendant, et de jouir d'une liberté consacrée par le sang du peuple de cette île; et après avoir recueilli les avis, a demandé que chacun des généraux assemblés prononçât le serment de renoncer à jamais à la France, de mourir plutôt que de vivre sous sa domination, et de combattre jusqu'au dernier soupir pour l'indépendance.

Les généraux, pénétrés de ces principes sacrés, après avoir donné d'une voix unanime leur adhésion au projet bien manifesté d'indépendance, ont tous juré à la postérité, à l'univers entier, de renoncer à jamais à la France, et de mourir plutôt que de vivre sous sa domination.

Fait aux Gonaïves, ce 1er janvier 1804 et le 1er de l'Indépendance d'Haïti.

Signé : Dessalines, général en chef; Christophe, Pétion, Clervaux, Geffrard, Vernet, Gabart, généraux de division; P. Romain, E. Gérin, F. Capoix, Daut, J.L. François, Férou, Cangé, L. Bazelais, Magloire Ambroise, J.J. Herne, Toussaint Brave, Yayou, généraux de brigade; Bonnet, F. Papalier, Morelly, Chevalier, Marion, adjudants-généraux; Magny, Roux, chefs de brigade; Charéron, B. Loret, Qenez, Makajoux, Dupui, Carbonne, Diaquoi aîné, Raphaël, Mallet, Derenoncourt, officiers de l'armée; et Boisrond Tonnerre, secrétaire.

Appendix 2

L'HYMNE NATIONAL DE LA REPUBLIQUE D'HAITI
LA DESSALINIENNE

I

Pour le Pays
Pour les Ancêtres,
Marchons unis.
Dans nos rangs point de Traîtres,
Du sol soyons seuls maîtres.
Marchons unis,
Pour le Pays, pour les Ancêtres
Marchons unis,
Pour le Pays, pour les Ancêtres.

II

Pour les Aïeux,
Pour la Patrie,
Bêchons joyeux.
Quand le champ fructifie,
L'âme se fortifie,
Bêchons joyeux
Pour les Aïeux, pour la Patrie
Bêchons joyeux,
Pour les Aïeux, pour la Patrie.

III

Pour le Pays
Et pour nos Pères,
Formons des Fils.
Libres, forts et prospères,
Toujours nous serons frères,
Formons des fils,
Pour le Pays et pour nos Pères
Formons des fils,
Pour le Pays et pour nos Pères.

IV

Pour les Aïeux,
Pour la Patrie,
O Dieu des Preux!
Sous ta garde infinie
Prends nos droits, notre vie.
O Dieu des Preux!
Pour les Aïeux, pour la Patrie,
O Dieu des Preux!
Pour les Aïeux, pour la Patrie.

V

Pour le Drapeau,
Pour la Patrie,
Mourir est beau.
Notre passé nous crie:
"Ayez l'âme aguerrie."
Mourir est beau,
Pour le Drapeau, pour la Patrie,
Mourir est beau,
Pour le Drapeau, pour la Patrie.

Appendix 3

CONSTITUTION DE LA REPUBLIQUE D'HAITI
29 MARS 1987
Préambule

Le Peuple Haitien proclame la présente Constitution:

-Pour garantir ses droits inaliénables et imprescriptibles à la vie, à la liberté et à la poursuite du bonheur; conformément à son Acte d'Indépendance de 1804 et à la Déclaration Universelle des Droits de l'Homme de 1948.

-Pour constituer une nation haitienne socialement juste, économiquement libre, et politiquement indépendante.

-Pour rétablir un Etat stable et fort, capable de protéger les valeurs, les traditions, la souveraineté, l'indépendance et la vision nationale.

-Pour implanter la démocratie qui implique le pluralisme idéologique et l'alternance politique et affirmer les droits inviolables du peuple Haitien.

-Pour fortifier l'unité nationale, en éliminant toutes discriminations entre les populations des villes et des campagnes, par l'acceptation de la communautà de langues et de culture et par la reconnaissance du droit au progrès, à l'information, à l'éducation, à la santé, au travail et au loisir pour tous les citoyens.

-Pour assurer la séparation, et la répartition harmonieuse des pouvoirs de l'Etat au service des intèrêts fondamentaux et prioritaires de la Nation.

-Pour instaurer un régime gouvernemental basé sur les libertés fondamentales et le respect des droits humains, la paix sociale, l'équité économique, la concertation et la participation de toute la population aux grandes décisions engageant la vie nationale, par une décentralisation effective.

TITRE I

De la République d'Haiti
Son Emblême-Ses Symboles

CHAPITRE I

De la République d'Haiti

Article premier:
Haiti est une République, indivisible, souveraine, indépendante, coopératiste, libre, démocratique et sociale.

Article Premier-1:
La ville de Port-au-Prince est sa Capitale et le siège de son gouvernement. Ce siège peut être déplacé en cas de force majeure.

Article 2:
Les couleurs nationales sont: le bleu et le rouge.

Article 3:
L'emblème de la Nation Haitienne est le Drapeau qui répond à la description suivante:
a) Deux (2) bandes d'étoffe d'égales dimensions: l'une bleue en haut, l'autre rouge en bas, placées horizontalement;

b) Au centre, sur un carré d'étoffe blanche, sont disposées les Armes de la République;

c) Les Armes de la République sont: le Palmiste surmonté du Bonnet de la Liberté et ombrageant de ses Palmes, un Trophée d'Armes avec la Légende:

L' Union fait la Force.

Article 4:
Le devise nationale est : Liberté, Egalité, Fraternité.

Article 4-1:
L' Hymne National est: La Dessalinienne.

Article 5:

Tous les Haitiens sont unis par une Langue commune: Le Créole.

Le Créole et le Français sont les langues officielles de la République.

Article 6:

L' Unité Monétaire est: La Gourde. Elle est divisée en: Centimes.

Article 7:

Le culte de la personnalité est formellement interdit. Les effigies, les noms de personnages vivants ne peuvent figurer sur la monnaie, les timbres, les vignettes. Il en est de même pour les bâtiments publics, les rues et les ouvrages d'art.

Article 7-1:

L' utilisation d'effigie de personne décédée doit obtenir l'approbation du Corps Législatif.

CHAPITRE II

Du Territoire de la République d'Haiti.

Article 8:

Le Territoire de la République d'Haiti comprend:

a) La partie Occidentale de l'Ile d'Haiti ainsi que les Iles Adjacentes: La Gonâve, la Tortue, l'Ile à Vache, les Cayemittes, La Navase, La Grande Caye et les autres Iles de la Mer Territoriale;

Il est limité à l'Est par la République Dominicaine, au Nord par l'Océan Atlantique, au Sud et à l'Ouest par la mer des Caraïbes ou mer des Antilles;

b) La mer territoriale et la zone économique exclusive;

c) Le milieu aérien surplombant la partie Terrestre et Maritime.

Article 8-1:
Le territoire de la République d'Haiti est inviolable et ne peut être aliéné en tout, ni en partie par aucun Traité ou Convention.

Article 9:
Le Territoire de la République est divisé et subdivisé en Départements, Arrondissements, Communes, Quartiers et Sections Communales.

Article 9-1:
La loi détermine le nombre, les limites de ces divisions et subdivisions et en règle l'organisation et le fonctionnement.

TITRE II

De la Nationalité Haitienne

Article 10:
Les règles relatives à la Nationalité Haitienne sont déterminées par la loi.

Article 11:
Possède la Nationalité Haitienne d'origine, tout individu né d'un père haitien ou d'une mère haitienne qui eux-mêmes sont nés Haitiens et n'avaient jamais renoncé à leur nationalité au moment de la naissance.

Article 12:
La Nationalité Haitienne peut être acquise par la naturalisation.

Article 12-1:
Tout Etranger après cinq (5) ans de résidence continue sur le Territoire de la République peut obtenir la nationalité haitienne par naturalisation, en se conformant aux règles établies par la loi.

Article 12-2:
Les Haitiens par naturalisation sont admis à exercer leur droit de vote mais ils doivent attendre cinq (5) ans après la date de leur naturalisation pour être éligibles ou occuper des fonctions publiques

autres que celles réservées par la Constitution et par la Loi aux haitiens d'origine.

Article 13:
La Nationalité Haitienne se perd par:

a) La Naturalisation acquise en pays Etranger;

b) L'occupation d'un poste politique au service d'un Gouvernement Etranger;

c) La résidence continue à l'étranger pendant trois (3) ans d'un individu étranger naturalisé haitien sans une autorisation régulièrement accordée par l'Autorité compétente. Quiconque perd ainsi la nationalité haitienne, ne peut la recouvrer.

Article 14:
L'Haitien naturalisé étranger peut recouvrer sa Nationalité Haitienne, en remplissant toutes les conditions et formalités imposées à l'étranger par la loi.

Article 15:
La double Nationalité Haitienne et Etrangére n'est admise dans aucun cas.

TITRE III

Du Citoyen - Des Droits et Devoirs Fondamentaux

CHAPITRE I

De la Qualité de Citoyen

Article 16:
La réunion des Droits Civils et Politiques constitue la qualité de citoyen.

Article 16-1:
La jouissance, l'exercice, la suspension et la perte de ces droits sont réglés par la loi.

Article 16-2:
L'âge de la majorité est fixé à dix-huit (18) ans.

Article 17:
Les Haitiens sans distinction de sexe et d'Etat Civil, âgé de dix-huit (18) ans accomplis, peuvent exercer leurs Droits Civils et Politiques s'ils réunissent les autres conditions prévues par la Constitution et par la loi.

Article 18:
Les Haitiens sont égaux devant la Loi sous la réserve des avantages conférés aux Haitiens d'Origine qui n'ont jamais renoncé à leur nationalité.

CHAPITRE II

Des Droits Fondamentaux

SECTION A

Droit à la Vie et à la Santé

Article 19:
L' Etat a l' impérieuse obligation de garantir le Droit à la Vie, à la Santé, au Respect de la Personne Humaine, à tous les Citoyens sans distinction, conformément à la Déclaration Universelle des Droits de l'Homme.

Article 20:
La peine de mort est abolie en toute matière.

Article 21:
Le crime de Haute Trahison consiste à porter les armes dans une armée étrangère contre la République, à servir une Nation Etrangère en conflit avec la République, dans le fait par tout fonctionnaire de

voler les biens de l'Etat confiés à sa gestion ou toute violation de la Constitution par ceux chargés de la faire respecter.

Article 21-1:
Le crime de Haute Trahison est puni de la peine des Travaux forcés à perpétuité sans commutation de peine.

Article 22:
L' Etat reconnait le droit de tout citoyen à un logement décent, à l'éducation, à l'alimentation et à la sécurité sociale.

Article 23:
L' Etat est astreint à l'obligation d'assurer à tous les citoyens dans toutes les Collectivités Territoriales les moyens appropriés pour garantir la protection, le maintien et le rétablissement de leur santé par la création d'hôpitaux, centres de santé et de dispensaires.

SECTION B

De la Liberté Individuelle

Article 24:
La liberté individuelle est garantie et protégée par l'Etat.

Article 24-1:
Nul ne peut être poursuivi, arrêté ou détenu que dans les cas déterminés par la Loi et selon les formes qu'elle prescrit.

Article 24-2:
L'arrestation et la détention, sauf en cas de flagrant délit, n'auront lieu que sur un mandat écrit d'un fonctionnaire légalement compétent.

Article 24-3:
Pour que ce mandat puisse être exécuté, il faut:

a) Qu'il exprime formellement en créole et en français le ou les motifs de l'arrestation ou de la détention et la disposition de Loi qui punit le fait imputé;

b) Qu'il soit notifié et qu'il en soit laissé copie au moment de l'exécution à la personne prévenue;

c) Qu'il soit notifié au prévenu de son droit de se faire assister d'un avocat à toutes les phases de l'instruction de l'affaire jusqu'au jugement définitif;

d) Sauf en cas de flagrant délit, aucune arrestation sur mandat, aucune perquisition ne peut avoir lieu entre six (6) heures du soir et six (6) heures du matin;

e) La responsabilité est personelle. Nul ne peut être arrêté à la place d'un autre.

Article 25:
Toute rigueur ou contrainte qui n'est pas nécessaire pour appréhender une personne ou la maintenir en détention, toute pression morale ou brutalité physique notamment pendant l'interrogation sont interdites.

Article 25-1:
Nul ne peut être interrogé en l'absence de son avocat ou d'un témoin de son choix.

Article 26:
Nul ne peut être maintenu en détention s'il n'a comparu dans les quarante-huit (48) heures qui suivent son arrestation par devant un juge appelé à statuer sur la légalité de l'arrestation et si ce Juge n'a confirmé la détention par décision motivée.

Article 26-1:
En cas de contravention, l'inculpé est déféré par devant le Juge de Paix qui statue définitivement.

En cas de délit ou de crime, le prévenu peut, sans permission préalable et sur simple mémoire, se pourvoir par devant le Doyen du Tribunal de Première Instance du ressort qui, sur les conclusions du Ministère Public, statue à l'extraordinaire, audience tenante, sans remise ni tour de rôle, toutes affaires cessantes sur la légalité de l'arrestation et de la détention.

Article 26-2:
Si l'arrestation est jugée illégale, le Juge ordonne la libération immédiate du détenu et cette décision est exécutoire sur minute nonobstant appel, pourvoi en Cassation ou défense d'exécuter.

Article 27:
Toutes violations des dispositions relatives à la liberté individuelle sont des actes arbitraires. Les personnes lésées peuvent, sans autorisation préalable, se référer aux Tribunaux Compétents pour poursuivre les auteurs et les exécuteurs de ces actes arbitraires quelles que soient leurs qualités et à quelque Corps qu'ils appartiennent.

Article 27-1:
Les fonctionnaires et les employés de l'Etat sont directement responsables selon les Lois Pénales, Civiles et Administratives des actes accomplis en violation de droits. Dans ces cas, la responsabilité civile s'étend aussi à l'Etat.

SECTION C

De la Liberté d'Expression

Article 28:
Tout Haitien a le droit d'exprimer librement ses opinions, en toute matière par la voie qu'il choisit.

Article 28-1:
Le journaliste exerce librement sa profession dans le cadre de la Loi. Cet exercice ne peut être soumis à aucune autorisation, ni censure, sauf en cas de guerre.

Article 28-2:
Le journaliste ne peut être forcé de révéler ses sources. Il a toutefois pour devoir de vérifier l'authenticité et l'exactitude des informations. Il est également tenu de respecter l'éthique professionnelle.

Article 28-3:
Tout délit de Presse ainsi que les abus du Droit d'Expression relèvent du Code Pénal.

Article 29:
Le Droit de pétition est reconnu. Il est exercé personnellement par un ou plusieurs citoyens mais jamais au nom d'un Corps.

Article 29-1:
Toute pétition adressée au pouvoir Législatif doit donner lieu à la procédure réglementaire permettant de statuer sur son objet.

SECTION D

De la Liberté de Conscience

Article 30:
Toutes les Religions et tous les Cultes sont libres. Toute personne a le droit de professer sa Religion et son Culte, pourvu que l'exercice de ce droit ne trouble pas l'ordre et la paix publics.

Article 30-1:
Nul ne peut être contraint à faire partie d'une association ou à suivre un enseignement religieux contraire à ses convictions.

Article 30-2:
La Loi établit les conditions de reconnaissance et de fonctionnement des Religions et des Cultes.

SECTION E

De la Liberté de Réunion et d'Association

Article 31:
La liberté d'Association et de Réunion sans armes à des fins politiques, économiques, sociales, culturelles ou à toutes autres fins pacifiques est garantie.

Article 31-1:
Les Partis et Groupements Politiques concourent à l'expression du suffrage. Ils se forment et exercent leur activité librement. Ils doivent respecter les principes de la Souveraineté Nationale et de la

Démocratie. La loi détermine leurs conditions de reconnaissance et de fonctionnement, les avantages et privilèges qui leur sont réservés.

Article 31-2:
Les Réunions sur la voie publique sont sujettes à notification préalable aux Autorités de Police.

Article 31-3:
Nul ne peut être contraint de s'affilier à une Association quelqu'en soit le caractère.

SECTION F

De l'education et de l'Enseignement

Article 32:
L'Etat garantit le Droit à l'Education. Il veille à la formation physique, intellectuelle, morale, professionnelle, sociale et civique de la Population.

Article 32-1:
L'Education est une charge de l'Etat et des Collectivités Territoriales. Ils doivent mettre l'Ecole gratuitement à la portée de tous, veiller au niveau de formation des Enseignants des Secteurs publics et privés.

Article 32-2:
La première charge de l'Etat et des Collectivités territoriales est la scolarisation massive, seule capable de permettre le développement du Pays. L'Etat encourage et facilite l'initiative privée en ce domaine.

Article 32-3:
L'Enseignement Primaire est obligatoire sous peine de sactions à déterminer par la Loi. Les fournitures classiques et le matériel didactique seront mis gratuitement par l'Etat à la disposition des élèves au niveau de l'Enseignement Primaire.

Article 32-4:
L'Enseignement Agricole, Professionnel, Coopératif et Technique est une responsabilité primordiale de l'Etat et des Communes.

Article 32-5:
La formation Pré-Scolaire et Maternelle ainsi que l'Enseignement Non-Formel sont encouragés.

Article 32-6:
L'accès aux Etudes Supérieures est ouvert en pleine égalité à tous, uniquement en fonction du mérite.

Article 32-7:
L'Etat doit veiller à ce que chaque Collectivité Territoriale, Section Communale, Commune, Département soit doté d'Etablissements d'Enseignement indispensables, adaptés aux besoins de son développement, sans toutefois porter préjudice à la priorité de l'Enseignement Agricole, Professionnel, Coopératif et Technique qui doit être largement diffusé.

Article 32-8:
L'Etat garantit aux handicapés et aux surdoués des moyens pour assurer leur autonomie, leur éducation, leur indépendance.

Article 32-9:
L'Etat et les Collectivités Territoriales ont pour devoir de prendre toutes les dispositions nécessaires en vue d'intensifier la Campagne d'Alphabétisation des Masses. Ils encouragent toutes initiatives privées tendant à cette fin.

Article 32-10
L'Enseignant a droit à un Salaire de base équitable.

Article 33:
L'Enseignement est libre à tous les degrés. Cette liberté s'exerce sous le contrôle de l'Etat.

Article 34:
Hormis les cas de flagrant délit, l'enceinte des Etablissements d'Enseignement est inviolable. Aucune force de l'ordre ne peut y pénétrer qu'en accord avec la Direction des dits Etablissements.

Article 34-1:
Cette disposition ne s'applique pas quand un Etablissement Scolaire est utilisé à d'autres fins.

SECTION G

De la Liberté du Travail

Article 35:
La liberté du travail est garantie. Tout citoyen a pour obligation de se consacrer à un travail de son choix en vue de subvenir à des besoins et à ceux de sa famille, coopérer avec l'Etat à l'établissement d'un système de sécurité sociale.

Article 35-1:
Tout employé d'une institution privée ou publique a droit à un juste salaire, au repos, au congé annuel payé et au bonus.

Article 35-2:
L'Etat garantit au travailleur, l'égalité des conditions de travail et de salaire quel que soit son sexe, ses croyances, ses opinions et son statut matrimonial.

Article 35-3:
La liberté syndicale est garantie. Tout travailleur des secteurs privés et publics peut adhérer au Syndicat de ses activités professionnelles pour la défense exclusivement de ses intérêts de travail.

Article 35-4:
Le syndicat est essentiellement apolitique à but non lucratif et non confessionnel. Nul ne peut être contraint d'y adhérer.

Article 35-5:
Le droit de grève est reconnu dans les limites déterminées par la Loi.

Article 35-6:
La Loi fixe la limite d'âge pour le travail salarié. Des Lois Spéciales réglementent le travail des enfants mineurs et des gens de maison.

SECTION H

De la Propriété

Article 36:
La Propriété Privée est reconnue et garantie. La Loi en détermine des modalités d'acquisition, de jouissance, ainsi que les limites.

Article 36-1:
L'Expropriation pour cause d'utilité publique peut avoir lieu moyennant le paiement ou la consignation ordonnée par justice aux ordres de qui de droit, d'une juste et préalable indemnité fixée à dire d'expert.

Si le projet initial est abandonné, l'expropriation est annulée et l'immeuble ne pouvant être l'objet d'aucune spéculation, doit être restitué à son propriétaire originaire, sans aucun remboursement pour le petit propriétaire. La mesure d'expropriation est effective à partir de la mise en oeuvre du projet.

Article 36-2:
La Nationalisation et la confiscation des biens, meubles et immeubles pour causes politiques sont interdites.

Nul ne peut être privé de son droit légitime de propriété qu'en vertu d'un jugement rendu par un Tribunal de Droit Commun passé en force de chose souverainement jugée, sauf dans le cadre d'une réforme agraire.

Article 36-3:
La Propriété entraine également des obligations. Il n'en peut être fait un usage contraire à l'intérêt général.

Article 36-4:
Le Propriétaire Foncier doit cultiver, exploiter le sol et le protéger notamment contre l'érosion. La sanction de cette obligation est prévue par la Loi.

Article 36-5:
Le Droit de propriété ne s'étend pas au Littoral, aux sources, rivières, cours d'eau, mines et carrières. Ils font partie du domaine public de l'Etat.

Article 36-6:
La Loi fixe des règles qui conditionnent la liberté de prospection et le droit d'exploiter les mines, minières et carrières du sous-sol, en assurant au propriétaire de la surface, aux concessionnaires et à l''tat Haitien une participation équitable au profit que procure la mise en valeur de ces ressources naturelles.

Article 37:
La Loi fixe les conditions de morcellement et de remembrement de la terre en fonction du plan d'aménagement du Territoire et du bien-être des communautés concernées, dans le cadre d'une réforme agraire.

Article 38:
La Propriété scientifique, littéraire et artistique est protégée par la Loi.

Article 39:
Les habitants des Sections communales ont un droit de préemption pour l'exploitation des terres du domaine privé de l'Etat situées dans leur localité.

SECTION I

Droit à l'Information

Article 40:
Obligation est faite à l'Etat de donner publicité par voie de Presse parlée, ecrite et télévisée, en langues créole et française aux Lois, Arrêtés, Décrets, Accords Internationaux, Traités, Conventions, à tout ce qui touche la vie nationale, exception faite pour les informations relevant de la sécurité nationale.

SECTION J

Droit à la Sécurité

Article 41:
Aucun individu de Nationalité Haïtienne ne peut être déporté ou forcé de laisser le Territoire National pour quelque motif que ce soit. Nul ne peut être privé pour des motifs politiques de sa capacité juridique et de sa nationalité.

Article 41-1:
Aucun Haïtien n'a besoin de visa pour laisser le Pays ou pour y revenir.

Article 42:
Aucun citoyen civil ou militaire ne peut être distrait des juges que la Constitution et les Lois lui assignent.

Article 42-1:
Le Militaire accusé de crime de Haute Trahison envers la Patrie est passible du Tribunal de Droit Commun.

Article 42-2:
La Justice Militaire n'a Juridiction que:

a) Dans les cas de violation des règlements du Manuel de Justice Militaire par des Militaires;

b) Dans les cas de conflicts entre les Membres des Forces Armées;

c) En cas de guerre.

Article 42-3:
Les cas de conflits entre Civils et Militaires, les abus, violences et crimes perpétrés contre un civil par un Militaire dans l'exercice de ses fonctions, relèvent des Tribunaux de Droit Commun.

Article 43:
Aucune visite domiciliare, aucune saisie de papier ne peut avoir lieu qu'en vertu de la Loi et dans les formes qu'elle prescrit.

Article 44:
Les détenus provisiores attendant d'ëtre jugés doivent être séparés de ceux qui purgent une peine.

Article 44-1:
Le régime des prisons doit répondre aux normes attachées au respect de la dignité humaine selon le Loi sur la matière.

Article 45:
Nulle peine ne peut être établie que par la Loi, ni appliquée que dans les cas que celle-ci détermine.

Article 46:
Nul ne peut être obligé en matière criminelle, correctionnelle ou de simple police, à témoigner contre lui-même ou ses parents jusqu'au quatrième degré de consanguinité au deuxième degré d'alliance.

Article 47:
Nul ne peut être contraint de prêter serment que dans les cas et dans les formes prévus par la Loi.

Article 48:
L'Etat veillera à ce qu'une caisse de Pension Civile de Retraite soit établie dans les Secteurs Privés et Publics. Elle sera alimentée par les contributions des Employeurs et Employés suivant les critères et modalités établis par la Loi. L'Allocation de la Pension est un droit et non une faveur.

Article 49:
La liberté, le secret de la correspondance et de toutes les autres formes de communication sont inviolables. Leur limitation ne peut se produire que par un acte motivé de l'Autorité
Judiciaire, selon les garanties fixées par la Loi.

Article 50:
Dans le cadre de la Constitution et de la Loi, le Jury est établi en matière criminelle pour les crimes de sang et en matière de délits politiques.

Article 51:
La Loi ne peut avoir d'effet rétroactif, sauf en matière pénale quand elle est favorable à l'accusé.

CHAPÌTRE III

Des Devoirs du Citoyen

Article 52:
A la qualité de citoyen se rattache le devoir civique. Tout droit est contrebalancé par le devoir correspondant.

Article 52-1:
Le Devoir Civique est l'ensemble des obligations du citoyen dans l'ordre moral, politique, social et économique vis-à-vis de l'Etat et de la Patrie.

Ces obligations sont:
a) Respecter la Constitution et l'Emblème National;
b) Respecter les Lois;
c) Voter aux Elections sans contrainte;
d) Payer ses taxes;
e) Servir de Juré;
f) Défendre le Pays en cas de guerre;
g) S'instruire et se perfectionner;
h) Respecter et protéger l'Environnement;
i) Respecter scrupuleusement les deniers et biens de l'Etat;
j) Respecter le bien d'autrui;
k) Oeuvrer pour le maintien de la Paix;
l) Fournir assistance aux personnes en danger;
m) Respecter les droits et la liberté d'autrui.

Article 52-2:
La dérogation à ces prescriptions est sanctionnée par la Loi.

Article 52-3:
Il est établi un Service Civique Mixte Obligatoire dont les conditions de fonctionnement sont établies par la Loi.

TITRE IV

Des Etrangers

Article 53:
Les conditions d'admission et de séjour des Etrangers dans le Pays sont établies par la Loi.

Article 54:
Les Etrangers qui se trouvent sur le Territoire de la République bénéficient de la même protection que celle qui est accordée aux Haïtiens, conformément à la Loi.

Article 54-1:
L'Etranger jouit des droits civils, des droits économiques et sociaux, sous la réserve des dispositions légales relatives au droit de propriété immobilière, à l'exercice des professions, au commerce de gros, à la représentation commerciale et aux opérations d'importation et d'exportation.

Article 55:
Le droit de propriété immobilière est accordé à l'Etranger résidant en Haïti pour les besoins de sa demeure.

Article 55-1:
Cependant, l'Etranger résidant en Haïti ne peut être propriétaire de plus d'une maison d'habitation dans un même Arrondissement. Il ne peut en aucun cas se livrer au trafic de location d'immeubles. Toutefois les sociétés étrangères de promotion immobilières bénéficient d'un statut spécial réglé par la Loi.

Article 55-2:
Le droit de propriété immobilière est également accordé à l'étranger résidant en Haïti et aux Sociétés étrangères pour les besoins de leurs entreprises agricoles, commerciales, industrielles, religieuses, humanitaires ou d'enseignement, dans les limites et conditions déterminées par la Loi.

Article 55-3:
Aucun étranger ne peut être propriétaire d'un immeuble borné par la frontière terrestre haïtienne.

Article 55-4:
Ce droit prend fin cinq (5) années après que l'étranger n'a cessé de résider dans le Pays ou qu'ont cessé les opérations de ces sociétés, conformément à la Loi qui détermine les règlements à suivre pour la transmission et la liquidation des biens appartenant aux étrangers.

Article 55-5:
Les contrevenants aux sus-dites dispositions ainsi que leurs complices seront punis conformément à la Loi.

Article 56:
L'étranger peut être expulsé du Territoire de la République lorsqu'il simmisce dans la vie politique du pays et dans les cas déterminés par la Loi.

Article 57:
Le droit d'asile est reconnu aux réfugiés politiques.

TITRE V

De la Souveraineté Nationale

Article 58:
La Souveraineté Nationale réside dans l'Universalité des citoyens.

Les citoyens exercent directement les prérogatives de la Souveraineté par:
a) L'Election du Président de la République;

b) L'Election des Membres du Pouvoir Législatif;

c) L'Election des Membres de tous autres Corps ou de toutes Assemblées prévues par la Constitution et par la Loi.

Article 59:
Les citoyens délèguent l'exercice de la Souveraineté Nationale à trois (3) Pouvoirs:

1) Le Pouvoir Législatif;

2) Le Pouvoir Executif;

3) Le Pouvoir Judiciaire;

Le principe de la séparation des trois (3) Pouvoirs est consacré par la Constitution.

Article 59-1:
L'Ensemble de ces trois (3) Pouvoirs constitue le fondement essentiel de l'Organisation de l'Etat qui est civil.

Article 60:
Chaque Pouvoir est indépendant des deux (2) autres dans ses attributions qu'il exerce séparément.

Article 60-1:
Aucun d'eux ne peut, sous aucun motif, déléguer ses attributions en tout ou en partie, ni sortir des limites qui lui sont fixées par la Constitution et par la Loi.

Article 60-2:
La responsabilité entiére est attachée aux actes de chacun des trois (3) Pouvoirs.

CHAPITRE I

Des Collectivités Territoriales et de la Décentralisation

Article 61:
Les Collectivités Territoriales sont la Section Communale, la Commune et le Département.

Article 61-1:
La Loi peut créer toute autre Collectivité Territoriale.

SECTION A

De la Section Communale

Article 62:
La Section Communale est la plus petite entité Territoriale Administrative de la République.

Article 63:
L'Administration de chaque Section Communale est assurée par un Conseil de Trois (3) Membres élus au suffrage universel pour une durée de quatre (4) ans. Ils sont indéfiniment rééligibles.

Son mode d'Organisation et de Fonctionnement est réglé par la Loi.

Article 63-1:
Le Conseil d'Administration de la Section Communale est assisté dans sa tâche par une Assemblée de la Section Communale.

Article 64:
L'Etat a pour obligation d'établir au niveau de chaque Section Communale les structures propres à la Formation sociale, économique, civique et culturelle de sa population.

Article 65:
Pour être Membre du Conseil d'Administration de la Section Communale il faut:

a) Etre Haïtien et âgé de vingt-cinq (25) ans au moins;

b) Avoir résidé dans la Section Communale deux ans (2) avant les élections et continuer à y résider.

c) Jouir de ses droits Civils et Politiques et n'avoir jamais été condamné à une peine afflictive et infamante.

SECTION B

De la Commune

Article 66:
La Commune a l'autonomie Administrative et Financière. Chaque Commune de la République est administrée par un Conseil de trois (3) Membres élus au suffrage universel dénomé Conseil Municipal.

Article 66-1:
Le President du Conseil porte le titre de Maire. Il est assisté de Maires-Adjoints.

Article 67:
Le Conseil Municipal est assisté dans sa tâche d'une Assemblée Municipale formée notamment d'un représentant de chacune de ses Sections Communales.

Article 68:
Le Mandat du Conseil Municipal est de quatre (4) ans et ses Membres sont indéfiniment rééligibles.

Article 69:
Le mode d'Organisation et le fonctionnement de la Commune et du Conseil Municipal sont réglés par la Loi.

Article 70:
Pour être élu Membre d'un Conseil Municipal, il faut:

a) Etre Haïtien;

b) Etre âgé de vingt-cinq (25) ans accomplis;

c) Jouir de ses Droits Civils et Politiques;

d) N'avoir jamais été condamné à une peine afflictive et infamante;

e) Avoir résidé au moins 3 ans dans la Commune et s'engager à y résider pendant la durée de son mandat.

Article 71:
Chaque Conseil Municipal est assisté sur sa demande d'un Conseil Technique fourni par l'Administration Centrale.

Article 72:
Le Conseil Municipal ne peut être dissous qu'en cas d'incurie, de malversation ou d'administration frauduleuse légalement prononcée par le Tribunal Compétent.

En cas de dissolution, le Conseil Départemental supplée immédiatement à la vacance et saisit le Conseil Electoral Permanent dans les soixante (60) jours à partir de la date de la dissolution en vue de l'élection d'un nouveau Conseil devant gérer les intérêts de la Commune pour le temps qui reste à courir. Cette procédure s'applique également en cas de vacance pour toute autre cause.

Article 73:
Le Conseil Municipal administre ses ressources au profit exclusif de la Municipalité et rend compte à l'Assemblée Municipale qui elle-même en fait rapport au Conseil Départemental.

Article 74:
Le Conseil Municipal est gestionnaire privilégié des biens fonciers du domaine privé de l'Etat situés dans les limites de sa Commune. Ils ne peuvent être l'objet d'aucune transaction sans l'avis préalable de l'Assemblée Municipale.

SECTION C

De l'Arrondissement

Article 75:
L'Arrondissement est une division Administrative pouvant regrouper plusieurs Communes. Son organisation et son Fonctionnement sont réglés par la Loi.

SECTION D

Du Département

Article 76:
Le Département est la plus grande Division Territoriale. Il regroupe les Arrondissements.

Article 77:
Le Département est une personne morale. Il est autonome.

Article 78:
Chaque Département est administré par un Conseil de trois (3) Membres élus pour quatre (4) ans par l'Assemblée Départementale.

Article 79:
Le Membre du Conseil Départemental n'est pas forcément tiré de l'Assemblée mais il doit:

a) Etre Haïtien et âgé de vingt-cinq (25) ans au moins;

b) Avoir résidé dans le Département trois (3) ans avant les élections et s'engager à y résider pendant toute la durée du mamdat.

c) Jouir de ses Droits Civils et Politiques et n'avoir jamais été condamné à une peine afflictive et infamante.

Article 80:
Le Conseil Départemental est assisté dans sa tâche d'une Assemblée Départementale formée: d'un (1) Représentant de chaque Assemblée Municipale.

Article 80-1:
Ont accès aux réunions de l'Assemblée avec voix consultative.

a) Les Députés et Sénateurs du Département;

b) Un (1) Représentant de chaque Association Socio-Professionnelle ou Syndicale;

c) Le Délégué départmental;

d) Les Directeurs des Services Publics du Département.

Article 81:
Le Conseil Départmental élabore en collaboration avec l'Administration Centrale le plan de développement du Département.

Article 82:
L'Organisation et le Fonctionnement du Conseil Départemental et de l'Assemblée Départementale sont réglés par la Loi.

Article 83:
Le Conseil Départemental administre ses ressources financières au profit exclusif du Département et rend compte à l'Assemblée Départementale qui elle-même en fait rapport à l'Administration Centrale.

Article 84:
Le Conseil Départemental peut-être dissous en cas d'incurie, de malversations ou d'administration frauduleuse légalement constatées par le Tribunal Compétent.
En cas de dissolution, l'Administration centrale nomme une commission Provisiore et saisit le Conseil Electoral Permanent en vue de l'élection d'un nouveau Conseil pour le temps à courir dans les soixante (60) jours de la dissolution.

SECTION E

Des Délégués et Vice-Délégués

Article 85:
Dans chaque Chef-Lieu de Département, le Pouvoir Exécutif nomme un Représentant qui porte le titre de Délégué. Un Vice-Délégué placé sous l'autorité du Délégué est également nommé dans chaque Chef-Lieu d'Arrondissement.

Article 86:
Les Délégués et vice-Délégués assurent la coordination et le contrôle des Services Publics et n'exercent aucune fonction de Police repressive.

Les autres attributions des Délégués et Vice-Délégués sont déterminées par la Loi.

SECTION F

Du Conseil Interdépartemental

Article 87:
L'Executif est assisté d'un (1) Conseil Interdépartemental dont les Membres sont désignés par les Assemblées Départementales à raison d'un (1) par Département.

Article 87-1:
Ce représentant choisi parmi les Membres des Assemblées Départementales sert de liaison entre le Département et le Pouvoir Executif.

Article 87-2:
Le Conseil Interdépartemental, de concert avec l'Exécutif, étudie et planifie les projets de décentralisation et de développement du pays au point de vue social, économique, commerciale, agricole et industriel.

Article 87-3:
Il assiste aux séances de travail du Conseil des Ministres lorsqu'elles traitent des objets mentionnés au précédent paragraphe avec voix délibérative.

Article 87-4:
La décentralisation doit être accompagnée de la déconcentration des Services Publics avec Délégation de Pouvoir et du décloisonnement industriel au profit des Départements.

Article 87-5:
La Loi détermine l'Organisation et le fonctionnement du Conseil Interdépartemental ainsi que la fréquence des séances du Conseil des Ministres auxquelles il participe.

CHAPITRE II

Du Pouvoir Législatif

Article 88:
Le Pouvoir Législatif s'exerce par deux (2) Chambres représentatives. Une (1) Chambre des Députés et un (1) Sénat qui forment le Corps Législatif ou Parlement.

SECTION A

De la Chambre des Députés

Article 89:
La Chambre des Députés est un Corps composé de Membres élus au suffrage direct par les citoyens et chargé d'exercer au nom de ceux-ci et de concert avec le Sénat les attributions du Pouvoir Législatif.

Article 90:
Chaque Collectivité Municipale constitue une Circonscription Electorale et élit un (1) Député.

La Loi fixe le nombre de Députés au niveau des grandes agglomérations sans que ce nombre n'excède trois (3).

En attendant l'application des alinéas précédents, le nombre de Députés ne peut être inférieur à soixante-dix (70).

Article 90-1:
Le Député est élu à la majorité absolue des suffrages exprimés dans les Assemblées Primaires, selon les conditions et le mode prescrits par la loi électorale.

Article 91:
Pour être Membre de la Chambre des Députés, il faut:

1) Etre Haitien d'Origine et n'avoir jamais renoncé à sa Nationalité;

2) Etre âgé de vingt-cinq (25) ans accomplis;

3) Jouir de ses Droits Civils et Politiques et n'avoir jamais été condamné à une peine afflictive et infamante pour un crime de droit commun.

4) Avoir résidé au moins deux (2) années consécutives précédant la date des élections dans la Circonscription Electorale à représenter;

5) Etre propriétaire d'un immeuble au moins dans la circonscription ou y exercer une profession ou une industrie;

6) Avoir reçu décharge, le cas échéant, comme gestionnaire de Fonds Publics.

Article 92:
Les Députés sont élus pour quatre (4) ans et sont indéfiniment rééligibles.

Article 92-1:
Ils entrent en fonction le deuxième lundi de Janvier et siègent en deux (2) Sessions Annuelles. La durée de leur mandat forme une Législature.

Article 92-2:
La Première Session va du deuxième Lundi de Janvier au deuxième Lundi de Mai. La seconde, du deuxième Lundi du mois de Juin au deuxième Lundi de Septembre.

Article 92-3:
Le renouvellement de la Chambre des Députés se fait intégralement tous les quatre (4) ans.

Article 93:
La Chambre des Députés, outre les attributions qui lui sont dévolues par la Constitution en tant que branche du Pouvoir Législatif, a le

privilège de mettre en accusation le Chef de l'Etat, le Premier Ministre, les Ministres, les Secrétaires d'Etat par devant la Haute Cour de Justice, par une majorité des 2/3 de ses Membres. Les autres attributions de la Chambre des Députés lui sont assignées par la Constitution et par la Loi.

SECTION B

Du Sénat

Article 94:
Le Sénat est un Corps composé de Membres élus au suffrage direct par les Citoyens et chargé d'exercer en leur nom, de concert avec la Chambre des Députés, les attributions du Pouvoir Législatif.

Article 94-1:
Le nombre des Sénateurs est fixé à trois (3) Sénateurs par Département.

Article 94-2:
Le Sénateur de la République est élu au suffrage universel à la majorité absolue dans les Assemblées Primaires tenues dans les Départements Géographiques, selon les conditions prescrites par la Loi Electorale.

Article 95:
Les Sénateurs sont élus pour six (6) ans et sont indéfiniment rééligibles.

Article 95-1:
Le Sénat siège en permanence.

Article 95-2:
Le Sénat peut cependant s'ajourner, excepté durant la Session Législative. Lorsqu'il s'ajourne, il laisse un Comité permanent chargé d'expédier les affaires courantes. Ce comité ne peut prendre aucun Arrêté, sauf pour la convocation du Sénat.

Dans les cas d'urgence, l'Exécutif peut également convoquer le Sénat avant la fin de l'ajournement.

Article 95-3:
Le renouvellement du Sénat se fait par tiers (1/3) tous les deux (2) ans.

Article 96:
Pour être élu Sénateur, il faut;
1) Etre Haitien d'Origine et n'avoir jamais renoncé à sa Nationalité;

2) Etre âgé de trente (30) ans accomplis;

3) Jouir de ses Droits Civils et Politiques et n'avoir jamais été condamné à une peine afflictive et infamante pour un crime de droit commun.

4) Avoir résidé dans le Département à représenter au moins quatre (4) années consécutives précédant la date des élections;

5) Etre Propriétaire d'un immeuble au moins dans le Département ou y exercer une profession ou une industrie;

6) Avoir obtenu décharge, le cas échéant, comme gestionnaire de Fonds Publics.

Article 97:
En addition aux responsabilités qui lui sont inhérentes en tant que branche du Pouvoir Législatif, le Sénat exerce les attributions suivantes:
1) Proposer à l'Executif la liste des Juges de la Cour de Cassation selon les prescriptions de la Constitution;

2) S'ériger en Haute Cour de Justice;

3) Exercer toutes attributions qui lui sont assignées par la présente Constitution et par la Loi.

SECTION C

De l'Assemblée Nationale

Article 98:
La réunion en une seule Assemblée des deux (2) branches du Pouvoir Législatif constitue l'Assemblée Nationale.

Article 98-2:
Les Pouvoirs de l'Assemblée Nationale sont limités et ne peuvent s'étendre à d'autres objets que ceux qui lui sont spécialement attribués par la Constitution.

Article 98-3:
Les attributions sont:

1) De recevoir le serment Constitutionnel du Président de la République;

2) De ratifier toute décision, de déclarer la guerre quand toutes les tentatives de conciliation ont échoué;

3) D'approuver ou de rejeter les Traités et Conventions Internationaux;

4) D'amender la Constitution selon la procédure qui y est indiquée;

5) De ratifier la décision de l'Executif, de déplacer le siège du Gouvernement dans les cas déterminés par l'Article de la Présente Constitution;

6) De statuer sur l'opportunité de l'Etat de siège, d'arrêter avec l'Executif les garanties Constitutionnelles, à suspendre et de se prononcer sur toute demande de renouvellement de cette mesure;

7) De concourir à la formation du Conseil Electoral Permanent conformément à l'article 192 de la Constitution;

8) De recevoir à l'ouverture de chaque Session, le Bilan des activités du Gouvernement.

Article 99:
L'Assemble Nationale est présidée par le Président du Sénat assisté du Président de la Chambre des Députés en qualité de Vice-Président. Les Secrétaires du Sénat et ceux de la Chambre des Députés sont les Secrétaires de l'Assemblée Nationale.

Article 99-1:
En cas d'empêchement du Président du Sénat, l'Assemblée Nationale est présidée par le Président de la Chambre des Députés, le Vice-President du Sénat devient alors Vice-Président de l'Assemblée Nationale.

Article 99-2:
En cas d' empêchement des deux (2) Présidents, les deux (2) Vice-Présidents y suppléent respectivement.

Article 100:
Les séances de l'Assemblée Nationale sont publiques. Néanmoins, elles peuvent avoir lieu à huis clos sur la demande de cinq (5) Membres et il sera ensuite décidé à la majorité absolue si la séance doit être reprise en public.

Article 101:
En cas d'urgence lorsque le Corps Legislatif n'est pas en session, le Pouvoir Exécutif peut convoquer l'Assemblée Nationale à l'Extraordinaire.

Article 102:
L'Assemblée Nationale ne peut siéger ou prendre des décisions et des résolutions sans la preesence en son sein de la majorité de chacune des deux (2) Chambres.

Article 103:
Le Corps Législatif a son siège à Port-au-Prince. Néanmoins, suivant les circonstances, ce siège peut être transféré ailleurs au même lieu et en même temps que celui du Pouvoir Exécutif.

SECTION D

De l'Exercice du Pouvoir Législatif

Article 104:
La Session du Corps Législatif prend date dès l'ouverture des deux (2) chambres en Assemblée Nationale.

Article 105:
Dans l'intervalle des Sessions Ordinaires et en cas d'urgence, le Président de la République peut convoquer le Corps Législatif en Session Extraordinaire.

Article 106:
Le Chef du Pouvoir Exécutif rend compte de cette mesure par un message.

Article 107:
Dans le cas de Convocation à l'Extraordinaire du Corps Législatif, il ne peut décider sur aucun objet étranger au motif de la convocation.

Article 107-1:
Cependant, tout Sénateur ou Député peut entretenir l'Assemblée à laquelle il appartient de question d'intérêt général.

Article 108:
Chaque Chambre vérifie et valide les pouvoirs de ses Membres et juge souverainement les contestations qui s'élèvent à ce sujet.

Article 109:
Les Membres de chaque Chambre prêtent le serment suivant:

> "Je jure de m'acquitter de ma tâche, de maintenir et de sauvegarder les droits du Peuple et d'être fidèle à la Constitution."

Article 110:
Les séances des deux (2) Chambres sont publiques. Chaque Chambre peut travailler à huis clos sur la demande de cinq (5) Membres et décider ensuite à la majorité si la Séance doit être reprise en public.

Article 111:
Le Pouvoir Législatif fait des lois sur tous les objets d'intérêt public.

Article 111-1:
L'initiative en appartient à chacune des deux (2) Chambres ainsi qu'au Pouvoir Exécutif.

Article 111-2:
Toutefois, l'initiative de la Loi Budgétaire, des Lois concernant l'assiette, la quotité et le mode de perception des impôts et contributions, de celles ayant pour objet de créer les recettes ou d'augmenter les recettes et les dépenses de l'Etat est du ressort du Pouvoir Exécutif. Les Projets présentés à cet égard doivent être votés d'abord par la Chambre des Députés.

Article 111-3:
En cas de désaccord entre les deux (2) Chambres relativement aux Lois mentionnées dans le précédent paragraphe, chaque Chambre nomme au scrutin de liste et en nombre égal une Commission parlementaire qui résout en dernier ressort le désaccord.

Article 111-4:
Si le désaccord se produit à l'occasion de toute autre Loi, celle-ci sera ajournée jusqu'à la Session suivante. Si, à cette Session et même en cas de renouvellement des Chambres, la Loi étant présentée à nouveau, une entente ne se réalise pas, chaque Chambre nomme au scrutin de liste et en nombre égal, une Commission Parlementaire chargée d'arrêter le texte définitif qui sera soumis aux deux (2) Assemblées, à commencer par celle qui avait primitivement voté la Loi. Et si ces nouvelles délibérations ne donnent aucun résultat, le Projet ou la Proposition de Loi sera retiré.

Article 111-5:
En cas de désaccord entre le Pouvoir Législatif et le Pouvoir Exécutif, la Commission de Conciliation prévue à l'Article 206 ci-après, est saisie du différend sur demande de l'une des parties.

Article 111-6:
Si la Commission échoue dans sa mission, elle dresse un procès-verbal de non conciliation qu'elle transmet aux deux (2) hautes parties et en donne avis à la Cour de Cassation.

Article 111-7:
Dans la huitaine de la réception de ce procès-verbal, la Cour de Cassation se saisit d'office du différend. La Cour statue en Sections réunies, toutes affaires cessantes. La décision est finale et s'impose aux hautes parties.

Si entre temps, une entente survient entre les hautes parties, les termes de l'entente arrêteront d'office la procédure en cours.

Article 111-8:
En aucun cas, la Chambre des Députés ou le Sénat ne peut être dissous ou ajourné, ni le mandat de leurs Membres prorogé.

Article 112:
Chaque Chambre au terme de ses règlements nomme son personnel, fixe sa discipline et détermine le mode suivant lequel elle exerce ses attributions.

Article 112-1:
Chaque Chambre peut appliquer à ses Membres pour conduite répréhensible, par décision prise à la majorité des 2/3, des peines disciplinaires sauf celle de la radiation.

Article 113:
Sera déchu de sa qualité de Député ou de Sénateur, tout Membre du Corps Législatif qui, pendant la durée de son Mandat aura été frappé d'une condamnation prononcée par un Tribunal de Droit Commun qui a acquis autorité de chose jugée et entraîne l'inéligibilité.

Article 114:
Les Membres du Corps Législatif sont inviolables du jour de leur prestation de serment jusqu'a l'expiration de leur mandat, sous réserve des dispositions de l'Article 115
ci-après.

Article 114-1:
Ils ne peuvent être en aucun temps poursuivis et attaqués pour les opinions et votes émis par eux dans l'exercice de leur fonction.

Article 114-2:
Aucune contrainte par corps ne peut être exécutée contre un Membre du Corps Législatif pendant la durée de son mandat.

Article 115:
Nul Membre du Corps Législatif ne peut durant son Mandat, être arrêté en matière criminelle, correctionnelle ou de police pour délit de droit commun si ce n'est avec l'autorisation de la Chambre à laquelle il appartient, sauf en cas de flagrant délit pour faits emportant une peine afflictive et infamante. Il en est alors référé à la Chambre des Députés ou au Sénat sans délai si le Corps Législatif est en Session dans le cas contraire, à l'ouverture de la prochaine Session Ordinaire ou Extraordinaire.

Article 116:
Aucune des deux (2) Chambres ne peut siéger, ni prendre une résolution sans la présence de la majorité de ses Membres.

Article 117:
Tous les actes du Corps Législatif doivent être pris à la majorité des Membres présents, excepté s'il en est autrement prévu par la présente Constitution.

Article 118:
Chaque Chambre a le droit d'enquêter sur les questions dont elle est saisie.

Article 119:
Tout Projet de Loi doit être voté Article par Article.

Article 120:
Chaque Chambre a le droit d'amender et de diviser les Articles et Amendements proposés. Les Amendements votés par une Chambre ne peuvent faire partie d'un Projet de Loi qu'après avoir été votés par l'autre Chambre dans la même forme et en termes identiques.
Aucun Projet de Loi ne devient Loi qu'après avoir été voté dans la même forme par les deux (2) Chambres.

Article 120-1:
Tout projet peut-être retiré de la discussion tant qu'il n'a pas été définitivement voté.

Article 121:
Toute Loi votée par le Corps Législatif est immédiatement adressée au Président de la République qui, avant de la promulguer, a le droit d'y faire des objections en tout ou en partie.

Article 121-1:
Dans ce cas, le Président de la République renvoie la Loi avec ses objections à la Chambre où elle a été primitivement votée. Si la Loi est amendée par cette Chambre, elle est renvoyée à l'autre Chambre avec les objections.

Article 121-2:
Si la Loi ainsi amendée est votée par la seconde Chambre elle sera adressée de nouveau au Président de la République pour Ietre promulguée.

Article 121-3:
Si les objections sont rejetées par la Chambre qui a primitivement voté la Loi, elle est renvoyée à l'autre Chambre avec les objections.

Article 121-4:
Si la seconde Chambre vote également le rejet, la Loi est renvoyée au Preesident de la République qui est dans l'obligation de la promulguer.

Article 121-5:
Le rejet des objections est voté par l'une et l'autre Chambre à la majorité prévue par l'Article 117. Dans ce cas, les votes de chaque Chambre seront émis au scrutin secret.

Article 121-6:
Si dans l'une et l'autre Chambre, la majorité prévue à l'alinéa précédent n'est pas obtenue pour le rejet, les objections sont acceptées.

Article 122:
Le droit d'objection doit être exercé dans un délai de huit (8) jours francs à partir de la date de la réception de la Loi par le Président de la République.

Article 123:
Si dans les délais prescrits, le Président de la République ne fait aucune objection, la Loi doit être promulguée à moins que la Session du Corps Législatif n'ait pris fin avant l'expiration des délais, dans ce cas, la Loi demeure ajournée. La Loi ainsi ajournée est, à l'ouverture de la Session suivante, adressée au Président de la République pour l'exercice de son droit d'objection.

Article 124:
Un projet de Loi rejeté par l'une des deux (2) Chambres ne peut être présenté de nouveau dans la même Session.

Article 125:
Les Lois et autres Actes du Corps Législatif et de l'Assemblée Nationale seront rendus exécutoires par leur promulgation et leur publication au Journal Officiel de la République.

Article 125-1:
Ils sont numérotés, insérés dans le bulletin imprimé et numéroté ayant pour titre Bulletin des Lois et Actes.

Article 126:
La Loi prend date du jour de son adoption définitive par les deux (2) Chambres.

Article 127:
Nul ne peut en personne présenter des pétitions à la Tribune du Corps Législatif.

Article 128:
L'interprétation des Lois par voie d'Autorité, n'appartient qu'au Pouvoir Législatif, elle est donnée dans la forme d'une Loi.

Article 129:
Chaque Membre du Corps Législatif reçoit une indemnité mensuelle à partir de sa prestation de serment.

Article 129-1:
La fonction de Membre du Corps Législatif est incompatible avec toute fonction rétribuée par l'Etat, sauf celle d'enseignant.

Article 129-2:
Le droit de questionner et d'interpeller un Membre du Gouvernement ou le Gouvernement tout entier sur les faits et actes de l'Administration est reconnu à tout Membre des deux (2) Chambres.

Article 129-3:
La demande d'interpellation doit-être appuyée par cinq (5) Membres du Corps intéressé. Elle aboutit à un vote de confiance ou de censure pris à la majorité de ce Corps.

Article 129-4:
Lorsque la demande d'interpellation aboutit à un vote de censure sur une question se rapportant au programme ou à une déclaration de politique générale du Gouvernement, le Premier Ministre doit remettre au Président de la République, la démission de son Gouvernement.

Article 129-5:
Le Président doit accepter cette démission et nommer un nouveau Premier Ministre; conformément aux dispositions de la Constitution.

Article 129-6:
Le Corps Législatif ne peut prendre plus d'un vote de censure par an sur une question se rapportant au programme ou à une déclaration de politique générale du Gouvernement.

Article 130:
En cas de mort, de démission, de déchéance, d'interdiction judiciaire ou d'acceptation d'une fonction incompatible avec celle de Membre du Corps Législatif, il est pourvu au remplacement du Député ou du Sénateur dans sa Circonscription Electorale pour le temps seulement qui reste à courir par une élection partielle sur convocation de l'Assemblée Primaire Electorale faite par le Conseil Electorale Permanent dans le mois même de la vacance.

Article 130-1:
L'Election a lieu dans une période de trente (30) jours après la convocation de l'Assemblée Primaire, conformément à la Constitution.

Article 130-2:
Il en est de même à défaut d'élection ou en cas de nullité des élections prononcées par le Conseil Electoral Permanent dans une ou plusieurs Circonscriptions.

Article 130-3:
Cependant, si la vacance se produit au cours de la dernière Session Ordinaire de la Législature ou après la Session, il n'y a pas lieu à l'élection partielle.

SECTION E

Des Incompatibilités

Article 131:
Ne peuvent être élus Membres du Corps Législatif:

1) Les Concessionnaires ou Contractants de l'Etat pour l'exploitation des Services Publics;

2) Les Représentants ou Mandataires des Concessionnaires ou Contractants de l'Etat, Compagnies ou Sociétés Concessionnaires ou Contractants de l'Etat;

3) Les Délégués, Vice-Délégués, les Juges, les Officiers du Ministère Public dont les fonctions n'ont pas cessé six (6) mois avant la date fixée pour les élections;

4) Toute personne se trouvant dans les autres cas d'inéligibilité prévus par la présente Constitution et par la Loi.

Article 132:
Les Membres du Pouvoir Exécutif et les Directeurs Généraux de l'Administration Publique ne peuvent être élus Membre du Corps Législatif s'ils ne démissionnent un (1) an au moins avant la date des élections.

CHAPITRE III

Du Pouvoir Exécutif

Article 133:
Le Pouvoir Exécutif est exercé par:

a) Le Président de la République, Chef de l'Etat;

b) Le Gouvernement ayant à sa tête un Premier Ministre.

SECTION A

Du Président de la République

Article 134:
Le Président de la République est élu au suffrage universel direct à la majorité absolue des votants. Si celle-ci n'est pas obtenue au premier tour, il est procédé à un second tour.

Seuls peuvent s'y présenter les deux (2) candidats qui, le cas échéant, après retrait de candidats plus favorisés, se trouvent avoir recueilli le plus grand nombre de voix au premier tour.

Article 134-1:
La durée du mandat présidentiel est de cinq (5) ans. Cette période commence et se termine le 7 février, suivant la date des élections.

Article 134-2:
Les Elections Présidentielles ont lieu le dernier Dimanche de Novembre de la cinquième année du mandat présidentiel.

Article 134-3:
Le Président de la République ne peut bénéficier de prolongation de mandat. Il ne peut assumer un nouveau mandat, qu'après un intervalle de cinq (5) ans. En aucun cas, il ne peut briguer un troisième mandat.

Article 135:
Pour être élu Président de la République d'Haïti, il faut:

a) Etre Haïtien d'Origine et n'avoir jamais renoncé à sa Nationalité;

b) Etre âgé de trente-cinq (35) ans accomplis au jour des élections;

c) Jouir de ses Droits Civils et Politiques et n'avoir jamais été condamné à une peine afflictive et infamante pour crime de droit commun;

d) Etre propriétaire en Haïti d'un immeuble au moins et avoir dans le Pays une résidence habituelle;

e) Résider dans le Pays depuis cinq (5) années consécutives avant la date des élections;

f) Avoir reçu décharge de sa gestion si on a été comptable de deniers publics.

Article 135-1:
Avant d'entrer en fonction, le Président de la République prête devant l'Assemblée Nationale, le serment suivant:

"Je jure, devant Dieu et devant la Nation, d'observer et de faire observer fidèlement la Constitution et les Lois de la République, de respecter et de faire respecter les droits du Peuple Haïtien, de travailler à la grandeur de la Patrie, de maintenir l'indépendance Nationale et l'intégrité du Territoire."

SECTION B

Des Attributions du Président de la République

Article 136:
Le Président de la République, Chef de l'Etat veille au respect et à l'exécution de la Constitution et à la stabilité des Institutions. Il assure le fonctionnement régulier des Pouvoirs Publics ainsi que la continuité de l'Etat.

Article 137:
Le Président de la République choisit un Premier Ministre parmi les Membres du Parti ayant la majorité au Parlement. A défaut de cette majorité, le Président de la République choisit son Premier Ministre en consultation avec le Président du Sénat et celui de la Chambre des Députés.

Dans les deux (2) cas, le choix doit-être ratifié par le Parlement.

Article 137-1:
Le Président de la République met fin aux fonctions du Premier Ministre sur la présentation par celui-ci de la démission du Gouvernement.

Article 138:
Le Président de la République est le garant de l'Indépendance Nationale et de l'Intégrité du Territoire.

Article 139:
Il négocie et signe tous Traités, Conventions et Accords Internationaux et les soumet à la ratification de l'Assemblée Nationale.

Article 139-1:
Il accrédite les Ambassadeurs et les Envoyés Extraordinaires auprès des Puissances Etrangères, reçoit les Lettres de Créance des Ambassadeurs des Puissances Etrangères et accorde l'exéquatur aux Consuls.

Article 140:
Il déclare la guerre, négocie et signe les Traités de Paix avec l'approbation de l'Assemblée Nationale.

Article 141:
Le Président de la République, après l'approbation du Sénat nomme par Arrêté pris en conseil des Ministres, le Commandant en Chef des Forces Armées, le Commandant en Chef de la Police, les Ambassadeurs et les Consuls Généraux.

Article 142:
Par Arrêté pris en Conseil des Ministres, le Président de la République nomme les Directeurs Généraux de l'Administration Publique, les Délégués et Vice-Délégués des Départements et Arrondissements.

Il nomme également, après approbation du Sénat, les Conseils d'Administration des Organismes Autonomes.

Article 143:
Le Président de la République est le Chef Nominal des Forces Armées, il ne les commande jamais en personne.

Article 144:
Il fait sceller les Lois du Sceau de la République et les promulgue dans les délais prescrits par la Constitution. Il peut avant l'expiration de ce délai, user de son droit d'objection.

Article 145:
Il veille à l'exécution des décisions judiciaires, conformément à la Loi.

Article 146:
Le Président de la République a le droit de grâce et de commutation de peine relativement à toute condamnation passée en force de chose jugée, à l'exception des condamnations prononcées par la Haute Cour de Justice ainsi qu'il est prévu dans la Présente Constitution.

Article 147:
Il ne peut accorder amnistie qu'en matière politique et selon les prescriptions de la Loi.

Article 148:
Si le Président se trouve dans l'impossibilité temporaire d'exercer ses fonctions, le Conseil des Ministres sous le présidence du Premier Ministre, exerce le Pouvoir Exécutif tant que dure l'empêchement.

Article 149:
En cas de vacance de la Présidence de la République pour quelque cause que ce soit, le Président de la Cour de Cassation de la République ou, à son défaut, le Vice-Président de cette Cour ou à défaut de celui-ci, le juge le plus ancien et ainsi de suite par ordre d'ancienneté, est investi provisoirement de la fonction de Président de

la République par l'Assemblée Nationale dûment convoquée par le Premier Ministre. Le scrutin pour l'élection du nouveau Président pour un nouveau mandat de cinq (5) ans a lieu quarante-cinq (45) jours au moins et quatre-vingt-dix (90) jours au plus après l'ouverture de la vacance, conformément à la Constitution et à la Loi Electorale.

Article 149-1:
Ce Président Provisoire ne peut en aucun cas se porter candidat à la plus prochaine élection présidentielle.

Article 150:
Le Président de la République n'a d'autres pouvoirs que ceux que lui attribue la Constitution.

Article 151:
A l'ouverture de la Première Session Législative annuelle, le Président de la République, par un Message au Corps Législatif, fait l'Exposé Général de la situation. Cet Exposé ne donne lieu à aucun débat.

Article 152:
Le Président de la République reçoit du Trésor Public une indemnité mensuelle à partir de sa Prestation de Serment.

Article 153:
Le Président de la République a sa résidence officielle au Palais National, à la Capitale, sauf en cas de déplacement du siège du Pouvoir Exécutif.

Article 154:
Le Président de la République préside le Conseil des Ministres.

SECTION C

Du Gouvernement

Article 155:
Le Gouvernement se compose du Premier Ministre, des Ministres et des Secrétaires d'Etat. Le Premier Ministre est le Chef du Gouvernement.

Article 156:
Le Gouvernement conduit la politique de la Nation. Il est responsable devant le Parlement dans les conditions prévues par la Constitution.

Article 157:
Pour être nommé Premier Ministre, il faut:
1) Etre Haïtien d'Origine et n'avoir jamais renoncé à sa Nationalité;

2) Etre âgé de trente (30) ans accomplis;

3) Jouir de ses Droits Civils et Politiques et n'avoir jamais été condamné à une peine afflictive et infamante;

4) Etre propriétaire en Haïti ou y exercer une profession;

5) Résider dans le Pays depuis cinq (5) années consécutives;

6) Avoir reçu décharge de sa gestion si on a été comptable des deniers publics.

SECTION D

Des Attributions du Premier Ministre

Article 158:
Le Premier Ministre en accord avec le Président choisit les Membres de son Cabinet Ministériel et se présente devant le Parlement afin d'obtenir un vote de confiance sur sa déclaration de politique générale. Le vote a lieu au scrutin public et à la majorité absolue de chacune des deux (2) Chambres.

Dans le cas d'un vote de non confiance par l'une des deux (2) Chambres, la procédure recommence.

Article 159:
Le Premier Ministre fait exécuter les Lois. En cas d'absence, d'empêchement temporaire du Président de la République ou sur sa demande, le Premier Ministre préside le Conseil des Ministres. Il a le pouvoir réglementaire, mais il ne peut jamais suspendre, ni interpréter les Lois, Actes et Décrets, ni se dispenser de les exécuter.

Article 159-1:
De concert avec le Président de la République, il est responsable de la Défense Nationale.

Article 160:
Le Premier Ministre nomme et révoque directement ou par délégation les fonctionnaires publics selon les conditions prévues par la Constitution et par la Loi sur le statut général de la Fonction Publique.

Article 161:
Le Premier Ministre et les Ministres ont leurs entrées aux Chambres pour soutenir les Projets de Lois et les objections du Président de la République ainsi que pour répondre aux interpellations.

Article 162:
Les actes du Premier Ministre sont contresignés, le cas échéant par les Ministres chargés de leurs exécutions. Le Premier Ministre peut être chargé d'un portefeuille ministériel.

Article 163:
Le Premier Ministre et les Ministres sont responsables solidairement tant des actes du Président de la République qu'ils contresignent que de ceux de leurs Ministères. Ils sont également responsables de l'exécution des Lois, chacun en ce qui le concerne.

Article 164:
La fonction de Premier Ministre et celle de Membre du Gouvernement sont incompatibles avec mandat parlementaire. Dans un tel cas, le parlementaire opte pour l'une ou l'autre fonction.

Article 165:
En cas de démission du Premier Ministre, Le Gouvernement reste en place jusqu'à la nomination de son successeur pour expédier les affaires courantes.

SECTION E

Des Ministres et des Secrétaires d'Etat

Article 166:
Le Président de la République préside le Conseil des Ministres. Le nombre de ceux-ci ne peut être inférieur à dix (10).

Le Premier Ministre quand il le juge nécessaire adjoindra aux Ministres, des Secrétaires d'Etat.

Article 167:
La Loi fixe le nombre des Minitères.

Article 168:
La Fonction Ministérielle est incompatible avec l'exercice de tous autres emplois publics, sauf ceux de l'enseignement Supérieur.

Article 169:
Les Ministres sont responsables des actes du Premier Ministre qu'ils contresignent. Ils sont solidairement responsables de l'exécution des Lois.

Article 169-1:
En aucun cas, l'ordre écrit ou verbal du Président de la République ou du Premier Ministre ne peut soustraire les Ministres à la responsabilité attachée à leurs fonctions.

Article 170:
Le Premier Ministre, les Ministres et les Secrétaires d'Etat perçoivent des indemnités mensuelles établies par la Loi Budgétaire.

Article 171:
Les Ministres nomment certaines catégories d'agents de la Fonction Publique par délégation du Premier Ministre, selon les conditions fixées par la Loi sur la Fonction Publique.

Article 172:
Lorsque l'une des deux (2) Chambres, à l'occasion d'une interpellation met en cause la responsabilité d'un Ministre par un vote de censure

pris à la majorité absolue de ses Membres, l'Executif renvoie le Ministre.

CHAPITRE IV

Du Pouvoir Judiciaire

Article 173:
Le Pouvoir Judiciaire est exercé par la Cour de Cassation, les Cours d'Appel, les Tribunaux de Première Instance, les Tribunaux de Paix et les Tribunaux Spéciaux dont le nombre, la composition, l'organisation, le fonctionnement et la Juridiction sont fixés par la Loi.

Article 173-1:
Les constetations qui ont pour objet les Droits Civils sont exclusivement du ressort des Tribunaux.

Article 173-2:
Nul Tribunal, nulle Juridiction Contentieuse ne peut être établie qu'en vertu de la Loi. Il ne peut être crée de Tribunal Extraordinaire sous quelque dénomination que ce soit.

Article 174:
Les Juges de la Cour de Cassation et des Cours d'Appel sont nommés pour dix (10) ans. Ceux des Tribunaux de Première Instance le sont pour sept (7) ans. Leur mandat commence à courir à compter de leur prestation de serment.

Article 175:
Les Juges de la Cour de Cassation sont nommés par le Président de la République sur une liste de trois (3) personnes par siège soumise par le Sénat. Ceux de la Cour d'Appel et des Tribunaux de Première Instance le sont sur une liste soumise par l'Assemblée Départementale concernée; les juges de Paix sur une liste préparée par les Assemblées Communales.

Article 176:
La Loi règle les conditions exigibles pour ètre Juge à tous les degrés. Une Ecole de la Magistrature est crée.

Article 177:

Les Juges de la Cour de Cassation, ceux des Cours d'Appel et des Tribunaux de Premiére Instance sont inamovibles. Ils ne peuvent être destitués que pour forfaiture légalement prononcée ou suspendus qu'à la suite d'une inculpation. Ils ne peuvent être l'objet d'affectation nouvelle, sans leur consentement, même en cas de promotion. Il ne peut être mis fin à leur service durant leur mandat qu'en cas d'incapacité physique ou mentale permanente dûment constatée.

Article 178:

La Cour de Cassation ne connait pas du fond des affaires. Néanmoins, en toutes matières autres que celles soumises au Jury lorsque sur un second recours, même sur une exception, une affaire se presentera entre les mêmes parties, la Cour de Cassation admettant le pourvoi, ne prononcera point de renvoi et statuera sur le fond, sections réunies.

Article 178-1:

Cependant, lorsqu'il s'agit de pourvoi contre les Ordonnances de Référé, les Ordonnances du Juge d'Instruction, les Arrêts d'Appel rendus à l'occasion de ces Ordonnances ou contre les sentences en dernier ressort des Tribunaux de Paix ou des décisions de Tribunaux Spéciaux, la Cour de Cassation admettant les recours statue sans renvoie.

Article 179:

Les fonctions de Juge sont incompatibles avec toutes autres fonctions salariées, sauf celle de l'Enseignement.

Article 180:

Les audiences des Tribunaux sont publiques. Toutefois, elles peuvent être tenues à huis clos dans l'intérêt de l'odre public et des bonnes moeurs sur décision du Tribunal.

Article 180-1:

En matière de délit politique et de délit de presse, le huis clos ne peut être prononcé.

Article 181:

Tout Arrêt ou Jugement est motivé et prononcé en audience publique.

Article 181-1:
Les Arrêts ou Jugements sont rendus et exécutés au nom de la République. Il portent le mandement exécutoire aux Officiers du Ministère Public et aux Agents de la Force Publique. Les actes des Notaires susceptibles d'execution forcée sont mis dans la même forme.

Article 182:
La Cour de Cassation se prononce sur les conflits d'attributions, d'après le mode réglé par la Loi.

Article 182-1:
Elle connait des faits et du droit dans tous les cas de décisions rendues par les Tribunaux Militaires.

Article 183:
La Cour de Cassation à l'occasion d'un litige et sur le renvoi qui lui en est fait, se prononce en Sections Réunies sur l'inconstitutionnalité des Lois.

Article 183-1:
L'interprétation d'une Loi donnée par les Chambres Législatives s'impose pour l'objet de cette Loi, sans qu'elle puisse rétroagir en ravissant des droits acquis.

Article 183-2:
Les Tribunaux n'appliquent les Arrêtés et les Réglements d'Administration Publique que pour autant qu'ils sont conformes aux Lois.

Article 184:
La Loi détermine les compétences des Cours et Tribunaux, régle la façon de procéder devant eux.

Article 184-1:
Elle prévoit également les sactions disciplinaires à prendre contre les Juges et les Officiers du Ministère Public, à l'exception des Juges de la Cour de Cassation qui sont justiciables de la Haute Cour de Justice pour forfaiture.

CHAPITRE V

De la Haute Cour de Justice

Article 185:
Le Sénat peut s'ériger en Haute Cour de Justice. Les Travaux de cette Cour sont dirigés par le Président du Sénat assisté du Président et du Vice-Président de la Cour de Cassation comme Vice-Président et Secrétaire, respectivement sauf si des Juges de la Cour de Cassation ou des Officiers du Ministère Public près cette Cour sont impliqués dans l'accusation, auquel cas, le Président du Sénat se fera assister de deux (2) Sénateurs dont l'un sera désigné par l'inculpé et les Sénateurs sus-visés n'ont pas voix délibérative.

Article 186:
La Chambre des Députés, à la majorité des deux tiers (2/3) de ses Membres, prononce la mise en accusation:

a) Du Président de la République pur crime de haute trahison ou tout autre crime ou délit commis dans l'exercice de ses fonctions;

b) Du Premier Ministre, des Ministres et des Secrétaires d'Etat pour crimes de haute Trahison et de malversations ou d'excès de Pouvoir ou tous autres crimes ou délits commis dans l'exercice de leurs fonctions.

c) Des Membres du Conseil Electoral Permanent et de la Cour Supérieure des Comptes et du Contentieux Administratif pour fautes graves commises dans l'exercice de leurs fonctions;

d) Des Juges et Officiers du Ministère Public près la Cour de Cassation pour forfaiture;

e) Du Protecteur du citoyen.

Article 187:
Les Membres de la Haute Cour de Justice prêtent individuellement et à l'ouverture de l'audience, le serment suivant:

"Je jure devant Dieu et devant la Nation de juger avec l'impartialité et la fermeté qui conviennent 'un homme probe et libre suivant ma conscience et mon intime conviction."

Article 188:
La Haute Cour de Justice, au scrutin secret et à la majorité absolue, désigne parmi ses Membres, une Commission chargée de l'instruction.

Article 188-1:
La décision sous forme de décret est rendue sur le rapport de la commission d'Instruction et à la majorité des deux tiers (2/3) des membres de la Haute Cour de Justice.

Article 189:
La Haute Cour de Justice ne siège qu'à la majorité des deux tiers (2/3) de ses Membres.

Article 189-1:
Elle ne peut prononcer d'autre peine que la destitution, la déchéance et la privation du droit d'exercer toute Fonction Publique durant cinq (5) ans au moins et quinze (15) ans au plus.

Article 189-2:
Toutefois, le condamné peut être traduit devant les Tribunaux Ordinaires, conformément à la Loi, s'il y a lieu d'appliquer d'autres peines ou de statuer sur l'exercice de l'action civile.

Article 190:
La Haute Cour de Justice, une fois saisie, doit siéger jusqu'au prononcé de la décision, sans tenir compte de la durée des Sessions du Corps Législatif.

TITRE VI

Des Institutions Indépendantes

CHAPITRE I

Du Conseil Electoral Permanent

Article 191:
Le Conseil Electoral Permanent est chargé d'organiser et de contrôler en toute indépendance, toutes les opérations électorales sur tout le Territoire de la République jusqu'à la proclamation des résultats du scrutin.

Article 191-1:
Il élabore également le Projet de Loi Electorale qu'il soumet au Pouvoir Exécutif pour les suites nécessaires.

Article 191-2:
Il assure de la tenue à jour des listes électorales.

Article 192:
Le Conseil Electoral Permanent comprend neuf (9) Membres choisis sur une liste de trois (3) noms proposés par chacun des Assemblées Départementales:

3 sont choisis par le Pouvoir Exécutif;
3 sont choisis par la cour de Cassation;
3 sont choisis par l'Assemblée National.

Les Organes sus-cités veillent, autant que possible à ce que chacun des Départements soit représenté.

Article 193:
Pour être Membre du Conseil Electoral Permanent, il faut:

1) Etre Haitien d'Origine;

2) Etre âgé au moins de quarante (40) ans révolus;

3) Jouir de ses Droits Civils et Politiques et n'avoir jamais été condamné à une peine afflictive et infamante;

4) Avoir reçu décharge de sa gestion si on a été comptable de deniers publics;

5) Avoir résidé dans le Pays au moins trois (3) ans avant sa nomination.

Article 194:
Les Membres du Conseil Electoral Permanent sont nommés pour une Période de neuf (9) ans non renouvelable. Ils sont inamovibles.

Article 194-1:
Le Conseil Electoral Permanent est renouvable par tiers tous les trois (3) ans. Le Président est choisi parmi les Membres.

Article 194-2:
Avant d'entrer en fonction, les Membres du Conseil Electoral Permanent prêtent le serment suivant devant la Cour de Cassation:

"Je jure de respecter la Constitution et les dispositions de la Loi Electorale et de m'acquitter de ma tâche avec dignité, indépendance, impartialité et patriotisme."

Article 195:
En cas de faute grave commise dans l'exercice de leur fonction, les Membres du Conseil Electoral Permanent sont passibles de la Haute Cour de Justice.

Article 195-1:
Le siège du Conseil Electoral Permanent se trouve à la Capitale. Sa juridiction s'etend sur tout le Territoire de la République.

Article 196:
Les Membres du Conseil Electoral Permanent ne peuvent occuper aucune fonction publique, ni se porter candidat à une fonction élective pendant toute la durée de leur mandat.

En cas de démission, tout Membre du Conseil doit attendre trois (3) ans avant de pouvoir briguer une fonction élective.

Article 197:
Le Conseil Electoral Permanent est le Contentieux de toutes les contestations soulevées à l'occasion soit des élections, soit de l'application ou de la violation de la Loi Electorale, sous réserve de toute poursuite légale à entreprendre contre le ou les coupables par devant les Tribunaux Compétents.

Article 198:
En cas de vacance créée par décès, démission ou toute autre cause, il est pourvu au remplacement du Membre, suivant la procédure fixée par l'Article 192 pour le temps qui reste à courir, compte tenu du Pouvoir qui avait désigné le Membre à remplacer.

Article 199:
La loi détermine les règles d'organisation et de Fonctionnement du Conseil Electoral Permanent.

CHAPITRE II

De la Cour Supérieure des Comptes et du Contentieux Administratif

Article 200:
La Cour Supérieure des Comptes et du Contentieux Administratif est une Juridiction financière, administrative, indépendante et autonome. Elle est chargée du contrôle administratif et juridictionnel des recettes et des dépenses de l'Etat, de la vérification de la Comptabilité des Entreprises d'Etat ainsi que de celles des collectivités territoriales.

Article 200-1:
La Cour Supérieure des Comptes et du Contentieux Administratif connait des litiges mettant en cause l'Etat et les Collectivités Territoriales, l'Administration et les Fonctionnaires Publics, les Services Publics et les Administrés.

Article 200-2:
Ses décisions ne sont susceptibles d'aucun recours, sauf le pourvoi en Cassation.

Article 200-3:

La Cour Supérieure des Comptes et du Contentieux Administratif comprend deux (2) Sections:

1) La Section du Contrôle Financier;
2) La Section du Contentieux Administratif.

Article 200-4:

La Cour Supérieure des Comptes et du Contentieux Administratif participe à l'élaboration du Budget et est consultée sur toutes les questions relatives à la Législation sur les Finances Publiques ainsi que sur tous les Projets de Contrats, Accords et Conventions à caractère Financier ou Commercial auxquels l'Etat est partie. Elle a le droit de réaliser les audits dans toutes les Administrations Publiques.

Article 200-5:

Pour être Membre de la Cour Supérieure des Comptes et du Contentieux Administratif il faut:

a) Etre Haitien et n'avoir jamais renoncé à sa Nationalité;

b) Etre âgé de trente-cinq (35) ans accomplis;

c) Avoir reçu décharge de sa gestion lorqu'on a été comptable de deniers publics;

d) Etre licencié en droit ou être comptable agréé ou détenteur d'un diplôme d'Etudes Supérieures d'Administration Publique, d'Economie ou de Finances Publiques;

e) Avoir une expérience de cinq (5) années dans une Administration Publique ou Privée;

f) Jouir de ses Droits Civils et Politiques.

Article 200-6:

Les candidats à cette fonction font directement le dépôt de leur candidature au Bureau du Sénat de la République. Le Sénat élit les dix (10) Membres de la Cour, qui parmi eux désignent leurs Président et Vice-Président.

Article 201:
Ils sont investis d'un (1) mandat de dix (10) années et sont inamovibles.

Article 202:
Avant d'entrer en fonction, les Membres de la Cour Supérieure des Comptes et du Contentieux Administratif prêtent devant une Section de la Cour de Cassation, le serment suivant:

> "Je jure de respecter la Constitution et les Lois de la République, de remplir mes fonctions avec exactitude et loyauté et de me conduire en tout avec dignité."

Article 203:
Les Membres de la Cour Supérieure des Comptes et du Contentieux Administratif sont justiciables de la Haute Cour de Justice pour les fautes graves commises dans l'exercice de leur fonction.

Article 204:
La Cour Supérieure des Comptes et du Contentieux Administratif fait parvenir chaque année au Corps Législatif dans les trente (30) jours qui suivent l'ouverture de la Première Session Législative, un rapport complet sur la situation financière du Pays et sur l'efficacité des dépenses publiques.

Article 205:
L'organisation de la Cour sus-mentionnée, le statut de ses Membres, son mode de fonctionnement sont établis par la Loi.

CHAPITRE III

De la Commission de Conciliation

Article 206:
La Commission de Conciliation est appelée à trancher les differends qui opposent le Pouvoir Exécutif et le Pouvoir Législatif ou les deux (2) branches du Pouvoir Législatif. Elle est formée ainsi qu'il suit:

a) Le Président de la Cour de Cassation - Président;

b) Le Président du Sénat - Vice-Président;
c) Le Président de la Chambre des Députés - Membre
d) Le Président du Conseil Electoral Permanent- Membre;
e) Le Vice-Président du Conseil Electoral Permanent-Membre;
f) Deux (2) Ministres désignés par le Président de la République - Membres.

Article 206-1:
Le mode de fonctionnement de la Commission de Conciliation est déterminé par la Loi.

CHAPITRE IV

De la Protection du Citoyen

Article 207:
Il est crée un office dénomé Office de la Protection du Citoyen dont le but est de protéger tout individu contre toutes les formes d'abus de l'Administration Publique.

Article 207-1:
L'office est dirigé par un citoyen qui porte le titre de Protecteur du Citoyen. Il est choisi par consensus entre le Président de la République, le Président de Sénat et le President de la Chambre des Députés. Il est investi d'un mandat de sept (7) ans, non renouvelable.

Article 207-2:
Son intervention en faveur de tout plaignant se fait sans frais aucun, quelle que soit la juridiction.

Article 207-3:
Une loi fixe les conditions et les réglements de fonctionnement de l'office du Protecteur du Citoyen.

CHAPITRE V

De l'Université - De l'Académie - De la Culture

Article 208:
L'Enseignement Supérieur est libre. Il est dispensé par l'Université d'Etat d'Haiti qui est autonome et par des Ecoles Supérieures Publiques et des Ecoles Supérieures Privées agréées par l'Etat.

Article 209:
L'Etat doit financer le fonctionnement et le développement de l'Université d'Etat d'Haiti et des Ecoles Supérieures Publiques. Leur organisation et leur localisation doivent être envisagées dans une perspective de développement régional.

Article 210:
La création de Centres de Recherches doit être encouragée.

Article 211:
L'autorisation de fonctionner des Universités et des Ecoles Supérieures Privées est subordonnée à l'approbation technique du Conseil de l'Université d'Etat, à une participation majoritaire haitienne au niveau du Capital et du Corps Professoral ainsi qu'à l'obligation d'enseigner notamment en langue officielle du Pays.

Article 211-1:
Les Universités et Ecoles Supérieures Privées et Publiques dispensent un Enseignement Académique et pratique adapté à l'évolution et aux besoins du développement national.

Article 212:
Une Loi Organique réglemente la création, la localisation et le fonctionnement des Universités et des Ecoles Supérieures Publiques et Privées du Pays.

Article 213:
Une Académie Haitienne est instituée en vue de fixer la langue créole et de permettre son développement scientifique et harmonieux.

Article 213-1:
D'autres Académies peuvent être créées.

Article 214:
Le titre de Membre de l'Académie est purement honorifique.

Article 214-1:
La Loi détermine le mode d'organisation et de fonctionnement des Académies.

Article 215:
Les richesses archéologiques, historiques, culturelles et folkloriques du Pays de même que les richesses architecturales, témoin de la grandeur de notre passé, font partie du Patrimoine Nationale.

En conséquence, les monuments, les ruines, les sites des grands faits d'armes de nos ancêtres, les centres réputés de nos croyances africaines et tous les vestiges du passé sont placés sous la protection de l'Etat.

Article 216:
La Loi détermine pour chaque domaine les conditions spéciales de cette protection.

TITRE VII

Des Finances Publiques

Article 217:
Les Finances de la République sont décentralisées. La gestion en est assurée par le Ministère y afférent. L'Exécutif assisté d'un Conseil Interdépartemental élabore la Loi qui fixe la portion et la nature des revenus publics attribués aux Collectivités Territoriales.

Article 218:
Aucun impôt au profit de l'Etat ne peut être établi que par une Loi. Aucune charge, aucune imposition soit Départementale, soit Municipale, soit de Section Communale, ne peut être établie qu'avec le consentement de ces Collectivités Territoriales.

Article 219:
Il ne peut être établi de privilège en matière d'impôts.

Aucune exception, aucune augmentation, diminution ou suppression d'impôt ne peut être établie que par la Loi.

Article 220:
Aucune pension, aucune gratification, aucune allocation, aucune subvention, à la charge du Trésor Public, ne peut être accordée qu'en vertu d'une Loi. Les pensions versées par l'Etat sont indexées sur le coût de la vie.

Article 221:
Le cumul des fonctions publiques salariées par l'Etat est formellement interdit, excepté par celles de l'Enseignement, sous réserve des dispositions particulières.

Article 222:
Les procédures relatives à la préparation du Budget et à son Exécution sont déterminées par la Loi.

Article 223:
Le contrôle de l'exécution de la Loi sur le Budget et sur la comptabilité Publique est assuré par la Cour Supérieure des Comptes et du Contentieux Administratif et par l'Office du Budget.

Article 224:
La Politique Monétaire Nationale est déterminée par la Banque Centrale conjointement avec le Ministère de l'Economie et des Finances.

Article 225:
Un Organisme public Autonome jouissant de la personalité juridique et de l'autonomie financière remplit les fonctions de Banque Centrale. Son statut est déterminé par la Loi.

Article 226:
La Banque Centrale est investie du privilège exclusif d'émettre avec force libératoire sur tout le Territoire de la République, des billets représentatifs de l'Unité Monétaire, la monnaie divisionnaire, selon le titre, le poids, la description, le chiffre et l'emploi fixés par la Loi.

Article 227:
Le Budget de chaque Ministère est divisé en Chapitres et Sections et doit être voté Article par Article.

Article 227-1:
Les valeurs à tirer sur les allocations budgétaires ne pourront en aucun cas dépasser le douzième de la dotation pour un mois déterminé, sauf en Décembre à cause du bonus à verser à tous Fonctionnaires et Employés Publics.

Article 227-2:
Les Comptes Généraux des recettes et des dépenses de la République sont gérés par le Ministre des Finances selon un mode de Comptabilité établi par la Loi.

Article 227-3:
Les Comptes Généraux et les Budgets prescrits par l'article précédent, accompagnés du rapport de la Cour Supérieure des Comptes et du Contentieux Administratif doivent être soumis aux Chambres Leegislatives par le Ministre des Finances au plus tard dans les quinze (15) jours de l'ouverture de la Session Législative.

Il en est de même du bilan annuel et des opérations de la Banque Centrale, ainsi que de tous autres comptes de l'Etat Haitien.

Article 227-4:
L'Exercice Administratif commence le premier Octobre de chaque année et finit le trente (30) Septembre de l'année suivante.

Article 228:
Chaque année, le Corps Législatif arrête:

a) Le Compte des recettes et des dépenses de l'Etat pour l'année écoulée ou les années précédentes;

b) Le Budget Général de l'Etat contenent l'aper'cu et la portion des fonds alloués pour l'année à chaque Ministère.

Article 228-1:
Toutefois, aucune proposition, aucun amendement ne peut être introduit au Budget à l'occasion du vote de celui-ci sans la prévision correspondante des voies et moyens.

Article 228-2:
Aucune augmentation, aucune réduction ne peut être apportée aux appointements des fonctionnaires publics que par une modification des Lois y afférentes.

Article 229:
Les Chambres Législatives peuvent s'abstenir de tous Travaux Législatifs tant que les documents sus-visés ne leur sont pas présentés. Elles refusent la décharge aux Ministres lorsque les comptes présentés ne fournissent pas par eux-mêmes ou les pièces à l'appui, les éléments de vérification et d'appréciation nécessaires.

Article 230:
L'examen et la liquidation des Comptes de l'Administration Générale et de tout Comptable de deniers publics se font suivant le mode établi par la Loi.

Article 231:
Au cas où les Chambres Législatives pour quelque raison que ce soit, n'arrêtent pas à temps le Budget pour un ou plusieurs Départements Ministèriels avant leur ajournement, le ou les Budgets des Départements intéressés restent en vigueur jusqu'au vote et adoption du nouveau Budget.

Article 231-1:
Au cas où par la faute de l'Exécutif, le Budget de la République n'a pas été voté, le Président de la République convoque immédiatement les Chambres Législatives en Session Extraordinaire à seule fin de voter le Budget de l'Etat.

Article 232:
Les Organismes, les Entreprises Autonomes et les Entités subventionnés par le Trésor Public en totalité ou en partie sont régis par des budgets Spéciaux et des systèmes de traitements et salaires approuvés par le Pouvoir Exécutif.

Article 233:
En vue d'exercer un contrôle sérieux et permanent des dépenses Publiques, il est élu au scrutin secret, au début de chaque Session Ordinaire, une Commission Parlementaire de Quinze (15) Membres dont neuf (9) Députés et six (6) Sénateurs chargée de rapporter sur la gestion des Ministres pour permettre aux deux (2) Assemblées de leur donner décharge.

Cette Commission peut s'adjoindre des Spécialistes pour l'aider dans son contrôle.

TITRE VIII

De la Fonction Publique

Article 234:
L'Administration Publique Haitienne est l'instrument par lequel l'Etat concrétise ses missions et objectifs. Pour garantir sa rentabilité, elle doit être gérée avec honnêteté et efficacité.

Article 235:
Les Fonctionnaires et Employés sont exclusivement au service de l'Etat. Ils sont tenus à l'observance stricte des normes et éthique déterminées par la Loi sur la Fonction Publique.

Article 236:
La Loi fixe l'organisation des diverses structures de l'Administration et précise leurs conditions de fonctionnement.

Article 236-1:
La Loi règlemente la Fonction Publique sur la base de l'aptitude, du mérite et de la discipline. Elle garantit la sécurité de l'emploi.

Article 236-2:
La Fonction Publique est une carrière. Aucun fonctionnaire ne peut être engagé que par voie de concours ou autres conditions prescrites par la Constitution et par la Loi, ni être révoqué que pou des causes spécifiquement déterminées par Loi. Cette révocation doit être prononcée dans tous les cas par le Contentieux Administratif.

Article 237:
Les Fonctionnaires de carrière n'appartiennent pas à un service public déterminé mais à la Fonction Publique qui les met à la disposition des divers Organismes de l'Etat.

Article 238:
Les Fonctionnaires indiqués par la Loi sont tenus de déclarer l'état de leur patrimoine au Greffe du Tribunal Civil dans les trente (30) jours qui suivent leur entrée en fonction. Le Commissaire du Gouvernement doit prendre toutes les mesures qu'il juge nécessaires pour vérifier l'exactitude de la déclaration.

Article 239:
Les Fonctionnaires et Employés Publics peuvent s'associer pour défendre leurs droits dans les conditions prévues par la Loi.

Article 240:
Les Fonctions ou Charges POlitiques ne donnent pas ouverture à la carrière administrative, notamment les fonctions de Ministre et de Secrétaire d'Etat, d'Officier du Ministère Public, de Délégué et de Vice-Délégué, d'Ambassadeur, de Secrétaire Privé du Président de la République, de Membre de Cabinet de Ministre, de Directeur Général de Département Ministèriel ou d'Organisme Autonome, de Membres de Conseil d'Administration.

Article 241:
La Loi sactionne les infractions contre le fisc et l'enrichissement illicite. Les Fonctionnaires qui ont connaissance de tels faits ont pour devoir de les signaler à l'Autorité Compétente.

Article 242:
L'enrichissement illicite peut être établi par tous les modes de preuves, notamment par présomption de la disproportion marquée entre les moyens du fonctionnaire acquis depuis son entrée en fonction et le montant accumulé du Traitement ou des Emoluments auxquels lui a donné droit la charge occupée.

Article 243:
Le Fonctionnaire coupable des délits sus-désignés ne peut bénéficier que de la prescription vicennale. Cette prescription ne commence à

courir qu'à partir de la cessation de ses fonctions ou des causes qui auraient empêché toute poursuite.

Article 244:
L'Etat a pour devoir d'éviter les grandes disparités d'appointements dans l'Administration Publique.

TITRE IX

CHAPITRE I

De l'Economie - De l'Agriculture

Article 245:
La liberté économique est garantie tant qu'elle ne s'oppose pas à l'intérêt social. L'Etat protège l'entreprise privée et vise à ce qu'elle se développe dans les conditions nécessaires à l'accroissement de la richesse nationale de manière à assurer la participation du plus grand nombre au bénéfice de cette richesse.

Article 246:
L'Etat encourage en milieu rural et urbain, la formation de coopérative de production, la transformation de produits primaires et l'esprit d'entreprise en vue de promouvoir l'accumulation du Capital National pour assurer la permanence du développement.

Article 247:
L'Agriculture, source principale de la richesse nationale, est garantie du bien-être des populations et du progrès socio-économique de la Nation.

Article 248:
Il est créé un Organisme Spécial dénommé: Institut National de la Réforme Agraire en vue d'organiser la refonte des structures foncières et de mettre en oeuvre une réforme agraire au bénéfice des réels exploitants de la terre. Cet Institut élabore une politique agraire axée sur l'optimisation de la productivité au moyen de la mise en place d'infrastructure visant la protection et l'aménagement de la terre.

Article 248-1:
La Loi détermine la superficie minimale et maximale des unités de base des exploitations agricoles.

Article 249:
L'Etat a pour obligation d'établir les structures nécessaires pour assurer la productivité maximale de la terre et la commercialisation interne des denrées. Des unités d'encadrement technique et financières sont établies pour assister les agriculteurs au niveau de chaque Section Communale.

Article 250:
Aucun monopole ne peut être établi en faveur de l'Etat et des Collectivités Territoriales que dans l'intérêt exclusif de la Société. Ce monopole ne peut être cédé à un particulier.

Article 251:
L'importation des denrées agricoles et de leurs dérivés produits, en quantité suffisante sur le Territoire Nationale est interdite, sauf cas de force majeure.

Article 252:
L'Etat peut prendre en charge le fonctionnement des Entreprises de production, de biens et des services essentiels à la Communauté, aux fins d'en assurer la continuité dans le cas où l'existence de ces Etablissements serait menacée. Ces Entreprises seront groupées dans un système intégré de gestion.

CHAPITRE II

De l'Environnement

Article 253:
L'Environnement étant le cadre naturel de vie de la Population, les pratiques susceptibles de pertuber l'équilibre écologique sont formellement interdites.

Article 254:
L'Etat organise la mise en valeur des sites naturels en assure la protection et les rend accessible à tous.

Article 255:
Pour protéger les réserves forestières et élargir la couverture végétale, l'Etat encourage le développement des formes d'énergie propre: solaire, éolienne et autres.

Article 256:
Dans le cadre de la protection de l'Environnement et de l'Education Publique, l'Etat a pour obligation de procéder à la création et à l'entretien de jardins et zoologiques en certains points du Territoire.

Article 257:
La Loi détermine les conditions de protection de la faune et de la flore. Elle sanctionne les contrevenants.

Article 258:
Nul ne peut introduire dans le Pays des déchets ou résidus de provenances étrangères de quelque nature que ce soit.

TITRE X

De la Famille

Article 259:
L'Etat protège la Famille base fondamentale de la Société.

Article 260:
Il doit une égale protection à toutes les Familles qu'elles soient constituées ou non dans les liens du mariage. Il doit procurer aide et assistance à la maternité, à l'enfance et à la vieillesse.

Article 261:
La Loi assure la protection à tous les Enfants. Tout enfant a droit à l'amour, à l'affection, à la compréhension et aux soins moraux et matèriels de son père et de sa mère.

Article 262:
Un Code de la Famille doit être élaboré en vue d'assurer la protection et le respect des droits de la Famille et de définir les formes de la recherche de la paternité. Les Tribunaux et autres Organismes de l'Etat chargés de la protection de ces droits doivent être accessibles gratuitement au niveau de la plus petite Collectivité Territoriale.

TITRE XI

De la Force Publique

Article 263:
La Force Publique se compose de deux (2) Corps distincts:

a)   Les Forces Armées d'Haïti;
b)   Les Forces de Police.

Article 263-1:
Aucun autre Corps Armé ne peut exister sur le Territoire Nationale.

Article 263-2:
Tout Membre de la Force Publique prête lors de son engagement, le serment d'allégeance et de respect à la Constitution et au Drapeau.

CHAPITRE I

Des Forces Armées

Article 264:
Les Forces Armées comprennent les Forces de Terre, de Mer, de l'Air et les Services Techniques.

Les Forces Armées d'Haïti sont instituées pour garantir la sécurité et l'intégrité du Territoire de la République.

Article 264-1:
Les Forces Armées sont commandées effectivement par un officier Général ayant pour titre Commandant en Chef des Forces Armées d'Haïti.

Article 264-2:
Le Commandant en Chef des Forces Armées, conformément à la Constitution, est choisi parmi les Officiers Généraux en activité de Service.

Article 264-3:
Son mandat est fixé à trois (3) ans. Il est renouvelable.

Article 265:
Les Forces Armées sont apolitiques. Leurs Membres ne peuvent faire partie d'un groupement ou d'un parti politique et doivent observer la plus stricte neutralité.

Article 265-1:
Les Membres des Forces Armées exercent leur droit de vote, conformément à la Constitution.

Article 266:
Les Forces Armées ont pour attributions:

a) Défendre le Pays en cas de guerre;

b) Protéger le Pays contre les menaces venant de l'extérieur;

c) Assurer la surveillance des Frontières Terrestres, Maritimes et Aériennes;

d) Prêter main forte sur requête motivée de l'Exécutif, à la Police au cas où cette dernière ne peut répondre à sa tâche.

e) Aider la Nation en cas de désastre naturel.

f) Outre les attributions qui lui sont propres, les Forces Armées peuvent être affectées à des tâches de développement.

Article 267:
Les Militaires en activité de Service ne peuvent être nommés à aucune Fonction Publique, sauf de fa'con temporaire pour exercer une spécialité.

Article 267-1:
Tout Militaire en activité de Service, pour se porter candidat à une fonction élective, doit obtenir sa mise en disponibilité ou sa mise à la retraite un (1) an en avant la parution du Décret Electoral.

Article 267-2:
La carrière militaire est une profession. Elle est hiérarchisée. Les conditions d'engagement, les grades, promotions, révocations, mises à la retraite, sont déterminées par les règlements des Forces Armées d'Haïti.

Article 267-3:
Le Militaire n'est justiciable d'une Cour Militaire que pour les délits et crimes commis en temps de guerre ou pour les infractions relevant de la discipline militaire.

Il ne peut être l'objet d'aucune reevocation, mise en disponibilitee, à la réforme, à la retraite anticipée qu'avec son consentement. Au cas où ce consentement n'est pas accordé, l'intéressé peut se pourvoir par devant le Tribunal Compétent.

Article 267-4:
Le Militaire conserve toute sa vie, le dernier grade obtenu dans les Forces Armées d'Haïti. Il ne peut en être privee que par décision du Tribunal Compétent passée en force de chose souverainement jugée.

Article 267-5:
L'Etat doit accorder aux Militaires de tous grades des prestations garantissant pleinement leur sécurité matérielle.

Article 268:
Dans le cadre d'un Service National Civique mixte obligatoire, preevu par la Constitution à l'article 52-3, les Forces Armées participent à l'organisation et à la supervision de ce service.

Le Service Militaire est obligatoire pour tous les Haïtiens âgés au moins de dix-huit (18) ans.

La Loi fixe le mode de recrutement, la durée et les règles de fonctionnement de ces services.

Article 268-1:
Tout citoyen a droit à l'auto-défense armée, dans les limites de son domicile mais n'a pas droit au port d'armes sans l'autorisation expresse et motivée du Chef de la Police.

Article 268-2:
La détention d'une arme à feu doit être déclarée à la Police.

Article 268-3:
Les Forces Armées ont le monopole de la fabrication, de l'importation, de l'exportation, de l'utilisation et de la détention des armes de guerre et de leurs munitions, ainsi que du matériel de guerre.

CHAPITRE II

Des Forces de Police

Article 269:
La Police est un Corps Armé. Son fonctionnement relève du Ministère de la Justice.

Article 269-1:
Elle est créée pour la garantie de l'ordre public et la protection de la vie et des biens des citoyens.

Son organisation et son mode de fonctionnement sont réglés par la Loi.

Article 270:
Le Commandant en Chef des Forces de Police est nommé conformément à la Constitution, pour un mandat de trois (3) ans renouvelable.

Article 271:
Il est créé une (1) Académie et une (1) Ecole de Police dont l'organisation et le fonctionnement sont fixés par la Loi.

Article 272:
Des Sections spécialisées notamment l'Administration Pénitenciaire, le Service des Pompiers, le Service de la Circulation, la Police Routière, les Recherches Criminelles, le Service Narcotique et Anti-Contrebande... sont créés par la Loi régissant l'Organisation, le Fonctionnement et la Localisation des Forces de Police.

Article 273:
La Police en tant qu'auxiliaire de la Justice, recherche les contraventions, les délits et crimes commis en vue de la découverte et de l'arrestation de leurs auteurs.

Article 274:
Les Agents de la Force Publique dans l'exercice de leurs fonctions sont soumis à la responsabilité civile et pénale dans les formes et conditions prévues par la Constitution et par la Loi.

TITRE XII

Dispositions Générales

Article 275:
Le chômage de l'Administration Publique et Privée et du Commerce sera observé à l'occasion des Fêtes Nationales et des Fêtes Légales.

Article 275-1:
Les Fêtes Nationales sont:

1) La Fête de l'Indépendance Nationale le Premier Janvier;
2) Le Jour des Aieux le 2 Janvier;
3) La Fête de l'Agriculture et du Travail le Premier Mai;
4) La Fête du Drapeau et de l'Université le 18 Mai;
5) La Commémoration de la Bataille de Vertières Jour des Forces Armées, le 18 Novembre.

Article 275-2:
Les Fêtes Légales sont déterminées par la Loi.

Article 276:
L'Assemblée Nationale ne peut ratifier aucun Traité, Convention ou Accord Internationaux comportant des clauses contraires à la présente Constitution.

Article 276-1:
La ratification des Traités, des Conventions et des Accords Internationaux est donnée sous forme de Décret.

Article 276-2:
Les Traités ou Accords Internationaux, une fois sactionnés et ratifiés dans les formes prévues par la Constitution, font partie de la Législation du Pays et abrogent toutes les Lois qui leur sont contraires.

Article 277:
l'Etat Haïtien peut intégrer une Communauté Economique d'Etats dans la mesure où l'Accord d'Association stimule le développement eeconomique et social de la République d'Haïti et ne comporte aucune clause contraire à la Présente Constitution.

Article 278:
Aucune place, aucune partie du Territoire ne peut être déclarée en état de siège qu'en cas de guerre civile ou d'invasion de la part d'une force étrangère.

Article 278-1:
L'acte du Président de la République déclaratif d'état de siège, doit être contresigné par le Premier Ministre, par tous les Ministres et porter convocation immédiate de l'Assemblée Nationale appelée à se prononcer sur l'opportunité de la mesure.

Article 278-2:
L'Assemblée Nationale arrête le Pouvoir Exécutif, les Garanties Constitutionnelles qui peuvent être suspendues dans les parties du Territoire mises en état de siège.

Article 278-3:
L'Etat de siège devient caduc s'il n'est pas renouvelé tous les quinze (15) jours après son entrée en vigueur par un vote de l'Assemblée Nationale.

Article 278-4:
L'Assemblée Nationale siège pendant toute la durée de l'Etat de siège.

Article 279:
Trente (30) jours après son élection, le Preesident de la République doit déposer au greffe du Tribunal de Première Instance de son domicile, l'inventaire notarié de tous ses biens, meubles et immeubles, il en sera de même à la fin de son mandat.

Article 279-1:
Le Premier Ministre, les Ministres et Secrétaires d'Etat sont astreints à la même obligation dans les trente (30) jours de leur installation et de leur sortie de fonction.

Article 280:
Aucun frais, aucune indemnité généralement quelconques n'est accordé aux Membres des Grands Corps de l'Etat à titre des tâches spéciales qui leur sont attribuées.

Article 281:
A l'occasion des consultations nationales. l'Etat prend en charge proportionnellement un nombre de suffrages obtenus, une partie des frais encourus durant les campagnes électorales.

Article 281-1:
Ne sont éligibles à de telles facilités que les partis qui auront au niveau national obtenu dix pour cent (10%) des suffrages exprimés avec un plancher départemental de suffrage de cinq pour cent (5%).

TITRE XIII

Amendements à la Constitution

Article 282:
Le Pouvoir Législatif, sur la proposition de l'une des deux (2) chambres ou du Pouvoir Exécutif, a le droit de déclarer qu'il y a lieu d'amender la Constitution, avec motifs à l'appui.

Article 282-1:
Cette déclaration doit réunir l'adhésion des deux (2/3) tiers de chacune des deux (2) Chambres. Elle ne peut être faite qu'au cours de la dernière Session Ordinaire d'une Législature et est publiée immédiatement sur toute l'étendue du Territoire.

Article 283:
A la première Session de la Législature suivante, les Chambres se réunissent en Assemblée Nationale et statuent sur l'amendement proposé.

Article 284:
L'Assemblée Nationale ne peut siéger, ni délibérer sur l'amendement si les deux (2/3) tiers au moins des Membres de chacune des deux (2) Chambres ne sont présents.

Article 284-1:
Aucune décision de l'Assemblée Nationale ne peut être adoptée qu'à la majorité des deux (2/3) tiers des suffrages exprimés.

Article 284-2:
L'amendement obtenu ne peut entrer en vigueur qu'après l'installation du prochain Président élu. En aucun cas, le Preesident sous le gouvernement de qui l'amendement a eu lieu ne peut bénéficier des avantages qui en découlent.

Article 284-3:
Toute Consultation Populaire tendant à modifier la Constitution par voie de Referendum est formellement interdite.

Article 284-4:
Aucun amendement à la Constitution ne doit porter atteinte au caractère démocratique et républicain de l'Etat.

TITRE XIV

Des Dispositions Transitoires

Article 285:
Le Conseil National de Gouvernement reste et demeure en fonction jusqu'au 7 Février 1988, date d'investiture du Preesident de la République élu sous l'empire de la Présente Constitution, conformément au Calendrier Electoral.

Article 285-1:
Le Conseil National de Gouvernement est autorisé à prendre en Conseil des Ministres, conformément à la Constitution, des décrets ayant force de Loi jusqu'à l'entrée en fonction des députés et Sénateurs élus sous l'empire de la Présente Constitution.

Article 286:
Tout Haïtien qui a adopté une nationalité étrangère durant les vingt-neuf (29) années précédant le 7 Février 1986 peut, par une déclaration faite au Ministère de la Justice dans un délai de deux (2) ans à partir de la publication de la Constitution, recouvrer sa nationalité haïtienne avec les avantages qui en découlent, conformément à la Loi.

Article 287:
Compte tenu de la situation des Haïtiens expatriés volontairement ou involontairement, les délais de résidence prévus dans la Présente Constitution, sont ramenés à une année révolue pour les plus prochaines élections.

Article 288:
A l'occasion de la prochaine Consultation Electorale, les mandats des trois (3) Sénateurs élus pour chaque Département seront établis comme suit:

a) Le Sénateur qui a obtenu le plus grand nombre de voix, bénéficiera d'un (1) mandat de six (6) ans;

b) Le Sénateur qui vient en seconde place en ce qui a trait au nombre de voix, sera investi d'un (1) mandat de quatre (4) ans;

c) Le troisième Sénateur sera élu pour (2) ans.

Dans la suite, chaque Sénateur élu, sera investi d'un (1) mandat de six (6) ans.

Article 289:
En attendant l'établissement du Conseil Electoral Permanent prévu dans la Présente Constitution, le Conseil National de Gouverneement forme un Conseil Electoral Provisoire de neuf (9) Membres, chargé de l'exécution et de l'élaboration de la Loi Electorale devant régir les prochaines élections et désigné de la façon suivante:

1) Un par l'Exécutif, non fonctionnaire;

2) Un par la Conférence Episcopale;

3) Un par le Conseil Consultatif;

4) Un par la Cour de Cassation;

5) Un par les Organismes de Défense des Droits Humains, ne participant pas aux compétitions électorales;

6) Un par le Conseil de l'Université;

7) Un par l'Association des Journalistes;

8) Un par les Cultes Réformés;

9) Un par le Conseil National des Coopératives.

Article 289-1:
Dans la quinzaine qui suivra la ratification de la Présente Constitution, les Corps ou Organisations concernés font parvenir à l'Exécutif le nom de leur représentant.

Article 289-2:
En cas d'abstention d'un Corps ou Organisation susvisé, l'Exécutif comble la ou les vacances.

Article 289-3:
La mission de ce Conseil Electoral Provisoire prend fin dès l'entrée en fonction du Président élu.

Article 290:
Les Membres du Premier Conseil Electoral Permanent se départagent par tirage au sort les mandats de neuf (9), six (6) et trois (3) ans, prévus pour le renouvellement par tiers (1/3) du Conseil.

Article 291:
Ne pourra briguer aucune fonction publique durant les dix (10) années qui suivront la publication de la Présente Constitution et cela sans préjudice des actions pénales ou en réparation civile:

a) Toute personne notoirement connue pour avoir été par ses excès de zèle un des artisans de la dictature et de son maintien durant les vingt-neuf (29) dernières annés;

b) Tout comptable des deniers publics durant les années de la dictature sur qui plane une présomption d'enrichissement illicite;

c) Toute personne dénoncée par la clameur publique pour avoir pratiqué la torture sur les prisoniers politiques, à l'occasion des arrestations et des enquêtes ou d'avoir commis des assassinats politiques.

Article 292:
Le Conseil Electoral Provisoire chargé de recevoir les dépôts de candidature, veille 'a la stricte application de cette disposition.

Article 293:
Tous les Décrets d'expropriation de biens immobiliers dans les zones urbaines et rurales de la Republique des deux (2) derniers Gouvernement Haïtiens au profit de l'Etat ou des sociétés en formation sont annulés si le but pour lequel ils ont été pris, n'a pas été exécuté au cours des dix (10) dernières années.

Article 293-1:
Tout individu victime de confiscation de biens ou de dépossession arbitraire pour raison politique, durant la période s'étendant du 22 Octobre 1957 au 7 Février 1986 peut récupérer ses biens devant le Tribunal compétent.

Dans ce cas, la procédure est accélérée comme pour les affaires urgentes et la décision n'est susceptible que du pourvoi en Cassation.

Article 294:
Les condamnations à des peines afflictives et infamantes pour des raisons politiques de 1957 à 1986, n'engendrent aucun empêchement à l'exercice des Droits Civils et Politiques.

Article 295:
Dans les six (6) mois à partir de l'entrée en fonction du Premier Président élu sous l'empire de la Constitution de 1987, le Pouvoir Exécutif est autorisé à procéder à toutes réformes jugées nécessaires dans l'Administration Publique en général et dans la Magistrature.

TITRE XV

Dispositions Finales

Articles 296:
Tous les Codes de Lois ou Manuels de Justice, toutes les Lois, tous les Décrets-Lois et tous les Décrets et Arrêtés actuellement en vigueur sont maintenus en tout ce qui n'est pas contraire à la présente Constitution.

Article 297:
Toutes les Lois, tous les Décrets-Lois, tous les Décrets restreignant arbitrairement les droits et libertés fondamentaux des citoyens notamment:

a) Le Décret-Loi du 5 Septembre 1935 sur les croyances superstitieuses;

b) La Loi du 2 Août 1977 instituant le Tribunal de la Sûreté de l'Etat;

c) La Loi du 28 Juillet 1975 soumettant les terres de la Vallée de l'Artibonite à un statut d'exception;

d) La Loi du 29 Avril 1969 condamnant toute doctrine d'importation;

Sont et demeurent abrogés.

Article 298:
La présente Constitution doit être publiée dans la quinzaine de sa ratification par voie référendaire. Elle entre en vigueur dès sa publication au Moniteur, Journal Officiel de la République.

Donné au Palais Législatif, à Port-au-Prince, siège de l'Assemblée Nationale Constituante, le 10 Mars 1987, ân 184ème de l'Indépendance.

Me Emile Jonassaint, président de l'Assemblée Constituante

Me Jean Supplice, Vice-président de l'Assemblée Constituante

Les Secrétaires:

Mme Bathilde Barbancourt
M. Jacques Saint-Louis
Me. Raphaël Michel Adelson

Les Membres:

M. Daniel Anglade
M. Karl Auguste
M. Yvon Auguste
M. Richard Baker
M. Jean Adler Bassin
Me. Fresnel Bélizaire
Me. Rigaud Th. Bois
Me. Nyll Calixte
Me. Hugo Charles
Me. Clavaroche Cherenfant
Me. Alcan Dorméus
Me. Chantal Hudicourt Ewald
Me. Rotchild François
M. Rick Garnier
Me. Reynold Georges
Me. Antoine Gilles
Dr. Georges Greffin
M. Alexis C. Guerrier
M. Louis Dominald Guerrier
M. Apollon Israël
Me. Athanase Jean-Louis
Me. Wilbert Joseph
M. Julio Larosilière
M. Guy Latortue
M. Gérard M. Laurent
M. Lavelanet Lindor
M. Jean Abraham Lubin

Me. Jean Léonidas Lucien
Me. François R. Magloire
Me. Jean Mainville
M. Volvick Mathieu
Me. Justin Mezile
Dr. Georges Michel
Me. Barbantès Moussignac
Me. Justin Obas
Me. Ménès Ovide
Me. Thalès Paul
M. Franck Paulché
M. Pierre Th. Pierre
M. Gustave Pierre-Louis
M. Réginald Riboul
Me. Gérard Romulus
Dr. Louis Roy
M. Gary Sajous
Me. Gracia Saint-Louis
M. Eddy Saint-Pierre
M. Pierre Saint-Rémy
M. Benoit Sanon
Me. Michel Félix Sapini
M. Jacques Séide
Me. Marc Sémervil
M. Jean Edmond Tida
M. Ecclésiaste Valcin
M. Serge Villard

SOURCES

Sources

The following sources were used in compiling this book.

Banque de la République d'Haïti. *Législation des Banques et des Institutions Financières*. B.R.H., Port-au-Prince, Haïti, 1985.

Bernardin, Ernst A. *L'Espace Rural Haïtien*. Editions des Antilles, Port-au-Prince, Haïti, 1991.

Berrou, Raphaël F. and Pradel Pompilus. *Histoire de la Littérature Haïtienne*, 3 vols. Editions Caraïbes, Port-au-Prince, Haïti, 1975, 1977 editions.

Blaustein, Albert P. and Gisbert H. Flanz, eds. *Constitutions of the Countries of the World*. Dobbs Ferry NY: Oceana.

Central Intelligence Agency. *The World Factbook 1991*. Public Affairs Division, Washington, D.C., August 1991.

Corvington, Georges. *Port-au-Prince au cours des Ans. La ville coloniale. 1743 - 1789*. Henri Deschamps, Port-au-Prince, Haïti, 1992 edition.

Delbeau, Colonel Jean-Claude. *Société culture et Médecine populaire traditionnelle*. Henri Deschamps, Port-au-Prince, Haïti, 1990.

Deshommes, Fritz. *Vie Chére*. L'Imprimeur II, Port-au-Prince, Haïti, 1992.

Dorsainvil, Dr. J.C. and F.I.C. *Histoire d'Haïti cours supérieur*. Henri Deschamps, Port-au-Prince, Haïti.

Etienne, Eddy V. *Institutions Financières et Administratives en Haïti*. Editions Etienne, Port-au-Prince, Haïti, 1988.

Etienne, Eddy V. *Monnaie & Banques*. Henri Deschamps, Port-au-Prince, Haïti, 1992.

Etienne, Eddy V. *La vraie dimension de la politique extérieure des premiers Gouvernements D'Haïti (1804-1843).* Editions Naaman, Québec, Canada, 1982.

Fayo. 3333 *Proverbs in Haitian Creole.* Editions Fardin, Port-au-Prince, Haïti.

FIC. *Cours de Géographie. Cours Elémentaire et Moyen.* Henri Deschamps, Port-au-Prince, Haïti, 1973 edition.

Fouchard, Jean. *Regards sur l'histoire.* Henri Deschamps, Port-au-Prince, Haïti, 1988.

Fouchard, Jean. *La Méringue danse nationale d'Haïti.* Henri Deschamps, Port-au-Prince, Haïti, 1988.

Honorat, Jean Jacques. *Haïti: l'Echec.* Le Natal, Port-au-Prince, Haïti, 1991.

Hyppolite, Michelson Paul. *Civilisation Haitienne,* 2 vols. Editions Fardin, Port-au-Prince, Haïti, 1983.

IHSI, Service Prospective et Démo-Economique (DARD).

Institut Haitien de Statistique and Département des Finances et des Affaires Economiques. *Guide Economique de la République D'Haïti.* 1971.

Institut Haïtien de Statistique et d'Informatique. Direction Géneral. Ministère de l'économie et des Finances.

ISPAN. *La Citadelle le palais de Sans Souci le site des Ramiers.* Imprimerie Le Natal, Port-au-Prince, Haïti, 1986.

Jean-Pierre, Jean Reynold. *Histoire D'Haïti Période Nationale, Tome I, Les Heros 1804-1843.* Editions des Antilles, Port-au-Prince, Haïti, 1992.

Jolibois, Gérard. *L'Exécution des Frères Coicou.* Imprimerie Le Natal, Port-au-Prince, Haiti, 1986.

Laguerre, Michel S. *The Complete Haitiana. A Bibliographic Guide to the Scholarly Literature 1900-1980.* Kraus International Publications, New York, 1982.

Lerebours, Michel Philippe. *Haïti et ses Peintres de 1804 à 1980,* 2 vols. L'Imprimeur II, Port-au-Prince, Haïti, 1989.

Lhérisson, Lélia J. *Les Heros de L'Indépendance dans l'histoire d'Haïti.* Port-au-Prince, Haïti, 1904.

Madiou, Thomas. *Histoire d'Haiti.* 8 volumes. Henri Deschamps. Port-au-Prince, Haïti,1989.

Mathon, Alix. *Haiti, un cas.* Le Natal, Port-au-Prince, Haïti, 1985.

Michel, Dr. Georges. *La Constitution de 1987: Souvenirs d'un Constituant.* Le Natal, Port-au-Prince, Haïti, 1992.

Michel, Dr. Georges. *Charlemagne Péralte.* Le Natal, Port-au-Prince, Haïti, 1989.

Milcent, Roger. *RETROSPECTIVE: 7 février 1986 - 7 février 1991: du CNG à Jean Bertrand Aristide.* Le Nouvelliste, No. 33.999 Vendredi 8 au Mercredi 13 Février 1991, p. 6- 10, Port-au-Prince, Haïti.

Milcent, Roger. *RETROSPECTIVE. 1990: Panorama de la vie nationale.* Le Nouvelliste Samedi 29 Décembre au Jeudi 3 Janvier 1991, p. 4-10, Port-au-Prince, Haïti.

Moïse, Claude. *Constitutions et Luttes de Pouvoir en Haïti.* 2 volumes. 1804-1987. Editions du Cidihca, Montréal, Québec, Canada, 1988, 1990.

Nadal, Marie-José and Gérald Bloncourt. *La Peinture Haïtienne/ Haitian Arts.* Nathan, Paris, France, 1989 edition.

Ott, Thomas O. *The Haitian Revolution. 1789 - 1804.* The University of Tennessee Press, Knoxville, 1973.

Prominex Haïti. *Guide de l'Investisseur.* Port-au-Prince, Haïti.

République d'Haïti Gouvernement de Consensus et de salut public. *Le Livre Blanc.* Henri Deschamps, Port-au-Prince, Haïti, 1992.

Revue de la Société Haitienne D'histoire de Géographie et de Géologie. *Bibliographie of Saint-Domingue especially for the period of 1700-1804* by M. W. Shannon. Volume 37, No: 125, Fardin, Port-au-Prince, Haïti, 1979.

Roy Fombrun, Odette. *L'Ayiti des Indiens.* Editions Henri Deschamps, Port-au-Prince, Haïti, 1992.

U.S. Department of Justice. Immigration and Naturalization Service. *Immigration Reform and Control Act. Report on the Legalized Alien Population.* March 1992

Valdman, Albert. *Haitian Creole-English Dictionary.* Indiana University, Creole Institute, Bloomington, 1981.

Wainwright, Joseph. *Agenda information Haïti 1993.* Port-au-Prince, Haïti, 1993.

INDEX

A

Abraham, Herard 57
Acau, Jean-Jacques 39
Administrative Structure of the Republic of Haiti **165**
    Branches of the State 165
    Permanent Electoral Council 167
    Public Forces 167
    Independent Government Agencies 168
Ailhaud 29
Alexis, Nord 44
Ardouin, Beaubrun 41
Aristide, Jean-Bertrand 57,58
Art Center (Centre d'Art) 49
Artists (Noted Haitian) **107**
    Abellard, Gesner 107
    Alix, Gabriel 107
    Allen, Ralph 107
    Ambroise, Jackson 107
    Antoine, Montas 107
    Armand, Gesner 107
    Auguste, Georges 108
    Bazile, Castera 108
    Benoit, Rigaud 108
    Bigaud, Wilson 108
    Blain, Roland 108
    Blaise, Fabolon 108
    Blaise, Saint-Louis 108
    Blaise, Serge Moléon 108
    Bloncourt, Gérald 108
    Booz, Ludovic 109
    Borno, Maurice 109
    Bottex, Jn Baptiste 109
    Bottex, Seymour Etienne 109
    Brésil, Henry-Robert 109
    Brierre, Murat 109
    Byron, Bourmond 109
    Castera, Jean Claude 110
    Cédor, Dieudonné 110
    Chapoteau, Ralf 110
    Chavannes, Etienne 110
    Denis, Villard (Davertige) 110

Desruisseaux, Rose-Marie 110
Dodard, Philippe 110
Dorcély, Roland 111
Dreux, Nicolas 111
Dubic, Abner 111
Ducasse, G. Emmanuel 111
Duffaut, Préfète 111
Duval-Carrié, Edouard 111
Etienne, Franck 103,111
Gabriel, Jacques 111
Garoute, Jean-Claude 112
Gerbier, Max 112
Gourgue, Jacques Enguerrand 112
Fombrun, Gérard 112
Grégoire, Alexandre 112
Hector, Georges P. 113
Hollant, Edith 113
Hyppolite, Hector 113
Jacques, Harry (Arijac) 113
Jean, Eugène 113
Jean, Jean-Baptiste 113
Jean-Louis, Eric 113
Jérôme, Jean-René 114
Joachim, Guy 114
Joseph, Antonio 114
Lamonthe, Gisou 114
Laurenceau, Lionel 114
Laurent, Peterson 114
Lazare, Luckner 115
Legagneur, Jean-Claude 115
Léontus, Adam 115
Liautaud, Georges 115
Louissant, Frank 115
Malbranche, Andrée 115
Malbranche, Elzire 115
Manès, Descollines 116
Mangonès, Albert 116
Manuel, Michèle 116
Mews, Ronald 116
Monosiet, Pierre 116
Mompremier, Madsen 117

Nadal-Gardère, Marie José 112
Normil, André 117
Obas, Charles 117
Obin, Philomé 117
Obin, Sénèque 117
Olivier, Raymond 117
Paquot, Néhémy Jean 113
Paillère, Pierre 117
Paul, Damien 117
Paul, Gérard 117
Philippe-Auguste, Salnave 118
Pierre, André 118
Pierre-Charles, Emmanuel 118
Pierre-Noel, Vergniaud 118
Pinchinat, Max 118
Poisson, Louverture 118
Price, Lucien 119
Remponneau, Georges 119
Rocher, Camy 119
Roy, Alix 119
Saint-Brice, Robert 119
Saint-Éloi, Lyonel 119
Sanon, Roosevelt 119
Savain, Pétion 120
Séjourné, Bernard 120
Sénatus, Jean-Louis 120
Similien, Émilcar 120
Stéphane, Micius 120
Télémaque, Hervé 120
Théard, Jean-Pierre 121
Théard, Karoll 121
Thébaud, Sacha 121
Torchon, Camille 121
Turnier, Luce 121
Valcin, Fravrange 121
Valcin, Gérard 121
Valcin, Pierre-Joseph 121
Vassor, Louis 121
Vilaire, Patrick 122
Vital, Maurice 121

Wah, Bernard 122
Williams, Hilda 122
Avril, Prosper 56
Auguste, Tancrède 45
Augustin, Father Rémy 50

B

Bâle, Treaty of 31
Banks (Major) **157**
    Government Banks 157
    Foreign Commercial Banks 157
    Private Banks 158
    Development Banks 158
    Other Banks 158
Battles
    Crête-à-Pierrot 33
    Pernier 28
    Ravine à Couleuvres 32
    Sibert 35
    Vertières, Battle of 34
Barbancourt, Dupré 4
Bauvais 32
Bazin, Marc Louis 58
Black Code (Code Noir) 26
Boisrond-Canal 42
Boisrond-Tonnerre, Louis 27
Borno, Louis 46
Boukman 28
Boyer, Jean-Pierre 37
Brunier, Charles (Marquis of Larnage) 26

C

Canal, Boisrond 42
Chavannes, Jean-Baptiste 28
Choucoune 43
Christophe, Henri 27,29,60
Constitutions 69

Constitution of the Republic of Haiti   173
Preamble   173
Emblem and Symbols   174
Territory of Haitian Republic   175
Haitian Nationality   176
Basic rights and duties of the citizen/
   Nature of Citizenship   177
Right to Life and Health   178
Individual Liberty   179
Freedom of Expression   181
Freedom of Conscience   182
Freedom of Assembly and Association   182
Education and Teaching   183
Freedom to Work   184
Property   185
Right to Information   187
Right to Security   187
Duties of the Citizen   189
Aliens   190
National Sovereignty   192
Territorial Divisions and Decentralization   193
Communal Sections   193
Communes   194
Arrondisements   196
Departments   196
Delegates and Vice Delegates   198
Interdepartmental Council   198
Legislative Branch   199
House of Deputies   200
Senate   201
National Assembly   201
National Assembly   203
Legislative Power   205
Incompatibilities   212
Executive Branch   213
President of the Republic   213
Duties of the President   215
The Government   218
Powers of the Prime Minister   219
Ministers and Secretaries of State   220
The Judiciary   221

High Court of Justice 224

Independent Institutions/Permanent
  Electoral Council 226

Superior Court of Auditors and
  Administrative Disputes 229

Conciliation Commission 231

Protection of Citizens 232

The University-Academy-Culture 232

Public Finance 234

Civil Service 237

Economics and Agriculture 239

Environment 241

Family 242

Armed Forces and Police Force 242,243,246

General Provisions 247

Amendments 249

Temporary Provisions 250

Final Provisions 253

Country Synopsis 2

Agriculture 11

Airports (Major) 10

Ancient Names 2

Beverages 13

Capital 4

Cities (Major) ....

Climate 3

Constitution Date 6

Free Trade Zones Industrial Sites 9

Ethnic Groups 5

Exchange Rate 9

Exports 10

Fiscal Year 6

Foreign Diplomatic Missions Accredited to Haiti   6

Haitian Representation in Foreign Countries ..   6

Higher Education 5

History of Name 2

Imports 10

Independence Date 4

Industries 10

International Clubs 9

International Organizations Represented in Haiti   8

Language 5
Literacy Rate 5
Location 3
Minimum Wage Rates 10
Monetary Unit 9
Music (Types) **11**
   Architects of Haitian Music 12
   Recording Groups 12
National Anthem 5
National Calendar 5
National Emblem 5
National Flag 5
National Slogan 5
Natural Mineral Resources 11
Newspapers (Major) 11
Official Designation 2
Phone Code 10
Population 4
Population Density 4
Population Growth 4
Popular Haitian Dishes 12
Ports 10
Principal Political Parties 7
Private Development Organizations 7
Radio Stations (Major) 11
Religion 5
Roads 10
Suffrage 6
Television Networks (Major) 11
Time Zone 10
Topography 3
Total Area 3
Trading Partners (Major) 10
Type of Government 6
Creole - English Lexicon 128
Creole Expressions 124
Creole Proverbs 142

D

Damiens' Agreement (Concordat of Damiens) 29
Dartiguenave, Sudre 45
Dauxion-Lavaysse 36
Delorme, Demesvar 41
Dessalines, Jean-Jacques 27,33,60
Domingue, Michel 42
Durand, Oswald 43
Duvalier, Dr. François 51,52
Duvalier, Jean-Claude 52,54

E

Embargo 58
d'Estaing, Count 27
English - Creole Lexicon 131
Estimé, Dumarsais 49

F

Faustin I 40
Fignolé, Daniel 51,54
Firmin, Anténor 43
First Civil Commission 29
Flon, Catherine 33
Fort de Joux 33

G

Galbaud 29
Geffrard, Fabre 40,41
Guerrier, Philippe 39
Guillaume Sam, Vilbrun 45
Guilloux, Jean-Marie 42

H

HASCO 44
Hédouville 31
Henri I 36

Hérard, Rivière 39
Historical Sites 79
   Citadel of Henri Christophe
     (Milot-Northern Haiti) 79
   City of Caracol (Northeast Region) 80
   Crête-à-Pierrot (Petite Rivière de l'Artibonite) . 80
   Forts Jacques & Alexandre
     (Fermathe, Hills behind Port-au-Prince) 79
   Heroes of Independence Square (Port-au-Prince) 80
   La Place des Heros
   Môle Saint-Nicolas (Northwest Region) 80
   Monument to the Unknown Maroon (Port-au-Prince)
   Monument du Marron Inconnu 80
   Palace of 365 Doors (Petite Rivière de
     l'Artibonite) 80
   Sans-Souci Palace (Milot, Northern Haiti) 79
   Vertières (Entrance of Cap-Haïtien) 79

Holidays 84
   National and Legal Holidays 84
   Other Celebrations 84
   Patron Saint Festivals 85
   Religious Holidays Which Change Every Year 84
   Roman Catholic Holidays Observed 84
Honorat, Jean-Jacques 58
Humidity (Average) 23
Hyppolite, Florvil 43,44

I
Islands (Surrounding) 20
   La Gonâve 20
   La Tortue 20
   L'Ile a Vache 20
   Les Cayemittes 20
   La Navase 20

J
Jacques I 34
Janvier, Louis-Joseph 43

L

La Dessalinienne 67
Lakes (Major) **22**
    Lake Azuei 22
    Lake Miragoâne 22
    Trou Caïman 22
Laleau, Léon 45
Laplume 32
Law of April 4, 1492 29
Leclerc 32,33
Leconte, Cincinnatus 44
Légitime, François Denys 43
Lescot, Elie 49
Ligondé, François Wolf 52
Literature (Haitian) **88**
    Alexis, Jacques Stephen 100
    Alexis, Stephen 99
    Ardouin, Beaubrun 90
    Ardouin, Céligni 91
    Ardouin, Coriolan 91
    Bellegarde, Dantès 100
    Bergeaud, Emeric 91
    Boisrond-Tonnerre, Louis 90
    Bonnet, Guy-Joseph 91
    Brierre, Jean-Fernand 100
    Brouard, Carl 100
    Brutus, Edner 101
    Brutus, Timoléon C. 101
    Camille, Roussan 101
    Chanlatte, Juste 88
    Charles, Christophe, ... 101
    Chauvet, Marie Vieux 101
    Cinéas, Jean-Baptiste 101
    Colimon, Marie-Thérèse 102
    Coicou, Massillon 93
    Corvington, Georges 102
    Delorme, Demesvar 94
    Dépestre, René 102
    Dorsainvil, Dr. Jean Chrysostome ... 102
    Dorsinville, Roger 102
    Dumesle, Hérard 88

Dupré, Antoine 88
Durand, Oswald 94
Ethéart, Liautaud 92
Etienne, Franck 103,111
Faubert, Pierre 92
Féry, Général Alibée 92
Firmin, Anténor 95
Fouchard, Jean 103
Gaillard, Roger 103
Hibbert, Fernand 97
Janvier, Louis-Joseph 96
Laforest, Edmond 97
Laleau, Léon 97
Léon, Dr. Rulx 104
Lhérisson, François Romain 89
Lhérisson, Justin 98
Madiou, Thomas 92
Marcelin, Frédéric 98
Mathon, Alix 104
Ménos, Solon 96
Mentor, Gérard 104
Milscent, Jules Solime 89
Morisseau-Leroy, Félix 104
Moravia, Charles 98
Nau, Emile 93
Nau, Ignace 93
Philoctète, René 104
Pompilus, Pradel 105
Price, Hannibal 96
Price-Mars, Dr. Jean 105
Romane, Jean-Baptiste 89
Roumain, Jacques 105
Roumer, Emile 105
Saint-Amand, Edris 106
St Juste, Laurore 106
Sannon, Horace Pauléus 106
Saint-Rémy, Joseph 93
Sylvain, Georges 99
Trouillot, Hénock 106
Turnier, Alain 106

Vastey, Pompée Valentin   90
Vilaire, Etzer   99

Louverture, François Dominique Toussaint   26,29,30,
. . . .   31,32,33,
. . . .   59,60

M
Mackandal   27
Mackau, Baron   38
Madiou, Thomas   40
Magloire, Paul E.   50
Maitland   31
Manigat, Leslie François   56
Medina, Franco de   36
Mirbeck   29
Mountains (Highest) **20**
    Morne la Selle   20
    Morne Macaya   20
    Morne du Cibao   20
    Morne Bois-Pin   20

N
Namphy, Henri   55,56
National Anthem - La Dessalinienne   67
National Council of Government (CNG)
(Conseil National de Gouvernement)   54
Nerette, Joseph C.   58

O
Ogé, Vincent   28
Ordinance of Charles X   38
Oreste, Michel   45

P
Pernier, Battle of   28
Pétion, Alexandre   33,61
Piquets   39

Pierre-Louis, Nemours   51
Pierrot, Jean-Louis   39,40
Polvérel   29
Pope Jean-Paul II   53
Population by Cities   75
Price, Hannibal   43
Price-Mars, Jean   46
Provisional Electoral Council
(Conseil Electoral Provisoire - CEP)   55

R

Ramirez de Fuente, Don Sebastián   25
Ravine à Couleuvres, Battle of   32
Riché, Jean Baptiste   39
Rigaud   32
Rivers (Major) **22**
Rivière Hérard   39
Rochambeau   34
Roumain, Jacques   47
Roume   29
Roy, Eugène   47
Ryswick, Treaty of   26

S

Saget, Nissage   41,42
Saint-Léger   29
Salomon Jeune, Lysius Félicité   42
Salnave, Sylvain   41
Sam, Tiresias Antoine Simon   44
Sam, Vilbrun Guillaume   45
Second Civil Commission   29
Sonthonax   29,30
Soulouque, Faustin   40
Sylvain, Franck   51

T
Temperature (Average) 23
Territorial Divisions of Haiti 15
    Artibonite Administrative Region
    (Département de l'Artibonite) 17
    Central Administrative Region
    (Département du Centre) 18
    Grand'Anse Administrative Region
    (Département de la Grand'Anse) 19
    Northeastern Administrative Region
    (Département du Nord-Est) 16
    Northern Administrative Region
    (Département du Nord) 16
    Northwestern Administrative Region
    (Département du Nord-Ouest) 17
    Southeastern Administrative Region
    (Département du Sud-Est) 18
    Southern Administrative Region
    (Département du Sud) 19
    Western Administrative Region
    (Département de l'Ouest) 15

Théodore, Davilmar 45
Third Civil Commission 31
Treaties
    Treaty of Bâle 31
    Treaty of Ryswick 26
Trouillot, Ertha Pascal 57

V
Valleys and Plains (Major) 21
Villatte Revolt (l'Affaire Villatte) 31
Vincent, Sténio 47

Z
Zamor, Oreste 45